» Women Reading
Women Writing

Self-Invention in **PAULA GUNN ALLEN**

GLORIA ANZALDÚA

and **AUDRE LORDE**

by AnaLouise Keating

Temple University Press

Philadelphia

Temple University Press, Philadelphia 19122
Copyright © 1996 by Temple University

Published 1996

Printed in the United States of America

⊖ The paper used in this publication meets the requirements of the American National Standard for Information Sciences—Permanence of Paper for Printed Library Materials, ANSI Z39.48-1984

Text design by Omega Clay

Library of Congress Cataloging-in-Publication Data
Keating, AnaLouise, 1961–
     Women Reading Women Writing: Self-Invention in Paula Gunn Allen, Gloria Anzaldúa, and Audre Lorde / by AnaLouise Keating.
         p. cm.
     Includes bibliographical references and index.
     ISBN 1-56639-419-8 (cloth : alk. paper).—ISBN 1-56639-420-1
(pbk : alk. paper)
     1. American literature—Women authors—History and criticism. 2. Women and literature—United States—History—20th Century. 3. American literature—20th century—History and criticism. 4. Allen, Paula Gunn—Criticism and interpretation. 5. Anzaldúa, Gloria—Criticism and interpretation. 6. Lorde, Audre—Criticism and interpretation. 7. Difference (Psychology) in literature. 8. Identity (Psychology) in literature. 9. Sex role in literature. 10. Invention (Rhetoric). 11. Self in literature.
     I. Title.
PS151.K43   1996
810.9'9287—dc20   95-39871

Contents

Acknowledgments

This book has benefitted from conversations and interactions with so many friends, colleagues, and students over the past few years that it's difficult to know how to begin, or what to say. A number of people have read and commented on portions of this book at various stages of its development. Thanks to Gloria Anzaldúa, Lois Banner, Mae Henderson, Karen Hollinger, Dan Keating, Ed Lynton, Debra Miller, Royal Prentice, and Margaret Willen; your insightful comments have forced me to push my thinking further. Thanks especially to Renae Bredin, Cynthia Hogue, and Bonnie Zimmerman who took time out of their own busy teaching and writing schedules to read and comment on the entire manuscript; your suggestions and your encouraging words have been invaluable. And thanks to Janet Francendesce, my editor at Temple, for your encouragement, your patience (even as I write these words, I *still* haven't come up with a satisfactory title!), and your sense of humor; and thanks to Jeannine Klobe for copy editing the entire manuscript not once but twice. Thanks to my parents, Tom and Joann Keating, for your confidence in me and the many provocative, stimulating books and articles on "blackness," "diversity," and related issues that you've sent me over the past few years; thanks especially, mom, for watching Jamitrice Kre-Chelle as I read the copy-edited manuscript. Thanks to the Eastern New Mexico University Office of Grants and Development for help with printing and photocopying; and my Spring 1995 U.S. Literature survey class for engaging in extensive discussions of literary "whiteness." Thanks also to Patrice Caldwell, Antony Oldknow, and the reference librarians at Golden Library: in various ways you've enabled me to make the most of my writing time. Thanks to Micki Muhlbauer for putting me in touch with Alex and Tim at very short notice. And last but definitely not least, thanks to Ed Lynton for so very much, including help with the cover art and author's photo.

One more thing: some of you might be wondering why my name on the cover is slightly different from the name that you've known me by. The change will make sense when you read the last chapter.

Women Reading
Women Writing

Threshold Identities

Not quite the Same, not quite the Other, she stands in that
undetermined threshold place where she constantly drifts in
and out.   TRINH MINH-HA

As self-identified[1] lesbians of color, Paula Gunn Allen, Gloria Anzaldúa, and Audre Lorde negotiate diverse, sometimes conflicting, sets of personal, political, and professional worlds. Allen, who refers to herself as a "multi-cultural event . . . raised in a Chicano village in New Mexico by a half-breed mother and a Lebanese-American father" ("Review," 127), is a well-known Native American scholar and poet, as well as a professor of English at UCLA; Anzaldúa, the daughter of sixth-generation *mexicanos* from the Rio Grande Valley of south Texas and a self-described "Chicana *tejana* feminist-dyke-*patlache* poet, fiction writer, and cultural theorist,"[2] has been a visiting professor at several universities and a doctoral student at the University of California, Santa Cruz; and Lorde, the daughter of working-class West Indian immigrants and a self-identified "Black woman warrior poet" was born and raised in New York City where she worked for over fifteen years as professor of English at Hunter College before 'returning' to the Caribbean where she spent the last years of her life. All three writers participate in a number of apparently separate worlds yet refuse to be contained within any single group or location. Instead, they move within, between, and among the specialized worlds of academia and publishing; the private spaces of family and friends; the politicized communities of Native Americans, Chicanas/Chicanos, and African Americans; and the overlapping yet distinct worlds of feminist, lesbian and gay, and U.S. women of color. To borrow Victor Turner's phrase, they are "threshold people" who "elude or slip through the network of classifications that normally locate states and positions in cultural spaces" (95).

I find this metaphor of threshold identities extremely suggestive, for it illustrates the potentially transformational implications of their work. Like thresholds—which mark transitional, in-between spaces where new beginnings and unexpected combinations can occur— Allen, Anzaldúa, and Lorde use their movements "betwixt and between" worlds to establish new connections among apparently different peoples.[3] Neither entirely inside nor fully outside any single community, they adopt ambivalent insider/outsider positions in relation to a variety of cultural, professional, gender, and sexual groups. The specific worlds each writer slips through and the revisionary tactics she deploys often reflect the specific details of her regional, ethnic, and economic background—as well as other differences like native language, religion, age, education, and skin color. Yet Allen, Anzaldúa, and Lorde mobilize their threshold positions in similar ways. They engage in to-and-fro movements between multiple worlds, thus illuminating the limitations in all pre-existing identities.

But threshold positions can be dangerous, uncomfortable locations—for both readers and writers. Thresholds mark crisis points, spaces where conflicting values, ideas, and beliefs converge, unsettling fixed categories of meaning. By locating themselves at the intersections of seemingly separate groups, Anzaldúa, Allen, and Lorde challenge people who view themselves as insiders—as permanent members of a single, unitary group—to reexamine the exclusionary terms used to define their own personal and social locations. But these challenges are rarely welcomed, and threshold people open themselves to multiple risks, including self-division, isolation, misunderstanding, rejection, and accusations of disloyalty. Take, for example, Anzaldúa's self-positioning in "La Prieta," an early autobiographical essay. She acknowledges the numerous forms of alienation she has experienced in her interactions with Mexican Americans, other people of color, feminists, lesbians, and gay men, yet refuses to sever her ties with these various groups. Instead, she locates herself on the thresholds:

> I am a wind-swayed bridge, a crossroads inhabited by whirlwinds. . . .
> "Your allegiance is to La Raza, the Chicano movement," say the members of my race. "Your allegiance is to the Third World," say my Black and Asian friends. "Your allegiance is to your gender, to women," say the feminists. Then there's my allegiance to the Gay movement, to the socialist revolution, to the New Age, to magic and the occult. And there's my affinity to literature, to the world of the artist. What am I? *A third world lesbian feminist with Marxist and mystic leanings.* They would chop me up into little fragments and tag each piece with a label. (205; her emphasis)

Significantly, Anzaldúa's threshold location includes ethnic- and gender-specific worlds she could be said to have entered by virtue of appearance and birth, as well as other worlds she has more consciously chosen to enter. Although each group makes full membership contingent on its own exclusionary sets of rules and demands based on ethnicity, gender, sexuality, class, ideology, or beliefs, Anzaldúa refuses these terms without disassociating herself from the various groups. By rejecting the need for unitary identities and exclusive, single-issue alliances, she challenges her readers—no matter how they identify—to reexamine and expand their own personal and social locations. Only then can they begin forming new threshold communities, or what she terms "*El Mundo Zurdo*, the left-handed world," where people marked as different work together to bring about individual and collective change:

> We are the queer groups, the people that don't belong anywhere, not in the dominant world nor completely within our own respective cultures. Combined we cover so many oppressions. But the overwhelming oppression is the collective fact that we do not fit, and because we do not fit, *we are a threat.* (209; her emphasis)

In Anzaldúa's *Mundo Zurdo*—a world entered by choice—the differences between members are transformed into new forms of commonality.

Allen and Lorde also risk numerous forms of alienation yet insist on the importance of multiple, at times contradictory, identities and locations. In *The Sacred Hoop*, her collection of scholarly essays on Native American literary and cultural traditions, Allen creates a threshold location based on her interactions with feminist, lesbian, academic, Native, and contemporary spiritual communities. By incorporating this threshold perspective into her work, she simultaneously challenges her readers to examine the ways homophobia, sexism, and racism have misshaped their perceptions of Native American cultures and expands existing definitions of Native, lesbian, gay, and female identities. Lorde mobilizes her own set of threshold maneuvers in her semi-autobiographical novel, *Zami: A New Spelling of My Name*, where she draws on the numerous forms of alienation she experienced as a black lesbian to complicate simplistic notions of commonality based on ethnic, gender, or sexual identities:

> *Being women together was not enough. We were different. Being gay-girls together was not enough. We were different. Being Black together was not enough. We were different. Being Black women together was not enough. We were different. Being Black dykes together was not enough. We were different.* (226; her emphasis)

As this passage suggests, Lorde insists that no matter how concise the identity markers might seem, they do not automatically unite people into self-affirming communities. Like Anzaldúa and Allen, however, she uses these differences among people to generate new forms of bonding.

For Allen, Anzaldúa, and Lorde, threshold locations are performative. Rather than deny the contradictions they experience as they negotiate among numerous groups, they explore them in writing. By thus translating their lives into words, they reinvent themselves and enact new forms of identity, nondual modes of subjectivity that blur the boundaries between apparently distinct peoples. This use of the written word draws on language's performative effects and deconstructs conventional western dualisms. Like other poststructuralist thinkers, Allen, Anzaldúa, and Lorde maintain that language does not simply reflect reality but instead reshapes it. Yet they take this belief in language's performative powers even further by associating it with precolonial nonwestern oral traditions. In so doing, they simultaneously spiritualize and politicize their words. More specifically, by drawing on Native American, Mexican Indian, and West African oral traditions, which posit a dialogic relationship between the human and nonhuman dimensions of life, they enact a variety of to-and-fro movements enabling them to combine cultural critique with the invention of new forms of culture. As they borrow from and rewrite precolonial belief systems, they simultaneously expose the limitations in existing definitions of ethnic, gender, and sexual identity and invent open-ended alternatives.

It is these transformational possibilities that distinguish the works of Allen, Anzaldúa, and Lorde from those of many other contemporary social actors, for in the process of reinventing themselves, they reinvent their readers. As they inscribe their threshold identities into their creative and critical writings, they challenge their readers to rethink the dominant culture's sociopolitical inscriptions—the labels that define each person according to gender, ethnicity, sexuality, class, and other systems of difference. More specifically, they employ what I call transformational identity politics. Unlike conventional identity politics—where social actors base their political theories and strategies on their personal sense of ethnic, gender, and sexual identity—transformational identity politics deconstructs all such notions of unified, stable identities. Although I discuss these two politics of identity in greater detail in Chapter 3, I want to point out the creative possibilities opened up by the latter, more flexible form. Rather than simply enabling alliances across differences, transformational identity politics employs these differences to generate new forms of commonality. This politics of identity relies on transformational epistemologies, nondual ways of thinking that destabilize the networks of classification that restrict us to static notions of personal and collective identity. In so doing, it opens up psychic spaces where alterations in consciousness can occur.

To emphasize the liberating potential in the new ways of thinking Allen, Anzaldúa, and Lorde invent, I want briefly to summarize conventional western knowledge systems. Based on Enlightenment principles, mainstream epistemologies share a number of unquestioned presuppositions, including: 1) the existence of a single, unchanging, universal truth; 2) a distinct separation between the knowing subject and the object under investigation that ensures the knower's unbiased access to this truth; 3) a neutral, transparent language system capable of accurately reporting these newly discovered truths; 4) objective, scientific conceptions of knowledge; and 5) the use of binary oppositions to develop intellectual structures so that reason, for example, is defined by what it excludes—it is the opposite of emotion. This dualistic framework has played a significant role in shaping contemporary western social structures, for it divides reality into a series of binary oppositions that separate subject from object, mind from body, and human beings from nature. Combined with the belief in a single, unchanging standard of truth, binary knowledge systems reinforce dominant/subordinate worldviews and restrictive forms of thinking that define difference as deviation from a single norm. Perhaps most importantly for my argument in *Women Reading Women Writing*, dualistic thinking leads to the construction of oppressive social and symbolic systems, where people marked as "different" because of appearance, lifestyle, or beliefs are viewed as inferior. They are dehumanized, objectified, and controlled by the so-called norm.

As I explain in the following chapters, by drawing on Native American, Mexican Indian, and West African worldviews, Allen, Anzaldúa, and Lorde create transformational epistemologies and embodied metaphysics that undermine these binary structures. Whether they call it "a spirit that pervades everything, that is capable of powerful song and radiant movement, and that moves in and out of the mind" (Allen), a "spirit world" (Anzaldúa), or the "divine principles" that move through our lives (Lorde), all three writers reinterpret non-western beliefs and invent nondual metaphysical systems that locate the spiritual in material and intellectual life. This revisionist approach to precolonial cultural traditions enables them to unite their critiques of existing social systems with visionary thinking: On the one hand, they critically analyze western culture's dualistic forms of thought and disrupt conventional social and symbolic structures; on the other hand, they construct transformational epistemologies that destabilize the boundaries between and within physical and nonphysical worlds, thus opening spaces where new forms of connection can occur.

This doubled gesture represents a significant theoretical shift in feminist theory, as well as a remarkable break from previous epistemologies. Whereas many liberal and conservative feminists have assumed that reason and other Enlightenment-based knowledge systems are neutral and can be expanded to include the experiences of women as well as men, Allen, Anzaldúa, and Lorde take a different approach. They move beyond the existing frameworks by exposing the hidden, masculine, Eurocentric biases that structure binary thinking. As I explain in the following chapter, they invent relational ways of knowing that unite subject with object, body with mind, and human beings with nature and the divine. Allen reinterprets Native ritual traditions and invents what I call *embodied mythic thinking*, a nondual way of knowing where thoughts, ideas, and beliefs take concrete material form, and matter itself is a special type of intelligence that can be continually reshaped by human beings. Anzaldúa draws on her own experiences of alienation and resistance as a Chicana queer and develops what she describes as *mestiza consciousness*, a fluid, transformational thinking process that breaks down the rigid boundaries between apparently separate categories of meaning. And Lorde incorporates the holism she finds in West African worldviews into her theory of the *erotic*, an embodied way of thinking that synthesizes multiple dimensions of thought. Unlike the radical separation of body and mind and the disembodied subjectivities found in Enlightenment thought systems, open-ended forms of thinking connect the intellect with the physical components of life. In so doing, they deconstruct binary structures from within.

These challenges to dualistic thinking resemble those made by Luce Irigaray, Adrienne Rich, Teresa de Lauretis, and other contemporary philosophers who simultaneously expose the hidden biases in existing knowledge systems and create new, embodied ways of knowing and theorizing. However, unlike the three writers I examine in this study, those philosophers focus almost entirely on the ways sexual difference has shaped knowledge structures. They argue that Enlightenment-based epistemologies are built upon a series of hierarchically ordered binarisms in which Man is associated with the intellect, spirit, and the divine, while Woman is associated with emotion, nature, and the body. According to Rosi Braidotti, by incorporating their experiences as women into their critiques, these "female feminists of sexual difference" invent genuinely new forms of thought; they are "counter-thinkers, claiming a new status for the activity of thinking itself" (*Patterns of Dissonance*, 175). Drawing on Teresa de Lauretis's formulation of "a new female feminist subjectivity," Braidotti associates the radical implications in these new theories with the irreducible, almost ineffable, sexualized difference they posit:[4]

> [T]he starting point for this redefinition of the female feminist subject is the notion of the asymmetry between the sexes, which results in the political and epistemological project of asserting difference in a non-hierarchical manner, refusing to disembody and therefore to desexualize the vision of the subject. The question then becomes: how to reconcile the recognition of the problematic nature of the construction of subjectivity with the political necessity of asserting women as subjects of another story? (*Patterns of Dissonance*, 281)

In other words, Braidotti's female feminists of sexual difference posit a conceptual gender-based[5] "separatism"—an elusive, nonhierarchical difference between Woman and Man that leads to radical epistemological and material changes.[6]

To my mind, however, this exclusive focus on the *sexualization* of patriarchal knowledges is too narrow and cannot entirely escape an underlying binary structure. Although Braidotti and other female feminists insist on the nonsymmetrical nature of this male/female difference, their repeated references to existing gender categories inadvertently reinforce heterosexual concepts of gender and dualistic forms of thinking. Norma Alarcón makes a similar point when she challenges mainstream U.S. feminists' "common denominator" theory, the belief that—despite the many differences among women—there is something distinctive about female identity that automatically unites all women. Drawing on the experiences of self-identified U.S. women of color, Alarcón argues that Anglo feminists' explorations of gender-based differences are too restrictive to bring about radical alterations in feminist theory. Like Braidotti, Alarcón uses Teresa de Lauretis's theory of "female feminist subjectivity" to explore the shift in feminist theorizing as women become the subjects, rather than the objects, of investigation. However, Alarcón is far less impressed with this female-feminist alteration.[7] Indeed, she suggests that the emphasis on female subjectivity inadvertently reinforces binary configurations of identity: "With gender as the central concept in feminist thinking, epistemology is flattened out in such a way that we lose sight of the complex and multiple ways in which the subject and object of possible experience are constituted. . . . There's no inquiry into the knowing subject beyond the fact of being a 'woman'" (361).

Although Irigaray and other female theorists of sexual difference do not flatten out feminist epistemologies to the extent Alarcón suggests, I, too, would argue that recent work by self-identified feminists of color leads to additional questions concerning the ways we talk and write about "Woman," "women," and the "feminine."[8] And although Alarcón restricts her analysis to U.S. feminists, I believe her critique applies to the international collection of radical female-feminist theorists Braidotti describes. Their reliance on dualistic (male/female) categories inhibits the production of alternative theories of subjectivity and reinforces the underlying heterosexist gender system, despite their acknowledgment of the many differences between and among women, their open-ended definitions of the "feminine," and their emphasis on a qualitative nonsymmetrical difference between "masculine" and "feminine." More importantly, by focusing exclusively on Eurocentric categories of thought, Braidotti and the female feminists she describes inadvertently restrict their own theorizing. This unacknowledged emphasis on European-based models serves as one of my own threshold locations in the following chapters: If interrogating sexual difference enables Irigaray and other radical female feminists to significantly alter western knowledge systems, what additional alterations occur when feminists incorporate an analysis of this Eurocentric bias into their theoretical perspectives?

II   As we make theory and offer it up to others, what do we assume is the connection between theory and consciousness? Do we expect others to read theory, understand it, believe it, and have their consciousnesses and lives thereby transformed? If we really want theory to make a difference to people's lives, how ought we to present it? Do we think people come to consciousness by reading? only by reading? Speaking to people through theory (orally or in writing) is a very specific context-dependent activity. That is, theory-makers and their methods and concepts constitute a community of people and of shared meanings. Their language can be just as opaque and foreign to those not in the community as a foreign tongue or dialect.

MARÍA LUGONES AND ELIZABETH SPELMAN

Must we always polarize in order to polemicise? Are we trapped in a politics of struggle where the representation of social antagonisms and historical contradictions can take no other form than a binarism of theory vs. politics?

HOMI BHABHA

I too am seduced by academic language.

GLORIA ANZALDÚA

What is the relationship between theory, consciousness, and concrete material change? As María Lugones and Elizabeth Spelman point out, contemporary theory can be a highly specialized, at times even elitist, endeavor. Like all forms of reading, writing, and speaking, it's a context-dependent activity, and theories relying on sophisticated terms, specific-meaning systems, and complex, intertextual references can create extremely restricted communities of readers and writers. Or as Anzaldúa puts it, jargonistic, abstract language can impede communication, making "the general listener/reader feel bewildered and stupid" ("Haciendo caras, una entrada," xxiii). This alienating effect results in the polarized opposition between theory and politics that Homi Bhabha describes in the second epigraph. The technical language, the excruciatingly long sentences, the unnecessarily difficult or obscure words, and the convoluted ideas, make it tempting to simply dismiss most contemporary theory—especially in its poststructuralist manifestations—as too removed from "real life" to be useful.

Yet I, too, am seduced by theory—seduced and transformed. Theory provides me with new tools in my own quest to bring about personal and collective change. And if, as I believe, language does not simply reflect reality but rather shapes our perspectives on life, theoretical writings can be creative, enabling us to generate alternate knowledge systems and new social actors. The challenge comes in trying to translate dense, exclusionary, theoretical language into practical, accessible terms capable of speaking to the experiences of self-identified women of color, lesbians, and other previously ignored groups.

So, in answer to Lugones's and Spelman's first question concerning the relationship between theory and consciousness, I would say that theory offers readers and writers catalysts for change. First, by revealing the contradictions in existing knowledges and beliefs, theory opens up new states of awareness within, between, and among writing or speaking subjects. Second, these alterations in consciousness lead to further transformations, including the construction of hybrid cultural identities and the establishment of transcultural connections between differently situated social actors. Anzaldúa makes a similar point in her introduction to *Making Face, Making Soul/Haciendo Caras*, where she underscores the potentially liberating roles theory plays in texts by self-identified women of color. She, too, associates theorizing with transformational politics by defining theory as specific modes of perception leading to concrete plans for action. Although she acknowledges the exclusionary nature of academic "high" theory, Anzaldúa does not reject all theoretical discourse. Instead, she maintains that because theory enables us to challenge oppressive belief systems, "it is *vital* that we occupy theorizing space" and begin reshaping it from within (xxv; her emphasis). Thus she calls for new types of theory that reinterpret and revise existing belief systems:

> Theory produces effects that change people and the way they perceive the world. Thus we need *teorías* that will enable us to interpret what happens in the world, that will explain how and why we relate to certain people in specific ways, that will reflect what goes on between inner, outer and peripheral "I"'s within a person and between the personal "I"'s and the collective "we" of our ethnic communities. *Necessitamos teorías* that will rewrite history using race, class, gender and ethnicity as categories of analysis, theories that cross borders, that blur boundaries—new kinds of theories with new theorizing methods. (xxv)

Because conventional theories contain hidden biases privileging restrictive gender, ethnic, sexual, and class norms, we need openly political theories that simultaneously expose these hidden biases and offer alternative perspectives.

Allen makes a related point in " 'Border' Studies: The Intersection of Gender and Color," where she maintains that academic literary and cultural theories are too restrictive to provide readers with insights into contemporary writings by self-identified U.S. women of color. She describes these women writers-of-color as *"las disappearadas"* to underscore their erasure in the existing canon of U.S. literature. Because they incorporate their multicultural experiences into their works, *"las disappearadas"* have developed multivoiced texts that cannot be interpreted according to conventional literary methods. Consequently, their work has not received the attention it merits. She calls for new, openly political forms of theory capable of exploring these multifaceted experiences:

> It is not merely biculturality that forms the foundation of our lives and work in their multiplicity, aesthetic largeness, and wide-ranging potential; rather, it is multiculturality, multilinguality, and dizzying class-crossing from the fields to the salons, from the factories to the academy, or from galleries and the groves of academe to the neighborhoods and reservations. The new field of study moves beyond the critical boundary set in Western academic circles and demands that the canonical massive walls be thinned and studded with openings so that criticism, like literary production itself, reflects the great variety of writerly lives and thought, particularly those in the American community. (305)

Anzaldúa's work illustrates the transformational, border-crossing, theoretical perspectives she and Allen call for. Take, for example, her use of autobiographical material to describe the Borderlands[9] as the convergence of apparently dissimilar peoples, places, and ideas. She begins with her own regional location and moves outward. By extending the geographical Texas/Mexico borderland and the conventional description of borders as boundaries between discrete locations to incorporate psychic, cultural, and sexual boundaries as well, Anzaldúa invents a metaphor that vividly illustrates threshold positionings. She thus constructs flexible, nonrestrictive subject positions for social actors. As she explains in *Borderlands/La Frontera*, people who dwell in the Borderlands do not define themselves in monolithic terms; they are hybrids, complex mixed-breeds who can neither be reduced to a single essence nor rigidly categorized.

Borderlands/La Frontera's hybrid form further illustrates these new theorizing methods. By combining autobiography with historical narrative, poetry, fantasy, and myth, Anzaldúa transgresses preestablished generic boundaries and blurs conventional forms of discourse. She replaces the humanist notion of a stable, unified self found in traditional western autobiographical works with a fluid, shifting subjectivity. Lourdes Torres describes this multifaceted self-positioning as a "politics of multiple identities" (273). As she explains in her discussion of recent Latina autobiographies, by incorporating their diverse personal experiences into their texts, Anzaldúa, Cherríe Moraga, and other U.S. Latina writers develop complex individual and communal identities:

> [They] create a new discourse which seeks to incorporate the often contradictory aspects of their gender, ethnicity, class, sexuality, and feminist politics. The radicalness of the project lies in the authors' refusal to accept any one position; rather, they work to acknowledge the contradictions in their lives and to transform difference into a source of power. They find being marginalized by multiple discourses, and existing in a borderland, compels them to reject prescriptive positions and instead leads them to create radical personal and collective identities. (275)

Anzaldúa's project, however, is even more radical than Torres suggests. Not only does she transform her *own* differences into a source of personal and textual power, she uses the differences between herself and her readers to generate new forms of commonality. This interplay between commonalities and differences functions as a catalyst for further change—alterations in self/worldviews that impact her readers as well as herself. Drawing on language's performative effects, Anzaldúa invents metaphors, such as the Borderlands and the new mestiza queers, enabling her to construct transformational, hybrid identities that reflect yet go beyond the specific details of her own cultural and sexual identity.

Similar comments apply to Allen's and Lorde's work as well. By employing politics of multiple identities that combine their interpretations of nonwestern and western traditions, they, too, create autobiographical, theoretical, and literary works capable of generating transformational interactions between writer, reader, and text. Their hybrid works bring together divergent perspectives, thus providing readers with new ways of perceiving themselves and their worlds. In *The Sacred Hoop*, for instance, Allen redefines feminism and lesbianism from a "Native" perspective and American Indian cultures from a lesbian-feminist point of view; in *Grandmothers of the Light* she merges ethnographic material from diverse Native cultures with New Age beliefs and creates transcultural forms of "medicine women," or what I describe as Indianized social actors. Lorde also enacts similar negotiations between diverse formal and cultural traditions. She describes *Zami: A New Spelling of My Name* as "biomythography"; like Anzaldúa, she synthesizes autobiography, biography, fiction, and myth into a hybrid literary form. In her poetry, fiction, and prose she uses revisionist myth to develop an interactional model of identity formation capable of transforming her readers as well as herself. By reinterpreting Yoruban and Fon myths from a twentieth-century black U.S. lesbian-feminist perspective, she constructs cross-cultural personal and collective Africanized identities.

One of Allen's, Anzaldúa's, and Lorde's greatest strengths is their ability to incorporate sophisticated theoretical perspectives into their poetry, fiction, and prose. They make theory accessible. They employ a variety of genres (including lectures, interviews, poetry, fiction, biomythography, and edited anthologies), borrow from diverse sets of culturally specific forms and themes (including Laguna, Sioux, Yoruban, Fon, Aztec, and Toltec), and incorporate U.S. feminist theories that untie concepts of unitary selves to address a broad readership. As I explain in the following chapters, this mixture of western and nonwestern literary, cultural, and theoretical forms occurs in—and indeed shapes—all three writers' transformational epistemologies as well. Allen incorporates the performative dimensions of Native American oral traditions into her embodied mythic thinking. Anzaldúa uses her experiences as a mestiza—especially the tactics she has developed to negotiate between Mexican, Indian, Spanish, and Anglo traditions—to create the differential forms of thinking found in mestiza consciousness. And Lorde combines her interpretation of West African-based metaphysics, as well as her critique of double consciousness, into her theory of the erotic.

All three writers invent what I would call threshold theories, theories that cross genres and mix codes, combining language with action, activism with aesthetics, and individual identity formation with collective cultural change. Anzaldúa makes a similar point in "Haciendo caras, una entrada" where she associates the transformational potential she finds in works by contemporary "theorists-of-color" with their desire to move beyond European-based theoretical models. By adopting nonwestern narrative and aesthetic traditions, they have begun creating alternate ways of thinking, writing, and perceiving that open "new positions in these 'in-between,' Borderland worlds of ethnic communities and academies, feminist and job worlds" (xxvi). They create hybrid texts in which "social issues such as race, class and sexual difference are intertwined with the narrative and poetic elements of a text, elements in which theory is embedded" (xxvi).

This mixture of narrative, poetry, and social critique has shaped my own approach in *Women Reading Women Writing*. Like Allen, Anzaldúa, and Lorde, I draw on a variety of theoretical perspectives, borrowing what's useful and leaving the rest. I set theories in dialogue—both with myself and with the three writers I examine: Allen's discussion of the perpetual liminality she finds in Native worldviews influences the way I read Anzaldúa's mestiza consciousness; Anzaldúa's theory of Aztec shamans' invoked art informs my theory of Lorde's interactional self-naming process; Lorde's use of West African *orisha*, which she describes as spiritual personifications of divine forces, shapes my interpretations of Allen's and Anzaldúa's revisionary myths. The following pages contain other threshold dialogues as well. In Chapter 4, I draw on Patricia Hill Collins's discussion of black-feminist standpoints to analyze Allen's use of Native belief systems; in Chapter 5, I build on Hélène Cixous's injunctions to "write the body" and explore Anzaldúa's theory of writing the body-soul; in Chapter 6, I borrow a bit from contemporary legal theory as I examine Lorde's interactional self-naming; and in Chapter 7, I return to "French feminist" theory and read Luce Irigaray's female genealogy in conversation both with my own desires and with Allen's, Anzaldúa's, and Lorde's revisionist myths. By setting these very different voices in dialogue with each other and with myself, I enact my own version of threshold theorizing.

Viewed from the perspective of cultural purity, my approach may seem rather irreverent—and, in fact, it is. Too often, however, the emphasis on authenticity reinforces the belief in self-contained identities and replicates already existing divisions. The boundaries between various groups of people—and, by extension, the theoretical perspectives designed to represent them—become rigid, inflexible, and far too restrictive. Generally we assume that cultural identities are permanent unchanging categories of meaning based on biology, family, history, and tradition. Although these components do have a significant impact on the ways others see us and the ways we define ourselves, this conception of self-contained cultural and ethnic identities is far less accurate than it seems. Take the rhetoric of authenticity that associates ethnic identity with the discovery of genuine, previously erased cultural and historic traditions. In such instances, meaning relies on unitary notions of an authentic past. However, I would argue that these authentic identities are created, not discovered. As Stuart Hall explains in "Cultural Identity and Diaspora," the complex interconnections between present and past can obscure the constructed nature of contemporary cultural identities:

> Cultural identities come from somewhere, have histories. But, like everything else which is historical, they undergo constant transformation. Far from being eternally fixed in some essentialized past, they are subject to the continuous "play" of history, culture and power. Far from being grounded in a mere "recovery" of the past, which is waiting to be found, and which, when found, will secure our sense of ourselves into eternity, identities are the names we give to the different ways we are positioned by, and position ourselves within, the narratives of the past. (325)

Similar comments could be made about gender and sexual identities as well. They, too, have histories, yet undergo continual transformations in complex interactions with other categories of meaning. In short, individual and collective identities are hybrid creations, not organic preexisting discoveries.

Allen's, Anzaldúa's, and Lorde's excursions into precolonial cultural traditions have, to a great degree, shaped my belief in the permeable shifting nature of all apparently stable identities and locations. As they borrow from and rewrite nonwestern mythic and spiritual traditions, they simultaneously position themselves in the narratives of the past Hall describes and invent new stories. And, by going 'back' to their Native American, Mexican Indian, or West African cultural "roots," they go forward and establish alternate theoretical perspectives and new bases for action in the sociopolitical present. Let me emphasize: Their revisionist mythmaking does not indicate the nostalgic desire to transcend or escape the socioeconomic problems facing contemporary social actors. In fact, it's the elements of nostalgia and essentialism so often associated with myth that makes an examination of their revisionist mythmaking particularly important for my argument in the following chapters. As they undertake to-and-fro movements between past, present, and future narratives, they enact a series of displacements that simultaneously affirm and disavow organic images of unitary selves and nonwestern cultural traditions. This interface—the slippage between their essentializing references to myth and their interventions into contemporary cultural and sexual politics—serves as my own threshold location in the following chapters.

⫸ 2   Mythic Ways of Knowing?

*I say mujer magica, empty yourself. Shock yourself into new
ways of perceiving the world. Shock your readers into the same.
Stop the chatter inside their heads.*   GLORIA ANZALDÚA

*New ways of seeing can indeed emancipate us. Literature, like
all art, can show us new meanings of constructing the world,
for it is by changing the images and structures through which
we encode meaning that we can begin to develop new scripts
and assign new roles to the heroines of the stories we recount in
order to explain and understand our lives.*

FRANÇOISE LIONNET

The rejection of traditional phallocentric values and
the subsequent search for descriptions of reality that affirm female experience have become major themes in twentieth-century U.S. wom-
en's poetry and fiction.[1] Whether they explore how the existing (masculine) discourse silences women or appropriates and transforms
conventional stories and myths, a number of contemporary feminist
writers have demonstrated the vital connection between narrative
control and female identity formation. In their works, only those
protagonists who can tell their own stories have the authority to redefine themselves.

One of the most effective strategies employed in this effort to reclaim the power of speech involves the revision of patriarchal myths.[2]
Because myths embody a culture's deep-seated, often unacknowledged (and therefore unquestioned) assumptions about human nature,[3] revisionist mythmaking enables women poets and novelists to
subvert negative depictions of female identity in two interrelated ways:
To borrow Rachael Blau DuPlessis' terms, they "displace" the narrative
voice by permitting the woman silenced in traditional accounts to tell
her side of the story, or they "delegitimate"—alter and rearrange—the

narrative events. According to DuPlessis and Alicia Ostriker, the motivating force behind women writers' revisionist myths is the subversion of the dominant ideology's hidden male bias. By rewriting the stories of Eve, Lilith, Medusa, and other mythic figures, women challenge patriarchal constructions of female identity. Such alterations transform the original myths' structure and content so extensively that, as Ostriker asserts,

> the old stories are changed, changed utterly, by female knowledge of female experience, so that they can no longer stand as foundations of collective male fantasy or as the pillars sustaining phallocentric "high" culture. Instead, they are corrections; they are representations of what women find divine and demonic in themselves; they are retrieved images of what women have collectively and historically suffered; in some cases they are instructions for survival. (215)

But what happens when women mythmakers reject both the "old stories" and the Graeco-Roman tradition they reflect? If changing the content transforms conventional myths into critiques of western civilization's masculinist bias, what implications arise when, instead of an "old vessel filled with new wine" (Ostriker, 212), both the container and the wine are replaced? Do the resulting myths still function primarily as "the challenge to and correction of gender stereotypes" (216)? Or do they oppose other representational systems as well? Perhaps more importantly, does the inclusion of nonwestern material enable women mythmakers to invent new, potentially liberating perspectives?

I want to explore the ways Allen, Anzaldúa, and Lorde use mythic traditions to introduce additional levels of complexity into their works. They reject the male bias found in conventional western narratives; however, they do not simply "displace" or "delegitimate" specific stories and myths. By incorporating precolonial creatrix figures such as the Laguna Pueblo Thought Woman, the Mesoamerican Coatlicue, and the Yoruban MawuLisa into their writings, they invent new images of female identity that affirm their experiences as U.S. lesbians of color. Yet their revisionist mythmaking goes beyond this challenge to existing definitions of womanhood. As they replace the Judeo-Christian worldview with modes of perception drawn from Native

American, Mexican Indian, and West African mythic traditions, they offer far-reaching critiques of western culture's binary structures. And more importantly, they use revisionist myths to invent alternate forms of knowledge that posit the interconnectedness of the spiritual and material dimensions of life. They create new ways of thinking that displace the boundaries between inner/outer, subject/object, spirit/matter, and other dichotomous terms. In short, they develop transformational writing and reading practices that simultaneously politicize and spiritualize their work.

This combination of politics, spirituality, and myth seems untenable to many contemporary academic critics. Even the term "nonwestern mythology" can be problematic, for it implies a nostalgic worldview and a metaphysics—a synthesis of psychic, supernatural, and material forces—often dismissed as irrelevant to twentieth-century concerns. Because western-trained readers frequently equate tribal myths with superstitious beliefs, they regard mythico-religious systems as unsophisticated, inaccurate, and naive.[4] Even theorists who recognize the importance of mythic tales often identify them with a timeless realm and universal truths disconnected from everyday life.[5] According to Victor Turner,

> Myths and liminal rites are not to be treated as models for secular behavior. Nor, on the other hand, are they to be regarded as cautionary tales, as negative models which should not be followed. Rather are they felt to be high or deep mysteries which put the initiand *temporarily* into close rapport with the primary or primordial generative powers of the cosmos, the acts of which *transcend rather than transgress* the norms of human secular society. In myth is a limitless freedom, a symbolic freedom of action which is denied to the norm-bound incumbent of a status in a social structure.[6]

This definition acknowledges myth's symbolic potential, however, it relies on a dualistic worldview that divides reality into two distinct parts: a transcendent, sacred, mythic space occupied by supernatural beings and an everyday world of history, social roles, and human actions. Yet by separating people's actions in the material world from the "symbolic freedom" in the mythical world, this dualistic perspective overlooks developing mythic images and narratives that simultaneously transcend and transgress contemporary models of human behavior. As Houston Baker notes, the dichotomy between "mythic/ literary and sociohistoric domains" posited by Turner and other scholars restricts myth and literature to an "ahistorical symbolic universe of discourse," areas of thought that remain almost entirely separated from history and human life (*Blues*, 116). Baker suggests that although these domains "*are distinguishable, they are not mutually exclusive*," and he locates Afro-American literary criticism at the "mediational juncture" of the literary/mythic and sociohistoric worlds of discourse (*Blues*, 116–17; his emphasis).

Although Baker revises Turner's definition of myth to demonstrate the "creative symbolic potency of Afro-American art," I believe his description of the critic's liminal status also illuminates the works of Allen, Anzaldúa, and Lorde. Like his "historically grounded critic" who functions as "a mediator—as an agent who summons and interprets for a human audience the symbolic force of literary or mythic narrative," these writers mediate between mythic, historic, and contemporary worlds. By rewriting Native American, Mexican Indian, and West African mythic traditions and incorporating these new myths into their works, they, too, locate themselves at cultural and interpretive crossroads "where new meanings are stunningly generated" (*Blues*, 117).

There are, however, at least two significant differences between the mediational juncture Baker describes and those developed by Allen, Anzaldúa, and Lorde. First, as I've already mentioned, their revisionist mythmaking contains a distinctively feminist component; consequently, the new meanings they create deconstruct conventional western gender categories, as well as cultural systems of difference. Second, they do not simply interpret the symbolic force of mythic narratives for their audience; instead, they invent new symbols designed to alter their readers as well as themselves. They are agents of transformation who use myth to bring about concrete material change. As they borrow from a variety of mythic and cultural traditions, they develop transformational writing practices that utilize the performative dimensions of verbal art. Like oral traditions, which are based on belief in the power of the spoken word, their theories of writing draw on language's creative powers—its ability to alter individual and collective identities. And because they maintain that changes in the social structure begin on a personal level, they describe writing as a dynamic, interactional process between writer, reader, and text. Thus, their revisionary myths become powerful tools for self-naming, community building, and social change.

---

11   Myth functions as an affirmation of self that transcends the temporal. It guides our attention to a view of ourselves, a possibility, that we might not otherwise encounter. It shows us our own ability to accept and allow the eternal to be part of ourselves. It allows us to image a marriage between our conscious and unconscious, fusing the twin dimensions of mind and society into a coherent, meaningful whole.   PAULA GUNN ALLEN

Whereas Turner describes the liminal period as a temporary stage concluding in the individual's "reaggregation," or return to the social structure, Paula Gunn Allen views liminality as a permanent (yet constantly changing) way of life. In a 1990 interview with Jane Caputi she associates her lesbianism with her Native American worldview and explains that "perversity (transformationality) . . . constitutes the sacred moment, the process of changing from one condition to another—*life-long* liminality" (quoted in Caputi, 56; Allen's emphasis). I find Allen's metaphor of perpetual liminality extremely suggestive for two reasons. First, perpetual liminality embodies a way of thinking that challenges conventional western forms of thought. Whereas European-based knowledge systems rely on a series of binary oppositions that divide reality into separate parts, perpetual liminality entails continuous movement between and among these apparently distinct categories. This emphasis on transitional movement facilitates change by breaking open the rigid boundaries between distinct groups.[7] Second, perpetual liminality implies a flexible model of individual and collective identity formation. Thus in the interview with Caputi, Allen associates lesbians and gay males with Coyote, the mythic southwestern Native trickster figure whose nonconventional actions unsettle existing social structures. Like Coyote, she explains, lesbians and gay males are agents of transformation who introduce revolutionary new perspectives into existing systems of gender and sexuality; they are sacred social actors engaged in an ongoing process of personal and cultural change. By underscoring the continual nature of these "perverse" changes, Allen develops a theory of subjectivity where each individual participates in a series of transformational processes. Indeed, Allen's entire cosmology reflects this perpetual liminality, or condition of life-long transformation and change, which she elsewhere describes as "the fluidity and malleability, or creative flux, of things" (*Sacred Hoop*, 68).

This belief in a dynamic, living universe shapes Allen's work as a poet, fiction writer, and literary scholar. She locates herself on the interface between apparently distinct internal and external realities and likens her writing process to a vision quest in which she attempts to "pull the vision out of" herself. The "trick," she maintains, "is to get back to our origin, to know what it knows or what she knows" (quoted in Eysturoy, 99). According to Allen, this search for "our origin"—an origin she often describes as "our mother," the Laguna Pueblo Thought Woman—does not imply a nostalgic retreat into a mythical, prehistorical past; it is, rather, a political act situated in the present. She believes that "the loss of tradition and memory"—the erasure of tribal, gynocentric belief systems—represents "the root of oppression" (*Sacred Hoop*, 210–13). Thus, Allen describes her attempts to recover the "feminine"[8] in Native traditions as an act of resistance with important implications for all contemporary social actors. As she asserts in her "Introduction" to *The Sacred Hoop*:

> Traditional tribal lifestyles are more often gynocratic than not, and they are never patriarchal. These features make understanding tribal cultures essential to all responsible activists who seek life-affirming social change that can result in a real decrease in human and planetary destruction and in a real increase in quality of life for all inhabitants of the planet earth. (2)

In other words, Allen maintains that the gynocentric values she finds embodied in more traditional Native American mythic systems offer significant models for social, political, and cultural change.

Although I'll explore the problematic nature of Allen's attempt to 'recover' authentic woman-centered, premodern traditions in Chapter 4, I want to point out the transgressive, transformational implications of her claims. To begin with, Allen insists that Native cultures can make significant contributions to contemporary U.S. social systems, thereby challenging stereotypical notions of American Indians as "wild savages" or uncivilized, primitive peoples. Moreover, as she encourages non-Indian social activists to adopt the values she attributes to indigenous North American peoples, she attempts to develop transcultural coalitions. Instead of reinforcing the boundaries between apparently separate cultural groups, she destabilizes them by establishing new commonalities. This mediational tactic can have far-reaching effects on readers. For example, echoing Allen's own assertions in *The Sacred Hoop*, Annette Van Dyke interprets Allen's claims to indicate an underlying commonality between Native Americans and other U.S. peoples. Van Dyke explains that "[b]ecause Indian values and culture have informed generations of Euro-Americans from the beginning of their emigration to America, and the Indian vision of a free and equal society has been the same as that of radical thinkers throughout history, to recover the Indian values is to recover our own most radical values" (341).[9]

By employing gynocentric myths to address culture- and gender-specific issues, Allen synthesizes social critique with the invention of transcultural communities. She draws parallels between the decimation of indigenous North American peoples, the systematic erasure of female-based ritual traditions, and the cross-cultural oppression of women in "Who Is Your Mother? The Red Roots of White Feminism" and "How The West Was Really Won." Similarly, she associates the heterosexism, ethnocentrism, and other distortions of woman-identified Native American myths with contemporary forms of oppression experienced by indigenous peoples and women of all colors in "When Women Throw Down Bundles: Strong Women Make Strong Nations" and "Kochinnenako in the Academe: Three Approaches to Interpreting a Keres Indian Tale." In these essays and others Allen reinterprets central female deities such as the Hopi's Spider Woman, the Navajo's Changing Woman, and the Laguna Pueblo's Thought Woman, making them significant for twentieth-century U.S. feminists of all cultural and ethnic backgrounds. By doing so, she attempts to enlist her readers in new forms of social action. Allen also exposes the ethnocentrism and racism behind stereotypes of Native women as beasts of burden, dumb squaws, or traitors to their own people.

Myth plays an essential role in the personal, social, and metaphysical changes Allen advocates. In "Something Sacred Going on Out There: Myth and Vision in American Indian Literature," she equates myth with metamorphosis by defining it as a unique mode of communication, "a language construct that contains the power to transform something (or someone) from one state or condition to another." Drawing on her knowledge of the oral literary tradition in Native cultures, she denounces western ethnocentric conceptions of mythology as regressive tales, mystifying falsehoods, or lies. She argues that mythic stories embody a highly complex metaphysics, as well as a sophisticated method of perceiving reality—or what she calls "the psychospiritual ordering of nonordinary knowledge"—shared by all human beings, "past, present, and to come" (*Sacred Hoop*, 104). For Allen, myths are "teleological statements" with direct bearing on how people conduct themselves in the physical world. Mythic tales provide human beings with new social roles and new possibilities for action, affirming each person's "most human and ennobling dimensions" (*Sacred Hoop*, 103–6). Whether she incites readers to action, intervenes in stereotypes of Native Americans, or invents alternate meaning systems, Allen's goal is transformation.

Allen attributes myth's transformative power to its liminality—its position betwixt and between societal conventions and established rules of behavior. Like the oral tradition itself, she maintains, mythic tales enable participants to explore "the universe of power and the interface between that universe and the world of mortals" (*Grandmothers*, 21). William Doty makes a similar point in his discussion of mythology's liminal status. He explains that by offering participants an alternate mode of perception, myths enable them to enter "realms other than the workaday." When listeners or readers imaginatively enter these mythic worlds, they can "play out alternate possibilities that would be impossible" in everyday life (130).

According to Allen, however, the alternate possibilities discovered in myth's liminal space *can* be embodied in daily life. She does not separate myth from the everyday world of human actions and social roles. Instead, she builds on the radical holism she finds in traditional Native cosmologies and invents an embodied metaphysics where the spiritual and material dimensions of life form a dynamic unity. Allen provides one of the most extensive discussions of her embodied metaphysics in "The Sacred Hoop: A Contemporary Perspective," where she draws from a wide variety of tribal mythic systems, including Cheyenne, Hopi, and Keres, to distinguish between Judeo-Christian and indigenous American worldviews. Whereas the former defines reality in dualistic, hierarchial terms that segment the world into parts, dividing the natural from the supernatural and the human from the divine, the latter does not:

> American Indian thought makes no such dualistic division, nor does it draw a hard and fast line between what is material and what is spiritual, for it regards the two as different expressions of the same reality, as though life has twin manifestations that are mutually interchangeable, and, in many instances, virtually identical aspects of a reality that is essentially more spirit than matter or, more correctly, that manifests its spirit in a tangible way. (*Sacred Hoop*, 60)

For Allen, then, traditional Native metaphysic systems signify an underlying dynamic intelligence—or what, borrowing from the Hopi, she describes as "what lives and moves and knows" (*Sacred Hoop*, 61)—that manifests itself in interchangeable spiritual and material forms.

Allen associates myth's transformational power with this holistic worldview. She maintains that mythic stories provide human beings with insights that can be translated into concrete action:

> Because of the basic assumption of the wholeness or unity of the universe, our natural and necessary relationship to all life is evident; all phenomena we witness within or "outside" ourselves are, like us, intelligent manifestations of the intelligent universe from which they arise, as do all things of earth and the cosmos beyond. Thunder and rain are specialized aspects of this universe, as is the human race. Consequently, the unity of the whole is preserved and reflected in language, literature, and thought, and arbitrary divisions of the universe into "divine" and "worldly" or "natural" and "unnatural" beings do not occur. (*Sacred Hoop*, 61)

By positing a cosmic intelligence that manifests itself in physical and nonphysical forms, Allen blurs the boundaries between apparently separate categories, such as inside/outside, natural/supernatural, and material/spiritual. Thus, the epistemological process she describes goes beyond conventional western logic to encompass what I call *embodied mythic thinking*: a nondualistic knowledge system in which thoughts, ideas, and beliefs have concrete material effects; and matter itself is a special form of intelligence that human beings can reshape. Like myth—which she describes as "a vehicle, a means of transmitting, of shaping paranormal power and using it to effect desired ends"[10] (*Grandmothers*, 7)—Allen's embodied mythic thinking employs language and narrative to generate personal and social change. In her epistemology, thinking is transformational: Just as Old Spider Woman thought and sang the material world and everything in it into existence, so real-life women—"embodied subjectivities" in Rosi Braidotti's phrase[11]—can, by directing their thought and using words in new ways, alter their physical surroundings as well as themselves. Unlike the radical separation of body and mind and the disembodied subjectivities found in Enlightenment thought systems, Allen's embodied mythic thinking posits an intimate interconnection between the psychic and physical dimensions of life, as well as a reciprocal relation between consciousness and bodily experience. As she asserts in the interview with Caputi, "consciousness has something to do with physicality. The body reflects consciousness" (54).

Allen gives an extensive illustration of her embodied mythic thinking in *Grandmothers of the Light: A Medicine Woman's Sourcebook.* Composed of an introductory section containing her reinterpretation of American Indian's "tribal" gynocentric worldview; her versions of Pueblo, Mayan, Cherokee, and other tribal mythic stories; and a brief overview of ten North American peoples' "mundane and spiritual" pre- and postcolonial histories, *Grandmothers of the Light* represents an astonishing departure from Allen's earlier, more academic work. Based on her belief in thought's "magical" power,[12] and targeted at a wide, multicultural, female audience, this text can easily be viewed as a mainstream self-help book. And indeed, Allen implies that—read from the proper mythic perspective—the Native American myths she retells function as a guidebook for any woman interested in learning to "walk the medicine path, . . . to live and think in ways that are almost but not quite entirely unlike our usual ways of living and thinking" (*Grandmothers*, 3). According to Allen: "The stories are guides and a handbook on how to be spiritual if you want to be spiritual. [*Grandmothers of the Light*] gives you stories you can use like recipes on how to act, what to do. These stories are about being medicine women" (quoted in Caputi, 66).

More specifically, the stories are about women's ability to attain personal and collective agency. As Allen explains in the preface, her stories demonstrate "the great power women have possessed, and how that power when exercised within the life circumstances *common to women everywhere* can reshape (terraform) the earth" (*Grandmothers*, xvi; my emphasis). She implies that by fully participating in the "sacred myths" collected in her anthology, twentieth-century English-speaking women of any ethnicity or cultural background can develop a *spiritual* mode of perception that would empower them to bring about psychic and *material* change.[13]

Given her remarks concerning the appropriation of Native religions and spirituality by non-Native peoples—or what she terms "spiritual genocide,"—Allen's project in *Grandmothers of the Light* is quite remarkable. According to Allen, "The very last thing that the Indian people have is their religion and white people do not get it; it's not theirs" (quoted in Caputi, 50). What, then, do we make of Allen's own attempts in *Grandmothers of the Light* and elsewhere? What distinguishes her revisionist Native spirituality from those versions developed by women who do not identify as "American Indian"? Although it's possible to accuse Allen of appropriating Native traditions, I see a different set of tactics at work. She does not place her non-Indian readers into an authentic American Indian context; instead, she creates a transcultural tribal system that draws from reconstructed Native customs and beliefs. Thus she enacts a process of reciprocal assimilation and develops an innovative form of thinking that relies on yet alters both indigenous and European beliefs.

Revisionist mythmaking plays several interconnected roles in the epistemological process Allen outlines in *Grandmothers of the Light*. By positing a cosmic "feminine" intelligence that manifests itself in mutually interchangeable physical and nonphysical forms, Allen affirms women's intellectual and creative capacities. In her epistemology thinkers are not passive receptacles waiting to be filled by a divine source of guidance; they are, rather, cocreators in an ever-changing reality: "Since all that exists is alive and must change as a basic law of existence, all existence can be manipulated under certain conditions and according to certain laws" (*Grandmothers*, 22). By focusing their thought and channeling its energy in specific ways, she maintains, women can effect material change. Allen stipulates, however, that to utilize this transformative dimension of thought, people brought up under western systems of knowledge must learn to perceive reality mythically. They must forego their usual reliance on empirical knowledge and rational, linear thinking to enter into a liminal space where alterations in consciousness can occur. Allen locates this liminal space within mythic narratives, at the interface between the sacred and mundane worlds invoked by the oral tradition.

By associating thought's transformational power with the oral tradition, Allen constructs a dialogic epistemology that draws on language's performative effects to generate personal and collective change. Based on a relational model requiring both storyteller and listeners to participate, oral narratives reinforce the communal, creative dimensions of thinking. As Richard Bauman notes, this conversational structure can lead to the creation of new social systems. He associates the "distinctive potential" found in oral narratives with a performative, interactive model of language use and explains that verbal art's communal nature potentially establishes a unique bond between performer and audience:

> It is part of the essence of performance that it offers to the participants a special enhancement of experience, bringing with it a heightened intensity of communicative interaction which binds the audience to the performer in a way that is specific to performance as a mode of communication. Through his performance, the performer elicits the participative attention and energy of his audience, and, to the extent that they value his performance, they will allow themselves to be caught up in it. (43)

For Allen as well, oral narratives function simultaneously as the expression and the active fulfillment of social needs. However, by incorporating her transcultural perspective into her description of oral traditions, she attempts to expand conventional anthropological definitions of the term:

> The oral tradition of all tribal people—whether Native American, Hindu, Greek, Celtic, Norse, Samois, Roman, or Papuan—is best seen as psychic literature. It cannot adequately be comprehended except in terms of the universe of power, for it speaks to the relationships among humans, animals of all kingdoms, supernaturals, and deities in a landscape that is subject to influences of thought, intention, will, emotion, and choice. (*Grandmothers*, 22)

This transition from oral to psychic literature underscores the transformational dimensions of Allen's embodied mythic thinking. Just as the mythic stories conveyed in oral narratives utilize participatory, performative speech acts to unify communities and bring about social change, her highly inventive, gynocentric myths in *Grandmothers of the Light* function as "verbal ritualization[s]" designed to transform her readers into "medicine women" (7). She explains that any reader who fully participates in the "ritual-magic-stories . . . moves into mythic space and becomes a voyager in the universe of power" (109).

Allen illustrates one form this verbal ritualization can take in *The Woman Who Owned The Shadows*, where her mixed-blood protagonist, Ephanie Atencio, remains alienated and unable to control her own life until she invents a mythic story that enables her to define herself. Ephanie struggles to understand the ways her identity has been shaped by childhood events, Anglo U.S. culture, Christianity, and Native American traditions. She moves several times, joins a therapy group, attends powwows, studies, and reads, yet physical and psychic health elude her. According to Allen, myth plays a pivotal role in her healing. It is only when Ephanie perceives the parallels between her own childhood and "the lives of the god-woman" that she can begin making sense of her life; she acquires "a point of entry into the ritual patterns of her people" (*Sacred Hoop*, 100). Allen explains that

> Ephanie's search for psychic unity is founded in ritual awareness which, in turn, is embedded within the adaptive and inclusive properties of the oral tradition as well as the ritual of her Guadalupe people.

Ephanie learns to understand how her life and the lives of her mother and grandmother parallel the tribal narratives. As she understands this and as she lives out the implications of that understanding, she is able to accept her place within the ritual tradition of her people and her responsibility to continue it. (*Sacred Hoop*, 100)

Although Allen herself associates Ephanie's "point of entry" with a specific tribal tradition, she constructs ritual and mythic patterns that combine elements from several distinct Native traditions. Indeed, because Ephanie's "people," the Guadalupe indians, have rejected her family for marrying "outside" tribal bloodlines, the story of the Iroquois Sky Woman most closely parallels Ephanie's. Consequently, Ephanie's mythic story does not signal escape into the past; instead, she brings the past into the present and creates a new future for herself. Past, present, and future converge in Ephanie's mythic story, thus illustrating Lorde's contention:

We have to deal with the strengths, the powers, and the weaknesses that come from the past and the intimations of that for a future. Once we stop seeing ourselves as the apex of a triangle and open it into a triad (that we are part of a whole line) it unburdens us of a great responsibility; yet, simultaneously, it makes us even more responsible in a positive sense. (quoted in Hammond, 27)

By placing herself in a woman-focused mythic and historic tradition that she reshapes to meet contemporary individual and communal needs, Ephanie achieves a liberating sense of agency. This insight transforms her; as she finally constructs a set of stories to explain her personal, collective, and mythic pasts, she learns how to live her life in the present:

Knowing that only without interference can the people learn and grow and become what they had within themselves to be. For the measure of her life, of all their lives, was discovering what she, they, were made of. What she, they, could do. And what consequences their doing created, and what they would create of these. (212)

More specifically, Ephanie develops a new self/worldview in which discovery and self-invention work together. She reinterprets the stories of Sky Woman, Kochinnenako, and Spider Woman to rewrite the story of her own life. Like Allen, who creates her own transcultural myths, Ephanie constructs her *own* "point of entry" into a multicultural community that she is partially responsible for creating.[14] Ephanie's story parallels the ongoing story Allen writes in *The Sacred Hoop, Grandmothers of the Light,* and *The Woman Who Owned the Shadows.* As Elizabeth Hanson asserts: "By discovering her own mode of American sacred, Allen creates her own myths; she reinvokes primordial sacred time with a contemporary profane time in order to recover and remake her self. That restored, renewed self suggests in symbolic terms a revival within Native American experience as a whole" (43). Allen takes this revival even further. As she reinterprets Laguna, Iroquois, and other Native mythic traditions, she writes new womanfocused myths that she shares with a multicultural audience.

III   I write the myths in me, the myths I am, the myths I want
       to become.   GLORIA ANZALDÚA

For Gloria Anzaldúa as well, revisionist mythmaking functions creatively, as a vehicle for the construction of individual and collective identities. She compares her task as a writer with that of the Aztec *nahual,* or shaman; she is a "shape-changer" who uses language's performative effects to reinvent herself, her readers, and her world.[15] Both in *Borderlands/La Frontera* and in *Making Face, Making Soul/ Haciendo Caras,* she tells her readers they also have access to this shamanic power: "You are the shaper of your flesh as well as of your soul."[16] This Nahuatl proverb illustrates her conviction that the inner and outer dimensions of life are intimately related. In fact, she implies that "making soul," writing, and building new forms of culture are almost synonymous: Just as the Aztecs believed "the religious, social and aesthetic purposes of art were all intertwined" (*Borderlands,* 66), so self-identified U.S. third world women artists are political activists who synthesize diverse elements to bring about spiritual, psychic, and social change. Anzaldúa makes a similar connection between politics, spirituality, and transformation in her discussion of the private and collective dimensions of artistic production. Because she believes that alterations in the social structure begin at the local level, she maintains that "[i]nherent in the creative act is a spiritual, psychic component— one of spiritual excavation, of (ad)venturing into the inner void, extrapolating meaning from it and sending it out into the world" ("Haciendo caras, una entrada" xxiv).

But what does it mean to undertake a "spiritual excavation"? And how does one extrapolate meaning from an "inner void"? Although Anzaldúa's terminology seems to indicate an inward journey resulting in the discovery of already existing truths, *Borderlands/La Frontera* suggests otherwise. In fact, this work can be read as her *Künstlerroman*, for in chapters such as "How to Tame a Wild Tongue," "*la herencia de Coatlicue/*The Coatlicue State," and "Tlilli, Tlapalli: The Path of the Red and Black Ink," Anzaldúa explores the difficulties she and other mestizas encounter in their efforts to write. Hers are not conventional accounts of an artist's private struggles to achieve self-autonomy. Rather, Anzaldúa's narrative blends autobiography with history and social protest with poetry and myth. Even her style—most notably her abrupt shifts between first- and third-person narration and her code-switching, her transitions from standard to working-class English to Chicano Spanish to Tex-Mex to Nahuatl—indicates the simultaneous growth of an individual and collective identity.[17]

Anzaldúa's discussion of language in "How to Tame a Wild Tongue" illustrates this interconnected development of personal and communal identities. As she describes her search for an adequate means of self-expression, she recounts the centuries of political, religious, and linguistic oppression experienced by Mexican-Indians and other dark-skinned peoples. She draws parallels between the "linguistic terrorism" she encountered as a child growing up in south Texas and the experiences of many other Mexican Americans by summarizing the evolution of Chicano Spanish—its status as an "illegitimate . . . bastard language" and the impact almost three hundred years of Spanish and Anglo colonization made on its development. She associates her own story—her linguistic inadequacy, her subsequent feelings of inferiority and shame, and her growing sense of pride in her "orphan tongue" (58)—with stories of other colonized peoples. Thus she speaks for herself yet offers a model to other self-identified mestizas when she boldly declares, "I will have my voice: Indian, Spanish, white; I will no longer suppress my woman's voice, my sexual voice, my poet's voice" (59).

By interweaving her own story with historical accounts, Anzaldúa rejects western culture's dichotomy between the private and public spheres of identity. As Chandra Mohanty notes, many autobiographies and testimonials produced by self-identified U.S. third world women challenge traditional Eurocentric theories of selfhood and sociality. These narratives do not focus exclusively on the development of a unified, individual self; instead, they suggest "the possibility, indeed the *necessity* of conceptualizing notions of collective selves and consciousness as the political practice of historical memory and writing by women of color and third world women" ("Cartographies," 36; her emphasis). Yet Anzaldúa's challenge to Eurocentric models of subjectivity goes further. Her conception of collective selves includes a spiritual component as well as the sociopolitical and historical elements Mohanty describes. It's this spiritual dimension that makes Anzaldúa's revisionist mythmaking so important to *Borderlands/La Frontera*.

By reclaiming and reinterpreting Coatlicue, Anzaldúa opens a space where historical and contemporary issues of spirituality, gender, culture, sexuality, and class converge: As she traces this Mesoamerican creatrix figure's descent from her pre-Columbian role as the all-encompassing, multi-gendered creator to her current status as the demonic Serpent Woman, she charts the transition to increasingly male-dominated, hierarchical social structures that occurred when the indigenous Indian tribes were conquered by the Aztecs and Spaniards. Stripped of her all-inclusive, cosmic powers, this god/dess[18]—who originally "contained and balanced the dualities of male and female, light and dark, life and death"—was doubly divided, first feminized then split in two: as Tlazolteotl/Coatlicue, she was banished to the underworld where she became the embodiment of darkness, materiality, and female evil; and as Tontantsi/Guadalupe, she was purified, Christianized, "desexed," and transformed into the holy virgin mother (*Borderlands*, 32).

Anzaldúa's description of Coatlicue's mythic fall should not be read as the nostalgic desire to return to some utopian, gynocentric state of epistemological innocence—to what Donna Haraway might skeptically call "a once-upon-a-time wholeness before language, before writing, before Man" (93). Nor does it imply what Judith Butler might describe as a deterministic trajectory, "a necessary and unilinear narrative that culminates in, and thereby justifies, the constitution of the law" (*Gender Trouble*, 36). Instead, Anzaldúa adopts this mythic figure to invent an ethnic-specific yet transcultural symbol that represents the particular forms of oppression experienced by Mexican Americans, as well as those experienced by third world peoples, western women of all colors, homosexuals, and others who differ from the dominant culture's norms. She associates Coatlicue's primary split with the double consciousness she experiences as a dark-skinned woman in contemporary U.S. culture and with the hierarchic division between reason and intuition found in Enlightenment-based knowledge systems. By rewriting Coatlicue's mythic fall, she synthesizes cultural critique with the invention of new ways of thinking. As she remembers and reinterprets Coatlicue, she deconstructs the binary oppositional mode of thought that divided this pre-Christian mythic figure into parts.

Anzaldúa's most extensive revisionist mythmaking occurs in "*la herencia de Coatlicue*," *Borderland/La Frontera*'s central chapter. Cherríe Moraga notes in her review of the book that the chapter is extremely perplexing: "[T]he prose disorients, jumping around from anecdote to philosophy to history to sueño, seldom developing a single topic" (152). It's true—"*la herencia de Coatlicue*" contains abrupt shifts and puzzling metaphors—but I believe an analysis of Anzaldúa's tactics reveals an underlying design. By adopting the figure of Coatlicue to represent what she calls the "Coatlicue state," she creates a metaphor that depicts her own development as an artist and offers her readers an alternative to western culture's emphasis on rational thought. The disorienting prose that Moraga finds so objectionable furthers Anzaldúa's metaphor, for it replicates the fragmentation that characterizes the Coatlicue state.

Just as her Coatlicue myths symbolize both the descent into double consciousness that occurred under colonial rule and the "fusion of opposites" she attempts to bring about in the present (44–47), the Coatlicue state represents periods of intense inner struggle that entail the juxtaposition and transmutation of contrary forces. Anzaldúa associates its earliest stages with the writing blocks that inhibit her creative energy and the resistance to growth that prevents her from achieving new states of awareness. These psychic conflicts are analogous to those she experiences as a Chicana; she explains that internalizing opposing Mexican, Indian, and Anglo worldviews leads to self-division, cultural confusion, and shame. On the one hand, she is drawn to nonrational Native traditions positing the validity of psychic events and the supernatural; on the other hand, she was trained to rely on reason and thus to dismiss all beliefs in nonempirical realities and events as "pagan superstitions." These two modes of perception—"the two eyes in her head, the tongueless magical eye and the loquacious rational eye"—seem to be mutually exclusive; they are separated by "an abyss that no bridge can span" (45).[19]

Anzaldúa's autobiographical description of her first encounter with Coatlicue suggests that this extreme dualism—coupled with subsequent feelings of personal inadequacy and cultural shame—led to the Coatlicue state. Near the chapter's opening she explains that she began menstruating at a very early age and felt that "[h]er body had betrayed her. She could not trust her instincts, her 'horses,' because they stood for her core self, her dark Indian self" (43). Anzaldúa's use of third-person pronouns to describe her own experience replicates the double consciousness that triggers the Coatlicue state, as well as the alienation resulting from this lack of self-trust. To gain distance from physical, emotional, and psychic pain, she began identifying herself—or what she calls "the conscious I"—exclusively with her rational mind. This self-division gave her a false sense of autonomy: Although she could not control her feelings, she could try to ignore them by severing herself from her body and focusing entirely on her conscious thoughts. This self-denial signals entry into the Coatlicue state.

Anzaldúa explains that each time she attempts to ignore her psychic or physical fears, she experiences extreme inner conflict that leads to depression, paralysis, and despair. Resolution cannot occur until she acknowledges and begins to explore these suppressed physical and emotional states. She does not *abandon* the "rational eye" in favor of the "magical eye," the emotional/intuitive mode of perception. Instead, she synthesizes these two ways of thinking and begins using her intellect differently: Rather than struggle to maintain self-control, she consciously struggles to let it go. Thus she opens "Letting Go" by asserting that

> It's not enough
> deciding to open.
>
> You must plunge your fingers
> into your navel, with your two hands
> split open,
> spill out the lizards and horned toads
> the orchids and the sunflowers
> turn the maze inside out.
> Shake it. (*Borderlands*, 164)

As this graphic imagery indicates, the transition from double consciousness to new states of awareness entails intense, often painful, self-reflection: She must "shake," "rip," and "split open" the protective false masks she normally wears. Only then can she truly "let go. / Meet the dragon's open face / and let the terror" engulf her. Although she "dissolve[s]" into her fear, this self-loss is only a temporary stage that initiates transformation; she has "crossed over" and entered an alien place: "All around [her] space. / Alone. With nothingness" and no one to save her, she must rely exclusively on herself. But she has entered a liminal space—a threshold location—where transformations can occur, and the self she relies on has changed: She is evolving new powers ("gills / grow on [her] breasts") that enable her to survive comfortably in this "vast terrain." This poem illustrates transitional states analogous to Allen's perpetual liminality, for it indicates an ongoing process. There is no ultimate arrival, no final truth; "letting go" and "crossing over" are not isolated, discrete events: "It's not enough / letting go twice, three times," or even "a hundred." Previous states of awareness have become "dull, unsatisfactory," and she repeatedly crosses over (*Borderlands*, 164–66).

Similarly, in "Poets have strange eating habits" Anzaldúa uses a series of metaphors such as horseback riding and human sacrifice to depict the poet's tactical use of conscious thought. She likens writing to a wild "nightride" over the edge of a cliff. Rather than surrender the reins and let her instincts or emotions control her, she must "coax and whip" the "balking mare / to the edge." Once again, the decision to "let go" is presented as a deliberate choice, and she asks:

> Should I jump   face tumbling
> down the steps of the temple
> heart offered up to the midnightsun.

Her conscious decision to abandon her conscious self makes change possible. She leaps over the edge and enters into a liminal space:

> Suspended in fluid sky
> I, eagle fetus, live serpent
>   feathers growing out of my skin

Anzaldúa again describes this transition in terms implying perpetual liminality: "Taking the plunge" becomes habitual, as "routine as cleaning [her] teeth," and "jumping off cliffs" turns into "an addiction" (*Borderlands*, 140–41). As the juxtaposition of eagle fetus with live serpent suggests, Anzaldúa, like Allen, associates this perpetual liminality with transformation and self-growth.

The conscious decision to "jump"—which, paradoxically, entails relinquishing conscious control—initiates what I describe as the second major phase of Anzaldúa's Coatlicue state. Anzaldúa's exploration of previously suppressed emotions leads to the development of new ways of thinking that synergistically combine rational and nonrational thought. In "*La conciencia de la mestiza*/Towards a New Consciousness," Anzaldúa describes this synergistic energy as a "third element," which she names "mestiza consciousness." She explains that the new mestiza learns to live with conflicting Indian, Mexican, and Anglo worldviews

> by developing a tolerance for contradictions, a tolerance for ambiguity. . . .She has a plural personality, she operates in a pluralistic mode—nothing is thrust out, the good the bad and the ugly, nothing rejected, nothing abandoned. Not only does she sustain contradictions, she turns the ambivalence into something else. (*Borderlands*, 79)

As in "Letting Go" and "Poets have strange eating habits," Anzaldúa maintains that this complex epistemological process often entails intense emotional and psychic pain as the new mestiza attempts to negotiate contradictory standpoints. It is the willingness to immerse herself in the cultural ambiguities—rather than simply reject or accept them—that enables her new mestiza to begin transforming ambivalence into a new state of awareness:

> This assembly is not one where severed or separated pieces merely come together. Nor is it a balancing of opposing powers. In attempting to work out a synthesis, the self has added a third element which is greater than the sum of its several parts. That third element is a new consciousness—a mestiza consciousness—and though it is a source of intense pain, its energy comes from continual creative motion that keeps breaking down the unitary aspect of each new paradigm. (*Borderlands*, 79–80)

I want to emphasize the fluid, transitional nature of Anzaldúa's mestiza consciousness. As the title of this essay suggests, Anzaldúa is working *toward* a new state of awareness; she maintains that "[a] massive uprooting of dualistic thinking is the *beginning* of a long struggle" (*Borderlands*, 80; my emphasis). She does not offer her readers a systematic, fully structured alternative to existing theories of knowledge. Instead, she provides us with a different perspective, a way to begin inventing new forms of thought. There is no single epistemological destination, no correct form of thinking we must strive to achieve. In a sense, then, Anzaldúa's mestiza consciousness could be described as a variation on Allen's perpetual liminality, for its constant movement between existing categories of meaning defies fixed boundaries and final goals. The energy Anzaldúa describes indicates an ongoing transformational process that breaks down the rigid, unitary elements in any new paradigm it constructs.

In many ways, Anzaldúa's mestiza consciousness resembles what Eve Tavor Bannet describes as the "feminist logic of both/and," a nondual epistemology based on women's experiential knowledge. I want to discuss both the similarities and differences between these two forms of thinking at some length to emphasize the radical potential in Anzaldúa's mestiza consciousness. By incorporating her threshold locations in her theory of mestiza consciousness, Anzaldúa creates an open-ended form of thinking that deconstructs binary structures from within. Whereas Bannet's exclusive focus on gender-based differences prevents her from avoiding binary categories, Anzaldúa's focus is more expansive and encompasses cultural and sexual differences as well.

According to Bannet, Luce Irigaray and other female feminists who focus on sexual difference have begun developing a new epistemological perspective that goes beyond the dominant "male stream" theoretical paradigm. Whereas patriarchal knowledge systems employ an exclusionary either/or logic that valorizes one term of a binary pair, both/and logic implies both the separation and the interdependence of opposites. Bannet argues that

> it is the male tradition which has taught us [women] to think dualistically, to think Either/Or, and to separate things out which for us have long been joined or inseparable. The both/and logic at work in feminist writings deconstructs such dualist thinking by speaking the complexities of women's experience where things which have been represented as opposed are present together, interdependent and intertwined. (3)

Both Anzaldúa's mestiza consciousness and Bannet's feminist logic of both/and open up intermediary spaces where opposites interact. Thus they provide alternatives to conventional forms of opposition and resistance. There are, however, significant differences in the interactional processes each theorist associates with her nondual mode of thought. According to Bannet, when opposites intermingle both terms are altered, yet the dualism itself remains. In the logic of both/and, each half of any binary "can exist both separately and interdependently" (4). Bannet attributes this emphasis on both separation and interdependence to "a politics of coexistence" that eschews critique and other patriarchal forms of opposition (16). Describing the critical, masculinized stance as "the conventional code of our culture" and "a standard weapon in the competition of goods, ideas, men, and interest groups," she maintains that "[w]omen's logic of both/and avoids negation." Bannet's women feminists participate in open-ended exchange—or what she names "a limitless both/and/and"—in which partial transformations and "possible cross-fertilization" can occur (16).

Anzaldúa, on the other hand, calls for more radical transformations. Although she, too, describes binary oppositional strategies as reactionary and ultimately ineffective, she does not reject them. Instead, she suggests they can be tactically useful:

> But it is not enough to stand on the opposite river bank, shouting questions, challenging patriarchal, white conventions. A counterstance locks one into a duel of oppressor and oppressed. . . . The counterstance refutes the dominant culture's views and beliefs, and, for this, it is proudly defiant. . . . Because the counterstance stems from a problem with authority—outer as well as inner—it's a step towards liberation from cultural domination. But it is not a way of life. At some point, on our way to a new consciousness, we will have to leave the opposite bank, the split between the two mortal combatants somehow healed so that we are on both shores at once and, at once, see through serpent and eagle eyes. (*Borderlands*, 78–79)

In this passage, Anzaldúa neither entirely accepts nor entirely rejects binary oppositional forms of resistance. Instead, she suggests that the counterstance between oppressor and oppressed can play a temporary role in liberating forms of thinking.

The distinction between Bannet's feminist logic of both/and and Anzaldúa's more flexible form of both/and thinking is contextual. Because Bannet focuses exclusively on the differences between masculine and feminine knowledge structures, she restricts her analysis to sexist forms of oppression. Anzaldúa develops her theory of mestiza consciousness in the context of multiple, overlapping, and sometimes conflicting oppressions; consequently, she incorporates cultural critique as well as other oppositional tactics into her deconstructive process. Thus in her discussion of sexism within Mexican American communities, Anzaldúa explores the ways gender-based differences intersect with cultural issues. She associates men's misogynist attitudes toward women with their own internalized racism and maintains that neither racism nor sexism can be tolerated:

> As long as woman is put down, the Indian and the Black in all of us is put down. . . . [A]s long as to be a *vieja* is a thing of derision, there can be no real healing of our psyches. We're half-way there—we have such

love of the Mother, the good mother. The first step is to unlearn the *puta/virgen* dichotomy and to see *Coatlapopeuh-Coatlicue* in the Mother, *Guadalupe*. (*Borderlands*, 84)

By exploring multiple systems of difference simultaneously, Anzaldúa combines acceptance with rejection. The both/and thinking employed to unlearn the virgin/whore dichotomy provides only a partial solution; it's the first step in constructing nonexclusionary communities.

Anzaldúa's tactical negations convert Bannet's feminist theoretical perspective into what I call the mestiza logic of both/and/neither/nor, a constantly shifting perspective that deploys various combinations of this fourfold constellation.[20] Take, for example, Anzaldúa's complex use of negations and affirmations in the following passage:

As a *mestiza* I have no country, my homeland cast me out; yet all countries are mine because I am every woman's sister or potential lover. (As a lesbian I have no race, my own people disclaim me; but I am all races because there is the queer of me in all races.) I am cultureless because, as a feminist, I challenge the collective cultural/religious male-derived beliefs of Indo-Hispanics and Anglos; yet I am cultured because I am participating in the creation of yet another culture. (*Borderlands*, 80–81)

Anzaldúa situates herself on a series of overlapping thresholds. As she shifts between ethnic, sexual, gender, and political identities, she simultaneously critiques existing social systems and creates new forms of identity incorporating differently positioned groups.

I want to differentiate between these feminist models of nonbinary thinking with two interrelated examples drawn from Bannet's discussions of revisionist mythmaking and gender. As part of her argument concerning female feminists' use of both/and thinking, Bannet examines the coexistence of opposites found in recent reinterpretations of "the Great Mother Goddess." She explains that

Whereas traditional and Jungian writings dichotomized the Great Mother (into the life-giving earth mother and the terrible devouring mother, for instance), feminists have shown that such dichotomies are only artificially differentiated aspects of the Mother and that they belong together. In feminist writings the Great Mother once again combines opposites: she is both womb and tomb, both beneficent and devouring. (2)

Although Bannet views these female-feminist combinations of opposites as nondualistic, the binary opposition between good and evil remains, only now they are embodied within a single image. I find a similar displacement of binary pairs in Bannet's discussion of male/female gender categories. According to her both/and model, when the two terms interact neither half of the binary stays the same, yet the dual categories themselves are not deconstructed; like other binary pairs, "[t]hey pursue their different paths, interdependent . . . but separate too" (10).

Anzaldúa also writes of male/female oppositions and uses revisionist mythmaking to redefine existing gender categories, but she approaches these dualities somewhat differently. By discussing mother goddesses and gender roles in the context of multiple systems of difference, she begins altering the binary pairs they represent. Take, for example, her description of Coatlicue in *Borderlands/La Frontera*: "Goddess of birth and death, *Coatlicue* gives and takes away life; she is the incarnation of cosmic processes" (46). Anzaldúa maintains that this precolonial mythic figure embodied the dualities of good and evil; however, unlike Bannet's feminists, she does not simply displace these binaries into a single image. Instead, she shifts from binary couples to "cosmic processes," displacing both halves of the binary by relocating them within a broader transitional context. Similarly, by incorporating this mythic figure of life and death into her depiction of the Coatlicue state, Anzaldúa transforms the coexisting binaries into a third element, a new transitional state of consciousness. She explains that "[s]imultaneously, depending on the person, [Coatlicue] represents: duality in life, a synthesis of duality, and a third perspective—something more than mere duality or a synthesis of duality" (46).

Although Anzaldúa does not specify what this "something more" might be, her discussion of Mexican American heterosexism, homophobia, and the *mita' y mita'* illustrates one form this nonbinary excess can take. She explains that "*mita' y mita'*" is a negative Mexicano term used to describe so-called sexual deviants: on the one hand, they are neither male nor female; on the other hand, they are both male and female. They are "half and half, . . . *neither* one *nor* the other but a strange doubling, a deviation of nature that horrified, a work of nature inverted" (*Borderlands*, 19; my emphasis). Whereas Bannet's feminist logic of both/and would allow the male and female energies to coexist both separately and together, Anzaldúa's both/and/neither/nor transitions begin transforming gender categories from within. This "strange doubling" opens a space for the development of threshold genders. Thus in "To live in the Borderlands means you" she depicts the border-dwelling *mita' y mita'* as the

> forerunner of a new race,
> half and half—*both* woman and man, *neither*
> a new gender (*Borderlands*, 194; my emphasis)

This ambivalent figure embodies a revolutionary potential. By simultaneously affirming and denying the *mita' y mita's* relationship to conventional gender roles, Anzaldúa deconstructs the binary gender system that reinforces the "heterosexual matrix."[21]

Anzaldúa's "both"/"neither" thinking, with its simultaneous acceptance and rejection of conventional western gender categories, represents a transformational model of oppositional consciousness that combines both/and assertions with neither/nor critical analyses of interlocking systems of oppression. As Chela Sandoval points out in "U.S. Third World Feminism," Anzaldúa's mestiza consciousness illustrates a distinct, yet generally unnoticed, oppositional theory and praxis, or what she calls "differential consciousness" (16). Sandoval uses this term to describe the nonbinary oppositional tactics effectively deployed by self-identified U.S. third world feminists in their efforts to confront racism, sexism, and other forms of oppression simultaneously. She outlines a "four-phase hegemonic typology" of traditional oppositional ideologies, which she labels "equal rights," "revolutionary," "supremacism," and "separatism," and describes differential consciousness as "a fifth form" that allows social actors to use the four existing oppositional strategies in new ways (3). Sandoval explains that differential consciousness represents a new subjectivity, a political revision that denies any one ideology as the final answer, while instead positing a tactical subjectivity with the capacity to recenter depending upon the kinds of oppression to be confronted. This is what the shift from hegemonic oppositional theory and practice to a U.S. third world theory and method of oppositional consciousness require. (14)

In other words, differential consciousness utilizes conventional oppositional readings of culture, but it does so selectively. When social actors employ differential consciousness, they convert binary forms of opposition into "ideological and *tactical* weaponry" capable of transforming oppressive social and political systems (14; her emphasis). By enabling movement "between and among" traditional binary oppositional strategies, differential consciousness "permits functioning within yet beyond the demands of the dominant ideology" (3).

I want to underscore the transcultural nature of these new ways of thinking. Sandoval associates differential consciousness with U.S. third world feminists, but she maintains that its mobile power is an acquired skill "accessible to all people."[22] Indeed, she believes that Anzaldúa, Lorde, and other twentieth-century, self-identified U.S. third world feminists have demonstrated that differential consciousness provides the most effective form of resistance for all contemporary social actors. Conventional "hegemonic" oppositional theories greatly restrict people's actions by establishing binary categories between dominant and subordinate groups and by demanding an internal consistency that eventually fractures resistance movements from within. Differential consciousness, however, remains flexible and acknowledges its partial containment in existing power structures.

This flexibility plays an important role in Anzaldúa's mestiza logic of both/and/neither/nor. It destabilizes the binary categories between oppressor and oppressed, allowing mobile speaking positions. Consider, for example, the transitions she makes in "La Prieta" or "En Rapport, In Opposition," where she challenges racism, sexism, and homophobia among people of color. Although she acknowledges the ways members of subjugated groups are oppressed, she rejects facile oppositions between oppressor and oppressed. Instead, she holds them accountable for oppressing others. Similarly, in "*la conciencia de la mestiza*" Anzaldúa questions simplistic stereotypes of the notorious "white" male as the ultimate oppressor when she argues that "[l]umping the males who deviate from the general norm with man, the oppressor, is a gross injustice." By distinguishing between the hegemonic masculinity that keeps "[m]en, even more than women, . . . fettered to gender roles" and the alternative masculinities gay men are attempting to develop, she implicitly challenges the binary male/female oppositions so many "*feministas y lesbianas*" automatically adopt (*Borderlands*, 80).

IV   The function of much of what I read about Africa and about Black women, that is meaningful to me, is frequently to keep me from feeling crazy. That's one of the horrors of being locked into the mouth of the dragon: not only do you not have any role models, but there's no resonance for your experience. That's what made me begin to think about writing what I've been writing. We (Black lesbian feminists) have been around a long time. . . . Yes, we do need role models. I wish I'd had some. It would have saved a lot of time.   AUDRE LORDE

Like Allen and Anzaldúa, Audre Lorde draws on nonwestern mythic traditions to develop a performative aesthetics and holistic worldview. As she explains in an interview with Claudia Tate, whereas European-based philosophical systems depict life as a series of conflicts,

> African tradition deals with life as an experience to be lived. In many respects, it is much like the Eastern philosophies in that we see ourselves as a part of a life force; we are joined, for instance, to the air, to the earth. . . . We live in accordance with, in a kind of correspondence with the rest of the world as a whole. And therefore living becomes an experience, rather than a problem, no matter how bad or painful it may be. Change will rise *endemically* from the experience fully lived and responded to. (112; my emphasis)

This statement illustrates the interactional model of identity formation and social change I see in Lorde's revisionist mythmaking. She posits an organic world in which all things are connected and change seems inevitable. Yet she also believes that transformation entails active participation; alterations only occur when the subject fully lives and responds to events. In Lorde's Africanized self/worldview, agency belongs partially to the individual social actor and partially to the external context.

This interactional model of personal and communal change plays an important role in Lorde's theory of writing. She posits an interconnection between her private experiences and an over-arching "life force" that establishes an interpretive context for her life: She can "read" each event that occurs as a lesson to be learned from rather than an obstacle to be overcome. Moreover, by maintaining that each person is similarly connected to this life force, Lorde finds the courage to explore her emotions as she writes and the confidence that this self-exploration leads inevitably to individual and collective change. In *The Cancer Journals*, for example, she uses writing to comprehend more fully the changes that occurred during her first experience with breast cancer. She explains that by exploring the anger, sorrow, and loss she felt after her mastectomy, she hopes to learn "who [she] was and was becoming throughout [that] time" (53). Because she sees her desire to comprehend her battle with cancer as "part of a continuum of women's work," she is confident that her words can be useful to others (17). This belief in a continuum of female experience motivates her writing. Thus she extends her own experience with breast cancer and a mastectomy outward to explore their implications for other women.[23]

Lorde's approach to life is not uniquely African, as she herself points out in the interview with Tate. Yet by attributing her organic worldview to her African ancestry, she underscores the political implications of her work. Her references to African cultural traditions enable her to resist dominant society's attempts to deny the existence of nurturing black communities. Patricia Hill Collins makes a similar point in her discussion of black U.S. women activists' strategies for survival: "By conserving and recreating an Afrocentric worldview, women . . . undermine oppressive institutions by rejecting the anti-

Black and anti-female ideologies they promulgate" (144). I see Lorde's transformational epistemology and her revisionist mythmaking as important dimensions of her own political activism. She incorporates her Afrocentric perspective in both her theory of the erotic and her revisionist myths, reconstructing a tradition that Judeo-Christian belief systems have almost entirely erased.[24]

This erasure parallels the experience of African American women's dehumanization—both by dominant U.S. culture and by their local communities—through a series of overwhelmingly negative stereotypes such as the matriarch, the welfare mother, and the sexually promiscuous woman. As Collins notes, although these doubly oppressive images make each woman "invisible as a fully human individual," many African American women have transformed their status as "invisible Other" into a source of tremendous inner strength (94). By developing a "private, hidden space of . . . consciousness," they have successfully defied externally imposed labels and maintained their authority to define themselves (92–93). Indeed, one of Collins's main arguments throughout *Black Feminist Thought* is the importance of self-definition. She maintains that African American women's ability to create unique self-expressed standpoints, or ways of knowing based on their own experiences as black U.S. women, has been essential to their survival. However, because they often use a doubled consciousness and mask their inward resistance with outward conformity, this inner dimension of their lives has received little recognition (91). As Collins suggestively notes, "far too many black women remain motionless on the outside . . . but inside?" (93; her ellipses).

Lorde uses revisionary mythmaking to *externalize* the "inside ideas" Collins sees as a hallmark of black U.S. women's resistance to dominant groups. As I'll explain in greater detail in Chapter 6, this transition from "inside ideas" to external forms indicates a radical departure from double consciousness and self-protective masks. In Lorde's work, West African mythic images serve as vehicles for establishing new definitions of womanhood, definitions that affirm the culturally specific components of black female identity yet go beyond this affirmation to provide all women with new models of subject formation. By expressing her own self-defined standpoints through the figures of Aido Hwedo, Seboulisa, and other Yoruban/Fon orisha,

Lorde simultaneously critiques previous conceptions of womanhood modeled on European beauty standards and social roles and offers her readers new ways to perceive themselves and new ways to act. It's this trajectory from "inside ideas" to outer forms she refers to in the interview with Tate. She describes her attempt to develop a voice "for as many people . . . who need to hear what I have to say—who need to use what I know." This desire to share her knowledge shapes her writing, and she "speak[s] from the center of consciousness, from the *I am* out to the *we are* and then out to the *we can*" (105; her emphasis).

Lorde's "we" is performative; it enables her to establish a personal/collective voice that she invites her readers to share. Lorde bases this shared sense of identity on an alternate mode of perception, or what she calls the erotic, "the sensual—those physical, emotional, and psychic expressions of what is deepest and strongest and richest within each of us" (*Sister Outsider*, 56). Like Allen's embodied mythic thinking and Anzaldúa's mestiza consciousness, Lorde's "erotic" indicates a nondual transformational epistemology that combines visionary language with cultural critique. Just as Allen's embodied mythic thinking enables her to synthesize spiritual, political, and material issues, Lorde's theory of the erotic enables her to unite alternate ways of thinking with material change: The erotic makes it possible to develop "new ways of understanding our experiences. This is how new visions begin, how we begin to posit a future nourished by the past. This is what I mean by matter following energy, and energy following feeling. Our visions begin with our desires" (quoted in Tate; 107). As this transition from feeling to energy to matter implies, Lorde's invention of the erotic integrates her Afrocentric spirituality with social protest and cultural change. Lorde locates this emotionally charged mode of perception within every individual—"in a deeply female and spiritual plane" (*Sister Outsider*, 53)—yet associates it with externally directed action. She says that

> when we begin to live from within outward, in touch with the power of the erotic within ourselves, and allowing that power to inform and illuminate our actions upon the world around us, then we begin to be responsible to ourselves in the deepest sense. For when we begin to recognize our deepest feelings, we begin to give up, of necessity, being

satisfied with suffering and self-negation, and with the numbness which so often seems like their only alternative in our society. Our acts against oppression become integral with self, motivated and empowered from within. (*Sister Outsider*, 58)

But what does it mean to "recognize our *deepest* feelings"? Or to act in ways that are "motivated and empowered from *within*"? We can interpret these references to inner guidance in two very different ways: Lorde's belief in an internal source of direction can be seen as a positive force for individual and collective change; or, her inward focus can be viewed more suspiciously, as a dangerously naive theory of autonomous self-identity. According to the first, more positive, interpretation, Lorde constructs an agent-centered collective subjectivity and an alternate knowledge system that subverts patriarchally defined concepts by affirming previously denigrated ways of knowing. A number of critics have argued that by locating the erotic within each human being, she encourages readers to reject external social inscriptions and define reality for themselves. Estella Lauter, for example, maintains that Lorde's erotic opens up new areas of human understanding and that by redefining the erotic Lorde "reappropriates the ground of creativity for women of all kinds" (398). Lauter also suggests that this theory of the erotic played a significant role in Lorde's own development as a writer: It gave her confidence in her own creativity and functioned as "a center of energy and authority from which she could break open the constraints imposed by patriarchal society and believe in a new future" (401).

However, when read from a poststructuralist perspective, Lorde's emphasis on the erotic's inward dimensions is quite problematic. According to this view, her valorization of "deep feelings" might imply a dangerously naive theory of subjectivity that overlooks the complex ways our emotional responses and "inner selves" are themselves shaped by external social forces. According to Kathy Ferguson, for instance, Lorde's references to depth and wholeness are highly suspicious, for they rely on biologically based notions of "woman's nature" that reinforce conservative stereotypes of female identity. She holds that Lorde's metaphoric language functions seductively and "privileges without actually making a case for a vision of the subject in which the superficial or imposed 'outside' is contrasted with the authentic and true 'inside' " (109). Thus Lorde overlooks the possibility that this authentic "inside" has been influenced by patriarchal discursive practices. In short, because our desires are themselves shaped by external institutions and standards, we cannot automatically assume that by looking within we attain a more truthful measure. Ferguson reasons that

> Lorde's arguments ride piggyback on the conventional contrast between inner truth and outer deception, between deep feeling and surface behavior. But what is left unsaid, and unsayable, in this familiar formulation? Is the "inside" really so innocent? Perhaps the notion that what is dearest to us is "deep" is the product of a discursive constitution of selfhood that obscures the workings of power on desire. (110)

To be sure, "[c]osmic metaphors of wholeness, depth, and completion" can, as Ferguson asserts, be "hopelessly mired in a serious essentialism" or in a "pervasive metaphysics of presence" that creates an artificial sense of closure and prevents "further questioning" (109–10). Indeed, Lorde's own language (say, for example, her references in *Sister Outsider* to "the lifeforce of women" or to "true knowledge") seems to indicate the "cosmic feminism" Ferguson deplores. However, I am not persuaded that the use of essentializing biologically based metaphors is necessarily hopeless;[25] nor do I believe that Lorde's references to organic wholeness and depth prevent further questioning. Although Lorde does at times employ a rhetoric of authenticity in her discussions of the erotic, her words are performative, not descriptive; they function to generate individual and collective change. Locating the erotic within each social actor invites her audience to adopt an epistemological process that opens additional areas for investigation.

Given the context in which Lorde first presented "Uses of the Erotic"—an academic conference composed primarily of women historians[26]—it's quite possible her words functioned performatively, as tactics designed to bring about specific changes in her audience. By positing a nonrational physical, psychic, and spiritual way of knowing, Lorde subtly criticized her listeners' compliance with the academic community's rigid beliefs concerning objective knowledge, analytical thinking, and empirical evidence. When women, including feminists, entered the academy, they achieved success by adhering to these already existing masculinist standards, and in their efforts to become respected members of the academic community, many women scholars separated their social activism from their intellectual work.[27] In such circumstances, it's unlikely that Lorde's discussion of a highly political, specifically feminine mode of perception uniting emotional responses with externally directed action would prevent further questioning.

Lorde's description of the erotic in the interview with Tate provides a useful gloss on the potentially open-ended nature of her epistemological process:

> Our thoughts are shaped by our tutoring. As black people, we have not been tutored for our benefit, but more often than not, for our detriment. We were tutored to function in a structure that already existed but that does not function for our good. Our feelings are our most genuine paths to knowledge. They are chaotic, sometimes painful, sometimes contradictory, but they come from deep within us. And we must key into those feelings and begin to *extrapolate from them, examine them for new ways of understanding our experiences.* (107; my emphasis)

Despite using metaphors of depth to emphasize the primary role emotions play in her theory of the erotic, Lorde does not make facile distinctions between "inner truths" and "outer deceptions." Nor does she contrast "deep feelings" with "surface behaviors." Instead, she describes a complicated series of layers that take into account the ways social structures, conscious thought, and personal belief have been shaped by oppressive discursive systems. Lorde underscores this complexity by emphasizing the contradictory, ambiguous nature of our "deep feelings."

Although Lorde associates the erotic with emotional, intuitive forms of thinking, she does not reject the usefulness of rational, analytical thought. Like Anzaldúa, she calls for a synergistic fusion of these two modes of perception.[28] And, just as Allen's embodied mythic thinking demonstrates the ongoing development of new states of awareness and alternate sociosymbolic structures, Lorde's erotic indicates directions for further investigation (or as she puts it, "our most genuine paths to knowledge"), not the spontaneous perception of preexisting truths. As Lorde's discussion of overlapping oppressions in a 1978 interview with Karla Hammond confirms, she bases her theory of the erotic on a sophisticated understanding of how power functions at multiple levels simultaneously to construct experience. By exploring our emotional responses to external events, we acquire additional information that enables us to more fully understand the diverse forms of internal and external oppression we experience.

I would suggest, then, that the epistemological process Lorde describes resists closure and indicates a standard of evaluation, a catalyst to further investigation. The metaphors of depth that Ferguson finds so seductive *are* seductive. But if Lorde's metaphors function performatively—to effect change in her audiences—the persuasiveness is a necessary element of her deconstructive tactics. As Barbara Christian asserts, Lorde's theory of the erotic addresses a complex issue, "one of the dilemmas of humanity. How do people get to the point where they not only recognize their own oppression but will initiate the changes necessary to free themselves?" (208). Lorde adopts metaphoric language to stimulate the self-reflection necessary for this recognition. As Ferguson herself points out, the relationship between metaphor and argument is implicitly political. Thus she cautions feminists to "attend as carefully as possible to the consequences of particular tropes and be wary of those that call on widely available cultural reassurances to make their case. Metaphors that are so familiar or legitimate that they sound like simple descriptions are the most powerful and dangerous of all" (108). Yet, by employing familiar metaphors to depict a subversive intellectual capacity that combines analysis of internal and external systems of control with visionary action, Lorde subverts the prevailing paradigms. Or, rather, she turns them against themselves.

Lorde's metaphoric emphasis on "depth" serves another purpose as well. She synthesizes emotional energy with rational thought, implicitly denouncing the Cartesian mind/body dualism, the commonly accepted belief that ideas and insights arise exclusively from mental processes. Like several other contemporary poststructuralists, she replaces this binary knowledge system with an embodied theory of knowing that posits an affective foundation for thought.[29] In Lorde's epistemology "thinking" represents an intimate, indivisible connection between body and mind. Ideas and insights have their source in physical, as well as intellectual, experiences.

Moreover, Lorde's revisionist use of the term "erotic" illustrates the cultural dimensions of her tactics, as well as her willingness to take risks. By selecting this word—with its allusions to sexuality—to describe her theory of knowledge, Lorde challenges one of the most damaging stereotypes applied to African American women: "Jezebel"—the highly sexed, aggressive woman. As Patricia Hill Collins explains, because "efforts to control Black women's sexuality lie at the heart of Black women's oppression," this stereotype has functioned since slavery to dehumanize African American women, erode their sense of agency, and justify their rapes and other forms of sexual violence committed against them (77). Lorde redefines the erotic without denying its sensual embodiedness, and so simultaneously subverts and transforms this oppressive image.

I want to emphasize the significance of Lorde's double gesture. "Jezebel," "Sapphire," and other derogatory images of black women circulating in U.S. culture have been used so extensively during the last three centuries that it is extremely difficult to move beyond them. Hortense Spillers makes a similar point in "Mama's Baby, Papa's Maybe." Speaking of her own experience as a dark-skinned woman in contemporary U.S. culture, she maintains that

> the names by which I am called in the public place render an example of signifying property *plus*. In order for me to speak a truer word concerning myself, I must strip down through layers of attenuated meanings, made an excess in time, over time, assigned by a particular historical order, and there await whatever marvels of my own inventiveness. (65; her emphasis)

These stereotypes are so deeply embedded in U.S. culture that many self-identified black women believe them to be true. As they internalize these negative images they see themselves and other black women as inferior. Instead of forming self-affirmative bonds with black women, they reject them. Thus in "Eye to Eye: Black Women, Hatred, and Anger" Lorde associates the lack of community among black U.S. women with this process of self-denial. She asserts that "[w]e have not been allowed to experience each other freely as Black women in america; we come to each other coated in myths, stereotypes, and expectations from the outside, definitions not our own" (*Sister Outsider*, 169–70).

Revisionist mythmaking plays an important role in Lorde's efforts to replace these externally imposed myths, stereotypes, and expectations with self-affirming images of female identity. By associating herself with Yemanja, Oshun, Oya, and other Yoruban/Fon orisha, she incorporates her erotic way of knowing into a complex self-naming process that combines the rejection of negative images with the invention of new identities. In "The Winds of Orisha" Lorde borrows from Yoruban myth to invent new images of Afrocentric female power. In this poem, she affirms her identity as a black woman warrior poet and lover of women. She creates an extended family of divine female figures, including Yemanja, mother of all the orisha; "the beautiful Oshun," orisha of beauty and love; and "Oya my sister my daughter," orisha of destruction and change. By associating her work as a writer with these West African spiritual forces, Lorde underscores the importance of her task, as well as her own creative power. Like Oya, who "destroys the crust of the tidy beaches," her words are forceful, designed to bring about positive change. And, her description of a sexual interchange between herself and Oshun affirms her own embodied erotic knowledge:

> the beautiful Oshun and I lie down together
> in the heat of her body truth my voice comes stronger.

As this fluid shift from the orisha's "body truth" to the poet's voice suggests, Lorde's revisionary myth enacts the erotic. She depicts an embodied, transformational way of knowing where "[i]mpatient legends speak through [her] flesh / changing this earths formation / spreading" (*Chosen Poems*, 48–49). In "October," for another example, she calls on Seboulisa to infuse her vision with power:

> give me the strength of your eyes
> to remember
> what I have learned
> help me to attend with passion
> these tasks at my hand for doing. (*Chosen Poems*, 108)

By aligning herself with this Dahomean creatrix figure, Lorde synthesizes language with action and memory with myth. She replaces the destructive images of Jezebel with an African-inspired tradition of strong women capable of transforming themselves and their world.

As she reinvents strong female images, Lorde invests her personal insights with collective meaning. Karla Holloway makes a similar point in her study of West African and African American women writers' use of nonwestern mythic material. By incorporating metaphoric ancestral and goddess figures into their work, contemporary black women writers have created both a gendered, culture-specific voice and a "collective consciousness" (30). Mythology serves as a cultural and linguistic bridge: it is "the meta-matrix for all uses of language and the primary source of a literature that would recover a historical voice that is at once sensual, visceral, and real" (107). Women writers of the diaspora cannot physically reclaim African cultures—the "language[s], religion[s], political independence, [and] economic polic[ies]"—lost during the Middle Passage and slavery; however, their revisionary myths enable them "spiritually" to remember and reconstruct their cultural pasts (20).

Although Holloway restricts her analysis to the aesthetic dimensions of fictional narratives, her emphasis on the interconnections between mythic metaphors, voice, and "spiritual memory" (20) has important implications for Lorde's poetry. In *The Black Unicorn*, Lorde's 1978 collection of poems thematically unified by references to Yoruban and Dahomean orisha, mythology serves as the "meta-matrix" for the invention of culture- and gender-specific voices. Lorde reshapes West African myth to define herself as a black woman warrior poet in the first section. Throughout the remaining sections, she enlarges this original definition to encompass a network of mythic, historic, contemporary, and imaginary women—extending from the Yoruban goddesses through the ancient Dahomean Amazons, her family, friends, and female lovers to the "mothers sisters daughters / girls" she has "never been" (48). Because myth provides the basis for "the community's shared meanings [and] interactions with both the spiritual and the physical worlds" (Holloway, 31), Lorde's retrieval of West African mythic figures enables her to intervene in existing systems of gendered meaning. She opens liminal spaces where new possibilities—new definitions of womanhood—can emerge. Thus Pamela Annas locates the poems in *The Black Unicorn* "at the *boundary* between unnaming and renaming" (23–24; my emphasis).

Lorde critiques existing definitions of womanhood and invents new definitions that more accurately reflect her own experiences as a woman of African descent. By replacing European-based, masculine images of a benign Mother Goddess with metaphors of Yoruban/Fon orisha, she simultaneously exposes the limitations in ethnocentric concepts of womanhood and begins constructing an alternate model of female identity formation. The title poem, for example, concludes with her "redefinition of woman, a necessary naming through unnaming, since in Western literature 'woman' has historically meant 'white' " (Annas, 24).

Lorde's revisionist mythmaking challenges other concepts of female identity as well. In "A Woman Speaks" she spurns the image of "womanly" power as a gentle nurturing force and warns readers to "beware [of her] smile": she is "treacherous" and angry, filled with "old magic" and "the noon's new fury" (5–6). And, like Allen's creatrix figures, Lorde's metaphors of Woman combine transcendence with immanence. In "The Women of Dan Dance with Swords in Their Hands," she rejects the dualistic notion of a transcendent deity, a disembodied spiritual power that exists elsewhere, in a nonphysical, supernatural place. She declares that her power, although divine, is not other-worldly: she "did not fall from the sky," nor does she descend gently "like rain." Instead, she "come[s] like a woman"—like an Amazon warrior woman—with a sword in her hand (14–15).

Whether she refers to Amazon women warriors dancing with swords in their hands or to goddesses "bent on destruction by threat" (88), Lorde's mythic figures represent an innovative departure from those reclaimed by a number of Anglo cultural feminists. These differences reflect the specific conditions faced by many contemporary black women and illustrate Holloway's contention that "[t]he African deity imaged in black women's literature is very different from the highly romanticized versions of goddesses rediscovered by Western feminists. The African deity is a figure of both strength and tragedy—like the women whose lives echo hers" (154–55).[30] In both "Dahomey" and "125th Street and Abomey" Lorde revises conventional western images of a bountiful mother goddess with her depiction of Seboulisa, the Dahomean creatrix figure,—"one breast / eaten away by worms of sorrow and loss" (10, 12). Yet these poems are not elegies; they are, rather, assertions of power in the face of tremendous cultural deprivations. Thus in the latter poem she names herself Seboulisa's "severed daughter," underscoring the cultural loss she experienced in the diaspora, the personal loss she experienced after her mastectomy, and her reconstruction of personal, communal, and mythic voices. In a stanza beautifully illustrating Collins's description of black women's "inside ideas," Lorde writes that, although separated by "[h]alf earth and time" from this single-breasted black goddess, her own "dream" reunites them. She has inscribed Seboulisa's image "inside the back of [her] head." This self-inscription demonstrates the performative, transformational dimensions of Lorde's revisionary mythmaking. Through imaginative reconstruction, she adopts the ravaged goddess's name as her own; in so doing, she enacts the erotic, "the woman strength / of tongue" that empowers her work. By redefining herself as Seboulisa, she synthesizes individual and collective concerns; she projects her speech outward and boldly declares that she will laugh "*our* name into echo / all the world shall remember" (12–13; my emphasis).

---

v

> The new mestiza queers have the ability, the flexibility, the amorphous quality of being able to stretch this way and that way. We can add new labels, names and identities as we mix with others.   GLORIA ANZALDÚA

Like these new mestiza queers, Allen, Anzaldúa, and Lorde develop spiritualized epistemologies, differential modes of consciousness enabling them to invent what I describe in the following chapter as transformational identity politics. They translate their liminality—their threshold locations—into their poetry, fiction, and prose, inventing new metaphors of female identity. I want to emphasize the liberating potential in their re-metaphorized images of Woman, which are culturally specific yet nonexclusive. Consider the cross-cultural alliances Lorde attempts to develop in her well-known letter to Mary Daly. She associates MawuLisa, Yemanja, and other orisha with "the

female bonding of African women" yet maintains that these "old traditions of power" are available to "*all women* who do not fear the reve-
lation of connection to themselves" (*Sister Outsider*, 69; my emphasis). She urges Daly to acknowledge this connection, to "re-member
what is dark and ancient and divine within yourself that aids your
speaking" (70). Similarly, Allen and Anzaldúa maintain that their
mythic metaphors of Woman have important implications for any
reader willing to acknowledge their own threshold identities and recognize that, "[a]s outsiders, we need each other for support and connection and all the other necessities of living on the borders" (70).[31]

By rewriting Native American, Mexican Indian, and West African
myth and inventing nondual ways of knowing, Allen, Anzaldúa, and
Lorde destabilize monolithic conceptions of female identity and create
flexible speaking subjects that reflect the voices of numerous groups.
As I argue in the following chapter, it is the refusal to acknowledge and
accept differences—rather than the reverse—that erects what Lorde
describes as "the wall that separates / our sameness" (*Chosen Poems*,
109) and prevents open dialogue between differently situated readers.
Although they acknowledge the walls that make each person or group
distinct, they do not present these markers as impenetrable barriers
separating people of diverse gendered, ethnic, sexual, or economic
backgrounds. Instead, they position themselves on these boundaries
and transform walls into thresholds. Like Anzaldúa, Lorde and Allen
choose to live "life on the borders, life in the shadows" (*Borderlands*,
87).

❯ 3   Transformational Identity Politics
Seeing "Through the Eyes of the Other"

---

*We have been organizing on the basis of identity, around
immutable attributes of gender, race and class for a long time,
and it doesn't seem to have worked.*   JUNE JORDAN

*I am who I am, doing what I came to do, acting upon you like
a drug or a chisel, to remind you of your me-ness, as I discover
you in myself.*   AUDRE LORDE

The word "sisterhood," when used in the context of
contemporary U.S. feminist movement,[1] is an extremely problematic
term. During the last two or three decades, U.S. feminists have become
increasingly aware of the many differences among women, differences
that make it difficult, if not impossible, to generalize concerning the
commonalities of "woman's" experience. Perhaps there are no commonalities. Perhaps, as Donna Haraway suggests, "[t]here is nothing
about being female that naturally binds women. There is not even
such a state as 'being' female, itself a highly complex category" (72).[2]

This challenge to monolithic conceptions of female identity has
been forcefully articulated by self-identified U.S. "radical women of
color."[3] Although they often acknowledge that all women are oppressed in male-dominated societies, they reject the assumption that
this gender-based oppression makes all women's experience identical.
By underscoring the many cultural, economic, ethnic, linguistic, physical, and sexual differences that shape each woman's experiences in
contemporary U.S. culture, self-identified feminists of color have
played a major role in demonstrating the problematic nature of the
pseudo-universal category "woman."[4]

This increased attention to the many differences among women marks a critical juncture in feminist theory, one that can lead either to further division as various groups splinter off and establish their own definitions of "woman" or to the creation of bonds between women of dissimilar backgrounds.[5] But to create these new bonds, we must go beyond self/other dichotomies and develop flexible forms of intersubjective dialogue enabling people of all genders, colors, classes, and sexual experiences to speak with—rather than for—each other. Thus Norma Alarcón cites the " 'Self/Other' theme" she finds deeply embedded in a number of Anglo feminists' works and insists that although *This Bridge Called My Back: Writings By Radical Women of Color* (the earliest anthology by self-identified U.S. third world feminists to receive a wide readership) has influenced individual lives, it has not brought about structural change. As I mentioned in Chapter 1, she argues that many Euro-American feminists have begun acknowledging that gender is socially constructed in relation to ethnicity, class, and other axes of difference, but this acknowledgment "has yet to effect a newer discourse" (358). Nor can it, until these feminists deconstruct female/male binary oppositions and recognize women of color as "highly complex" subjects in their own discourses.

In many ways, I agree with Alarcón's assessment of contemporary "white" feminism. The reluctance to explore how differences among women have been "purposefully constituted for the purpose of domination or exclusion" has greatly limited descriptions of feminist consciousness (359). However, I'm concerned by the contrasts she makes between "white women" and "women of color." Indeed, my initial reaction upon reading her critique was to draw on the African blood in my own heritage, disavow my Irish ancestry, and entirely separate myself from the "white" feminists she describes. But to do so is ineffective. It leaves the binary opposition between "white" feminists and "feminists of color" undisturbed. Just as male/female oppositional thinking "does not help us envision a world beyond binary restrictions" (362), rigid dichotomies between U.S. "third world feminists" and " 'white' feminists" prevent us from establishing dialogues among people of *all* colors.

Moreover, another variation of the self/other theme Alarcón finds in the works of "white" feminists can also be found in writings by self-identified feminists of color. Most U.S. women have internalized the dominant culture's binary thinking so extensively that, as Anzaldúa points out, many racially mixed feminists have begun "making our own people the Other" by adopting standards of "racial purity" and "ethnic superiority" that prevent us from accepting women whose lifestyles, ideologies, or even skin color differ from our own ("En Rapport," 143). Thus she challenges her readers to begin "identifying emotionally with a cultural alterity, with the Other" but stipulates that in order to do so we must "leave the permanent boundaries of a fixed self . . . and see . . . through the eyes of the Other" (145).

Although Anzaldúa's remarks in "En Rapport" are directed toward self-identified U.S. third world feminists, I believe her analysis of the barriers preventing women of color from establishing effective alliances has important implications for developing transformational identity politics, or the construction of differentially situated subjectivities that, deployed tactically, deconstruct self/other dichotomies from within. I would argue that Anzaldúa's invitation to "see . . . through the eyes of the Other" has important implications for *all* feminists, whether we identify as female or male; dark- or light-skinned; lesbian, gay, bisexual, heterosexual, or queer; poor, working-, middle-, or upper-class. But how do we learn to see through the eyes of the other? And what does this "seeing" entail?

This new form of vision calls for nondual configurations of identity that destabilize self/other dichotomies by challenging traditional humanist notions of a unitary self as well as the various forms it assumes in conventional identity politics.[6] All too often we view ourselves as isolated individuals with distinct boundaries separating us from others. Although we often believe these identities to be marked by gender, sexuality, and ethnicity, we generally assume these components are permanent, unchanging attributes. However, this conception of autonomous, self-contained identities is far less accurate than it seems. As Stuart Hall asserts, "[i]dentity is not as transparent or unproblematic as we think. Perhaps instead of thinking of identity as an already accomplished fact . . . we should think, instead, of *identity as a 'production,'* which is never complete, always in process, and always constituted within, not outside, representation" (222; my emphasis).

If, as Hall suggests, identity is always in process, then we are always open to further change. Anzaldúa makes a similar point in "To(o) Queer the Writer" where she insists that identity cannot be reduced to a compilation of discrete categories or to

> a bunch of little cubbyholes stuffed respectively with intellect, race, sex, class, vocation, gender. Identity flows between, over, aspects of a person. Identity is a river, a process. Contained within the river is its identity, and it needs to flow, to change to stay a river. (252–53)

Like Allen's theory of perpetual liminality, this view of identity as a fluid ongoing process encourages transformation. In this chapter I want to explore these transformational possibilities. My argument has two parts. First, continuing through an analysis of the various ways Allen, Anzaldúa, and Lorde deploy their personal experiences, I suggest that a model of nonbinary subject formation offers at least one alternative to the self/other dichotomies inhibiting contemporary feminist discourse. Second, I argue that their tactical shifts between apparently separate groups reveal the limitations of conventional identity politics and give social actors another option—transformational identity politics.

II

> You say my name is ambivalence? Think of me as Shiva, a many-armed and legged body with one foot on brown soil, one on white, one in straight society, one in the gay world, the man's world, the women's, one limb in the literary world, another in the working class, the socialist, and the occult worlds. A sort of spider woman hanging by one thin strand of web.   GLORIA ANZALDÚA

How does writing influence identity formation? If, as I've suggested in the previous chapters, language can have performative effects, self-writing becomes self-creation. In the epigraph to this section Anzaldúa uses the written word to position herself on the thresholds— simultaneously inside and outside a number of what seem to be mutually exclusive groups where identity is based on ethnicity, gender, sexuality, and beliefs. In the process, she creates a pluralized self-identity capable of interacting with many worlds. Similar comments can be made about Allen and Lorde as well. All three writers develop flexible models of subject positioning that enable them to establish points of similarity and difference among readers of diverse backgrounds. Instead of limiting herself to a single-voiced discourse on topics such as homophobia, racism, or sexism, each woman draws from her personal experiences and assumes complex speaking positions enabling her to explore issues crossing ethnic, sexual, national, and economic lines. This flexibility provides an important challenge to readers' generally more stable, essentialized notions of subjectivity and selfhood. As Trinh Minh-ha asserts,

> Essential difference allows those who rely on it to rest reassuringly on its gamut of fixed notions. Any mutation in identity, in essence, in regularity, and even in physical place poses a problem, if not a threat, in terms of classification and control. If you can't locate the other, how can you locate your-self? (*Moon*, 73)

Essential difference—or the belief in stable unchanging identities and permanent divisions between ourselves and others—provides a certain level of comfort and control. There is no need for self-reflection or change; we can rest assured in our sense of an authentic core self.

In various ways, and to varying degrees, Allen, Anzaldúa, and Lorde reject this belief in essential difference. By destabilizing all such beliefs in authenticity based in naturalized concepts of cultural, ethnic, gender, and sexual identity, their writings demonstrate the limitations of any fixed sociocultural inscription. They disrupt the restrictive networks of classification that inscribe us as racialized, engendered subjects, thus opening up psychic spaces where alterations in consciousness can occur. As they translate their threshold identities into their writings, they engage in what I call tactical renaming, or the construction of differentially situated subjectivities that, deployed contextually, deconstruct oppositional categories from within.[7] They take on multiple conflicts simultaneously, enacting a series of displacements that confound preestablished self/other divisions.

Lorde's intricate self-descriptions in *Sister Outsider* illustrate one form this tactical renaming process can take. As Gloria Hull notes, even the title indicates Lorde's decision to adopt "the extremes of a difficult identity" (154). Hull explains that

> we tend to read the two terms with a diacritical slash between them—
> in an attempt to make some separate, though conjoining, space. But
> Lorde has placed herself on that line between the either/or and
> both/and of "sister outsider"—and then erased her chance for rest or
> mediation. However, the charged field between the two energies re-
> mains strong, constantly suggested by the frequency with which
> edges, lines, borders, margins, boundaries, and the like appear as sig-
> nificant figures in her work. (154)

Like Anzaldúa, Lorde employs both/and/neither/nor thinking to situate herself in a liminal space that simultaneously divides and unites
sisters with outsiders. By rejecting simplistic identities and equally
simplistic solutions to the complex problems facing contemporary
social actors, she develops a diverse set of sometimes overlapping
speaking positions that she deploys differentially. In some pieces, such
as "Uses of the Erotic" and "Poetry is Not a Luxury," she focuses
almost exclusively on her gendered identity and speaks as a woman to
all women. In other essays, like "The Transformation of Silence into
Language and Action," she begins by foregrounding her ethnic and
sexual identity; she defines herself as a "Black lesbian poet" yet goes on
to draw parallels between her situation and those of heterosexually
identified black women and women of all colors as she urges her
audience to express their silent fears and open new dialogues with
each other.

Lorde's shifting self-definitions throughout *Sister Outsider* illustrate a sophisticated, use of identity politics. Indeed, I would suggest
that she uses potentially essentializing self-definitions tactically. As
Hull points out,

> Lorde's seemingly essentialist definitions of herself as a black/lesbian/
> mother/woman are not simple, fixed terms. Rather, they represent
> her ceaseless negotiations of a positionality from which she can speak.
> Almost as soon as she achieves a place of connection, she becomes
> uneasy at the comfortableness (which is, to her, a signal that some-
> thing critical is being glossed over) and proceeds to rub athwart the

smooth grain to find the roughness and the slant she needs to maintain her difference-defined, complexly constructed self. (155–56)

While I agree with Hull's assertion that Lorde defines herself
through her differences from others, I think it's also important to
note the way she utilizes these differences to generate commonalities
among differently situated readers. Consider her use of shifting subject positions in "Age, Race, Class, and Sex: Women Redefining Difference" to deconstruct the binary opposition between oppressor and
oppressed. In the opening paragraphs she describes herself as a "forty-
nine-year-old Black lesbian feminist socialist mother of two, including
one boy, and a member of an inter-racial couple" and asserts that this
diverse set of labels ensures her membership in a number of subjugated groups (*Sister Outsider*, 120). Although she draws on her own
experiences of oppression to discuss racism, heterosexism, and other
forms of discrimination, she does not become entrenched in any single position. Nor does she use her personal experiences to adopt a
superior stance, a type of epistemic privilege based on her marginaliz-
ation in U.S. culture. Instead, Lorde extends her experiences outward
to include anyone excluded from this country's "mythical norm":

> Institutionalized rejection of difference is an absolute necessity in a
> profit economy which needs outsiders as surplus people. As members
> of such an economy, we have *all* been programmed to respond to the
> human differences between us with fear and loathing and to handle
> that difference in one of three ways: ignoring it, and if that is not pos-
> sible, copy it if we think it is dominant, or destroy it if we think it is
> subordinate. (*Sister Outsider*, 115)

As she explores these socially enforced negative reactions to human
differences, Lorde makes her audience aware of an underlying commonality. Thus she blurs the boundary between oppressors and oppressed by locating herself, as well as her audience, in both groups.

Lorde's shifts are tactical and illustrate Trinh's contention that in
order to resist self-reification and closure, "[t]he challenge has to be
taken up every time a positioning occurs: for just as one must situate
oneself (in terms of ethnicity, class, gender, difference), one also re-

fuses to be confined to that location" (*Moon*, 229–30). Throughout her work Lorde positions herself in response to the specific audience she addresses and the particular social issues she confronts. By rejecting simplistic labels and "allowing power . . . to flow back and forth freely through all [her] different selves" (*Sister Outsider*, 120–21), she demonstrates that the recognition of differences can serve to unite, rather than divide, apparently dissimilar groups.

Although Allen's tactical renaming takes different forms, she too draws from her diverse personal experiences to explore complex sets of ethnic-, sexual-, and gender-related issues. In essays such as "Where I Come from Is Like This" and "Something Sacred Going on Out There" Allen utilizes her formal training as a literary scholar, her personal knowledge of Laguna traditions, and her experiences as a lesbian-feminist to examine the ways Eurocentric masculinist knowledge systems have distorted the histories of Native American and other non-European gynocentric cultures.

There is, however, a significant difference between Allen's politics of enunciation and Lorde's. Whereas Lorde draws on different elements of her experience and positions herself in a variety of ways, Allen generally draws from her Native ancestry and writes from the perspective of a halfbreed. As Elizabeth Hanson puts it, "Allen remains for herself and for us (*at least as she wishes us to know her*) the quintessential 'breed' " (15; my emphasis). Yet Allen's "breed" identity is no more static than Lorde's shifting positionality. As Hanson's comment indicates, Allen's renaming process is performative, not descriptive. Allen is not reconstructing a monolithic, gendered, ethnic-specific standpoint; instead, she redefines herself and other mixed-blood peoples in ways that challenge readers to rethink existing identity categories. At times, for example, Allen uses her "breed" identity to position herself at the juncture of diverse traditions. By so doing, she emphasizes the transmutational dimensions of her work. She explains in an interview that "half-breeds" function as catalysts to cultural change:

> We have a mediational capacity that is not possessed by either of the sides. What we are able to do is bridge variant realities because everybody is pissed off at us and we are pissed off at ourselves. What we are

able to do is move from flower to flower, so to speak, and get the pol-
len moved around among each of our traditions. Then we can plant
back into them. (quoted in Bruchac, 19)

At other times Allen destabilizes her own speaking position as well as
conventional notions of a unitary self by emphasizing the multiplicity
contained within this "breed" identity; she is a "multicultural event,"[8]
the "confluence"[9] of numerous, sometimes conflicting identities. As
she explains in another interview,

I am Lebanese-American, I am Indian, I am a breed, and I am New
Mexican and they have a lot to do with how I act and what I think and
how I interpret things. I was raised in a family and in a world that was
multicultural, multiethnic, multireligious, and multilinguistic, with a
number of social classes involved. . . . And then I have a kind of over-
laying or underlaying American or Anglo culture that I mostly picked
up in school. It is all me. It sometimes comes into conflict with itself,
but it is all me. (quoted in Eysturoy, 103)

Given this complex background it is, perhaps, not surprising that
Allen claims her Laguna/Sioux/Lebanese/Scottish/German ancestry
makes her "split, not in two but in twenty, and never . . . able to reconcile all the *places* that [she is]" (quoted in Bruchac, 18; my emphasis).

By describing herself as the convergence of apparently irreconcil-
able places, Allen distinguishes her ethnicity from more traditional
Native American views, which often associate place with a unified
location. As Arnold Krupat points out, the association of identity with
place is a common theme in contemporary Native American writings.
He asserts that "[t]he sense of rootedness seems extraordinarily per-
sistent in Native American peoples today, so there's really no place to
go, no matter where one travels for one purpose or another" (114).
But there is neither a single geographic location nor an internal sense
of located space capable of fully representing Allen's 'roots.' She is a
subject-in-process, always open to further change. One of the most
startling examples of this radical openness to additional transformation can be found in "Glastonbury Experience," where Allen describes
her travels to Glastonbury, a small southwestern town in England. In
this British landscape, so far from her southwestern U.S. birthplace—

or 'roots,'—Allen creates a new sense of home and an expanded context for self-definition: "I understood myself, my loves and longings, in ways I never would have otherwise, and more, I understood the dramatic, tragic, and very funny history of English-Native American history. It's not what anyone thinks, or writes, or says" (84).

The title character in Allen's novel, *The Woman Who Owned the Shadows*, reflects a similar multiplicity. A mixed-blood cut off from tribal traditions and educated at Catholic schools, Ephanie must painfully discover the ways her identity has been shaped by Native American, Mexican, and Anglo cultures. Like shadows, which are neither light nor dark but rather involve the interplay of both (*Sacred Hoop*, 244), Ephanie represents the mingling of apparent opposites. Although her mixed heritage prevents her from aligning herself with a single group, she uses it to deconstruct restrictive notions of cultural/ethnic purity and mediate between diverse peoples. As Allen notes, at the novel's conclusion Ephanie

> goes back to teach white people. So her resolution is that this is not about race; this is about vision. The people who live on this continent are Indians, that is to say, they live on the Indian continent, and what we must do is teach them how to live here. We tried and they kept killing us. That was then; but now maybe there are people here, lots of them, who are ready. (quoted in Eysturoy, 105)

I've quoted this remarkable passage at length because it provides an important key to understanding the performative dimensions of Allen's tactical renaming processes. Like Ephanie, Allen teaches "white people" how to live like Indians. Yet Allen takes this educational process further, for her lessons are designed to teach North American "white people" that they *are* "Indians." Throughout her scholarly writings, Allen draws on her mixed-blood heritage to authorize her position as "spokesperson within the scholarly community" (Hanson, 14). Consequently, readers generally assume she functions as a Native informer who simply reveals previously hidden aspects of American Indian life. Elizabeth Hanson, for example, relies heavily on Allen's biography. She associates Allen's work as a literary scholar with her mixed-blood heritage and contends that her literary criticism reflects "the alienation inherent in her self-portrait; both race and gender create dilemmas she seeks to explain to herself and her readers" (10). And indeed, Allen herself often reinforces this interpretation by presenting her literary and cultural criticism under the guise of *explaining* authentic Native American traditions to "outsiders." Yet she is at least equally concerned with developing new woman-centered "Native American" traditions capable of transforming her readers as well as herself. In other words, Allen does not simply attempt to explicate the intersection of gender and ethnicity in Native texts. Instead, she uses her gendered, ethnic identity performatively to alter her readers' self-perceptions, as well as their views of tribal cultures.

As coeditor of *This Bridge Called My Back* and editor of *Making Face, Making Soul/Haciendo Caras*, Anzaldúa is equally concerned with developing transformative dialogues between people of diverse backgrounds. She, too, maintains a "shifting and multiple identity" and speaks as "sister" and "outsider" by locating herself at the interface of Mexican, *indio*, Spanish, and Anglo cultures. In her poetry and prose she draws connections between diverse peoples and addresses issues including the dominant U.S. culture's oppression of people of color; Mexican Americans' hatred of their own Indian blood; sexism's harmful effects on *all* women; homophobia; and the disputes between self-identified Euro-American and U.S. third world feminists. Like Lorde, she converts simplistic binarisms between dominant and subordinate groups into complex interconnecting fields. Within the space of a single passage in *Borderlands/La Frontera*, she identifies herself with both the "oppressed" and the "oppressors"—with the "Chicano, *indio*, American Indian, *mojado*, *mexicano*, immigrant Latino, Anglo in power, working-class Anglo, Black, [and] Asian" as she describes the psychic struggles facing all twentieth-century peoples and insists that "[w]e need to meet on a broader communal ground" (87).

Anzaldúa's call for a broader communal ground, as well as her shifting, threshold identifications throughout *Borderlands/La Frontera*, vividly illustrate what she describes as the "new *mestiza* queers." As she explains in "To(o) Queer the Writer," "[t]he new *mestiza* queers have the ability, the flexibility, the amorphous quality of being able to stretch this way and that way. We can add new labels, names and identities as we mix with others" (249). Anzaldúa's new *mestiza* represents a hybrid, a complex mixed-breed who cannot be reduced to a single category nor rigidly classified according to a specific set of traits.[10] The product of two or more cultures—each with its own value system—the mestiza is a liminal figure existing in a "state of perpetual transition," attempting to reconcile, rather than reject, the many voices in her head. Indeed, Anzaldúa's new mestiza enacts Allen's theory of perpetual liminality. The continuous transitions she experiences as she synthesizes conflicting worldviews enable her to redefine herself and her world.

Perhaps not surprisingly, given Anzaldúa's emphasis on transition and change, her theory of *mestizaje* represents at least two significant departures from its earlier usage. First, by feminizing the term *mestizo*, her mestiza provides an important intervention into twentieth-century Chicano literary and theoretical movements that have been dominated by male-centered issues.[11] Second, by extending conventional definitions of the mestizo as a member of a specific biologically based cultural group to encompass the experiences of non-Mexican, non-Indian peoples as well, Anzaldúa de-essentializes and pluralizes culturally specific notions of identity. As Marcos Sanchez-Tranquilino points out, Anzaldúa's theory of mestizaje represents an innovative departure from earlier views:

> Her interpretation goes beyond the traditional concept of *mestizaje*. For Anzaldúa, that concept cannot ever again be thought of as a simple mixing of blood or cultures, but rather that what has always been in effect a mixing of identities many times over—beyond the old dualities be they gender, historical, economic, or cultural, etc. (568)

Anzaldúa rejects essentialized conceptions of identity that rely on blood quantum, physical appearance, or other biologically based components and constructs a transcultural, transgendered theory of hybrid subjectivities.

Anzaldúa explores the transformational process necessary for the development of mestiza subjectivity in *Borderlands/La Frontera*, where she emphasizes the difficulties this intermixing entails. The mestiza is torn within and without by conflicting worldviews. The Chicana, for example, has internalized a three-way battle where "commonly held beliefs of the white culture attack commonly held beliefs of the Mexican culture, and both attack commonly held beliefs of the indigenous culture" (78). Yet she cannot just reject these contradictory beliefs; she must learn to live with and transform the contradictions. Although she attempts to suppress her anger and deny her guilt, such feelings—along with isolation, shame, confusion, and fear—are familiar features in Anzaldúa's Borderlands. Indeed, she insists that such emotions must be explored, for they function as catalysts to alterations in consciousness. She explains in the introduction to *Making Face, Making Soul/Haciendo Caras*: "The intellect needs the guts and adrenaline that horrific suffering and anger . . . catapult us into. Only when all the charged feelings are unearthed can we get down to 'the work,' *la tarea, nuestro trabajo*—changing culture and all its oppressive interlocking machinations" (xviii).

Anzaldúa employs her mestiza logic of both/and/neither/nor as she attempts to alter oppressive social structures. She stipulates that in order to create new models of identity and nonhierarchical sociopolitical systems, the old forms cannot remain; they must be examined, evaluated, and transformed. As in Lorde's theory of the erotic, emotional energy plays a significant role in this process. By acknowledging the rage and fully exploring the pain and self-loathing, Anzaldúa's mestiza discovers how extensively she has internalized dominant U.S. cultural values. Only then can she undertake the deconstructive process capable of altering the Eurocentric, masculinist self/worldview.

Allen describes a similar combination of evaluation, selective rejection, and change in her fiction and poetry. In "New Birth," a poem filled with images of "war," "carnage," "anguish," and "tears," she writes that such "destruction" was necessary, for it

cleared away the useless
the senseless
the never-to-be-born
the stillborn
the walking dead
making clear
the way
for cleansing winds to blow. (*Skin and Bones*, 68–69)

Similarly, in "Recuerdo" Allen sorts through fragmented memories of personal, mythic, and collective pasts as she seeks an only partially remembered meaning—"that significance once heard and nearly lost." Rather than reject the physical and emotional fears these elusive memories evoke, she strives to establish a new relationship between past, present, and future. She confronts her fragmented memories, hoping to "find that exact hollow / where terror and comfort meet" (*Shadow Country*, 94–95).

Allen depicts this confrontational process again in *The Woman Who Owned the Shadows*, where Ephanie must fully experience her feelings of self-loathing, alienation, and guilt in order to change. The conflicting worldviews she has internalized led to fragmentation, and throughout almost the entire novel Ephanie undergoes a series of intense inner struggles as she tries to escape or transcend the "lifelong duality, dichotomy, twinning of her own self with a monstrous other" (133). It's not until she accepts this "monstrous other" as a part of herself and becomes immersed in the isolation she fears that she can reject this "lifelong duality" and develop a flexible, nondualistic self/ worldview.

Like Allen and Anzaldúa, Lorde acknowledges the self-destructive emotional effects of internalized oppression and insists that such feelings must be recognized and expressed. In "Eye to Eye: Black Women, Hatred, and Anger," she describes the conflicting values she was exposed to as a black girl growing up in "white," male-identified, heterosexist, urban U.S. culture and explains that, years later, she must still confront and work through "nightmare images" fighting within. In the essay she deconstructs self/other binaries by exploring how self-hatred is denied, externalized, and projected onto others. She insists that self-oppression leads to the oppression of others and locates the roots of black U.S. women's fury in their acceptance of the dualistic self/worldview that equates blackness and femaleness with inferiority. "[T]utored by hate" to distrust both their color and their sex, the women Lorde describes turn their self-loathing outward and reject their black sisters.[12] She urges black women to explore their self-hatred and recognize its source in the dominant culture's belief systems; only then can they work to reject such self-destructive values and begin channeling their anger into resistance and social change (*Sister Outsider*, 145–75).

Similarly, in "Between Ourselves" Lorde unsettles simplistic self/

other dichotomies, as well as the dogma of an "easy blackness" often found in nationalist thinking. As in the essays collected in *Sister Outsider*, she destabilizes facile oppositions between oppressor and oppressed by demonstrating their complex interconnections. In the following stanza, for example, she explores the role people from Africa played in their own enslavement:

> Under the sun on the shores of Elmina
> a black man sold the woman who carried
> my grandmother in her belly
> he was paid with bright yellow coin
> that shone in the evening sun
> and in the faces of her sons and daughters.
> When I see that brother behind my eyes
> his irises are bloodless and without color
> his tongue clicks like yellow coins
> tossed up on this shore
> where we share the same corner
> of an alien and corrupted heaven
> and whenever I try to eat
> the words
> of easy blackness as salvation
> I taste the color
> of my grandmother's first betrayal. (*Black Unicorn*, 112–13)

In Lorde's account, oppressed and oppressor are the same color, perhaps even from the same regional or ethnic group. By emphasizing the similarities between betrayer and betrayed, she undermines binary oppositions based on a rhetoric of authenticity. Again, Lorde does not valorize her own perspective with claims to epistemic privilege based on the multiple forms of oppression she experiences as a black woman. Although she begins by identifying herself with the woman sold into slavery by another African, this association is not static. She shifts locations and identifies herself with the "brother" oppressor as well. Rather than speak from a position of moral authority or complete victimhood, she oscillates between betrayer and betrayed, between self and other. This oscillation illustrates the challenge to her readers near the poem's conclusion when she declares that "we are all children of Eshu / god of chance and the unpredictable / and we each wear many changes / inside of our skin." Until we recognize these many faces as our own and "stop killing / the other / in ourselves / the self that we hate in others," we remain blinded by our own self-denial (*Black Unicorn*, 114).

But how do we discover the "other" in ourselves? And what can it mean to have "many changes" within "our skin"? In psychoanalytic terms, her challenge to recognize the other in ourselves entails a reversal and subsequent reincorporation of the displaced projections that occur during ego-splitting. I describe this nonbinary subject formation as re(con)ceiving the other to emphasize its twofold nature: We redefine the other as a part of ourselves by acknowledging our own otherness. Although Alicia Ostriker notes a similar process in the works of many contemporary U.S. women poets, there are several differences between the reintegration she describes and the re(con)ceived otherness I find in Lorde's work. As Ostriker suggests, women's attempts to reconcile "internal antinomies" necessitate the acceptance of previously denigrated characteristics:

> For many women writers, the quest to reintegrate a split self is simultaneously a drive to topple the hierarchy of the sacred and the profane, redeeming and including what the culture has exiled and excluded. To deny the other is to deny the self. Conversely, it is dread of what seems loathsome within the self that produces a projection of it onto another. (194–96)

Lorde expands this quest for reintegration in two ways. First, on a collective level, she extends the need for reintegration outward to encompass the specific forms of alienation experienced by people of the African diaspora. Second, on an individual level, she emphasizes that this quest for reintegration has particular resonance for people who, because of their ethnicity, gender, or sexuality, have been portrayed as the profane, especially if they have internalized this self-image. The myth of feminine evil, for example, often has further implications for dark-skinned women: Because the dominant ideology privileges male over female and light over dark, both their gender and their ethnicity seem to confirm their inferior status. As Virginia R. Harris and Trinity A. Ordoña explain, when dark-skinned women internalize this dualistic worldview and believe that "dark is inferior and evil and that woman is inferior, evil, and must be controlled sexually," they suppress themselves and distrust their ability to speak (306).

Anzaldúa enacts a related form of re(con)ceived otherness in "Speaking in Tongues" where she describes her own desire to write as a search for her ethnic/female identity, a

> quest for the self . . . which we women of color have come to think as "other"—the dark, the feminine. Didn't we start writing to reconcile this other within us? We knew we were different, set apart, exiled from what is considered "normal," white-right. And as we internalized this exile, we came to see the alien within us and, too often, as a result, we split apart from ourselves and each other. Forever after we have been in search of that self, that "other" and each other. (169)

As these complex interconnections between inner and outer forms of self/other alienation suggest, Anzaldúa's quest for the self-become-othered signifies more than a desire to reconcile internal antinomies. To my mind, her search represents an attempt to develop new models of individual and collective identity formation capable of reconciling *both* internal and external antinomies. Like Lorde, she implies that this re(con)ceived otherness, or recognition of the other in ourselves, makes possible the invention of nonbinary models of identity formation that open new interconnections among people. Yet she stipulates that this self-othering process entails a painful rebirth, a self-confrontation that requires both accepting and transforming the dominant society's label.

Anzaldúa's submersion into the Coatlicue state illustrates this interaction with the other as well as the painful rebirth it entails. As I mentioned in the previous chapter, Anzaldúa associates the Coatlicue state with the various forms of oppression she encounters as a Chicana queer and with her experiences as a writer. Not surprisingly, given her description of writing as a quest for the other, she bases her revisionist use of Coatlicue on the well-known patriarchal myth of feminine evil that casts Woman in the role of the other—the dangerous creature whose unholy, terrifying powers must be contained and controlled. Significantly, Anzaldúa uses culturally specific material to simultaneously accept, reject, and transform these cross-cultural myths of feminine evil. Like Mary Daly and other contemporary feminists, she claims her "Female/Elemental divinity"[13] by replacing conventional Judeo-Christian terminology with earlier woman-focused metaphors of the divine. Yet by identifying herself with Coatlicue, the pre-Columbian Mesoamerican serpent god/dess, Anzaldúa includes a cultural dimension that distinguishes her revisionist mythmaking from that of Daly and many other 'postpatriarchal' thinkers. She revitalizes (without 'lightening') the "'darkened' and disempowered" Serpent Woman (*Borderlands*, 38–39). Her description is worth quoting at length, for it illustrates the truly horrific nature of this mythic figure:

> She has no head. In its place two spurts of blood gush up, transfiguring into enormous twin rattlesnakes facing each other. . . . She has no hands. In their place are two more serpents in the form of eagle-like claws, which are repeated at her feet: claws which symbolize the digging of graves into the earth as well as the sky-bound eagle, the masculine force. Hanging from her neck is a necklace of open hands alternating with human hearts. . . . In the center of the collar hangs a human skull with living eyes in its sockets. Another identical skull is attached to her belt. (*Borderlands*, 47)

In Anzaldúa's revisionist mythmaking, Coatlicue remains a monstrous emblem of the other. As her submersion into the Coatlicue state reveals, however, it is only by confronting this other and re(con)ceiving it as a part of herself that she can begin stripping away the internalized oppression that led to the Coatlicue state. This process entails a doubled movement in which Anzaldúa simultaneously redefines this supposedly alien figure and incorporates it into her own self-definition. To paraphrase her words, the wound caused by the serpent must be cured by serpent (*Borderlands*, 50).

In poems such as "Creature of Darkness" and "that dark shining thing," Anzaldúa graphically depicts the highly emotional, terrifying nature of this confrontational process. In the former poem she speaks as a small animal with "[a] soft furry body / loose hanging skin" that has been immersed in total darkness for weeks. Rather than escape, she chooses "to sit here and pick at the scabs / watch the blood flow / lick the salt from [her] face." Her metamorphosis, when it finally begins in the *second* half of the *last* stanza, is not the movement into

light conventionally associated with new insight. Instead, she sinks
even "deeper / growing great with mouth / a creature afraid of the
dark / a creature at home in the dark." As this "growing . . . mouth"
suggests, however, her descent will empower her to speak, for she no
longer fears the dark as other than herself (*Borderlands*, 186–87).

Similarly, in "that dark shining thing" Anzaldúa recalls her own
experience as she observes and assists as another mestiza—"Colored,
poor white, latent queer / passing for white / seething with hatred,
anger"—enters the Coatlicue state. Like Lorde in "Eye to Eye," Anzaldúa depicts herself as the repository of other people's projected self-
hatred:

> I am the only round face,
> Indian-beaked, off-colored
> in the faculty lineup, the workshop, the panel
> and reckless enough to take you on.
> I am the flesh you dig your fingernails into
> mine the hand you chop off while still clinging to it
> the face spewed with your vomit
> I risk your sanity
> and mine. (*Borderlands*, 171)

Despite her desire to "turn [her] back" on this other woman, she does
not, for she recognizes the similarities between their situations:

> my feet know each rock you tread on
> as you stumble I falter too
> and I remember
> he/me/they who shouted
> push Gloria breathe Gloria
> feel their hands holding me up, prompting me
> until I'm facing that pulsing bloodied blackness
> trying to scream
> from between your legs (*Borderlands*, 171–72)

As she shifts between this other mestiza's situation in the present and
her own experiences in the past, Anzaldúa blurs self/other boundaries. Again she depicts the transition into an alternate mode of consciousness as acceptance, selective rejection, and transformation of the

dark. Re(con)ceiving the other entails a painful rebirth, and insight—although "numinous"—is "black." As in "Creature of Darkness," however, pain and fear begin to dissipate. In the poem's conclusion Anzaldúa describes a complex series of interconnections:

> I know that I am that Beast that circles your house
> peers in the window
> and that you see yourself my prey
>
> But I know you are the Beast
> its prey is you
> you the midwife
> you that dark shining thing (*Borderlands*, 172)

As the transitions from first- to second-person pronouns indicate, Anzaldúa sees herself through the eyes of the other. By identifying both herself and the other as the Beast, she enacts an intricate dance of transformation between preyer and preyed upon, self and other.

Anzaldúa's submersion into the Coatlicue state is similar to the inward journeys depicted by a number of twentieth-century women artists. Gloria Orenstein explains that in their works dark goddesses symbolize

> [t]he journey inward, . . . a journey to the underworld of the psyche, to the underworld of society, to the "scapegoated" aspects of women's strengths, to the "dark" Goddess of death, dismemberment, and ultimate rebirth, to the "ghetto of the unreal." This "dark" Goddess, then, also sheds light on the repressed and forgotten psychological characteristics (often strengths and powers that have been obscured or driven underground by patriarchal social systems). (32)

There are, however, two significant distinctions between the inward journeys Orenstein describes and those depicted by Anzaldúa. Unlike Orenstein's women writers, Anzaldúa challenges ethnocentrism as well as the masculinist bias informing contemporary U.S. society. By associating Coatlicue's "dismemberment" with the Aztec and Spanish conquests of gynocentric, indigenous Mesoamerican peoples, Anzaldúa's dark goddess represents both the erasure of Mexican-Indian culture and beliefs and the " 'scapegoated' aspects of women's strengths."

More importantly for my argument, Anzaldúa's inward journey goes beyond the recovery of repressed and forgotten aspects of female identity to illustrate an epistemological transformation. For Anzaldúa, this transformation entails the shift to differential, or mestiza, consciousness that occurs through an exploration of internalized oppression. In both "Creature of Darkness" and "that dark shining thing" the speaker feels psychic and emotional pain so intense that it forces her to confront her self-loathing. When she does, she faces her own dread of the other and discovers that this other is also part of herself. As she re(con)ceives the other into herself, she experiences the "violent shattering of the unitary sense of self" Chela Sandoval refers to in "U.S. Third World Feminism" (23). This self-splintering leads to the development of differential consciousness. As Sandoval explains,

> [d]ifferential consciousness is comprised of seeming contradictions and difference, which then serve as tactical interventions in the other mobility that is power. Entrance into the realm "between and amongst" the others demands a mode of consciousness once relegated to the province of intuition and psychic phenomena, but which now must be recognized as a specific practice. . . . Inside this realm resides the only possible grounds of unity across differences. Entrance into this new order requires an emotional commitment within which one experiences the violent shattering of the unitary sense of self as the skill which allows a mobile identity to form. (23)

This "violent shattering" enables social actors to recognize, evaluate, and transform contradictions and differences into tactical interventions.

Anzaldúa's depiction of the Coatlicue state indicates one way this mobile identity develops. By deconstructing self/other binaries and re(con)ceiving the other as herself, she constructs a flexible self/worldview enabling her to shift subject positions contextually. In *Borderlands/La Frontera* she uses this nonbinary mode of consciousness to redefine herself and her world. She creates a spiritualized mythos acknowledging her otherness—"the animal, the alien, the sub- or suprahuman, the me that has something in common with the wind and the trees and the rocks" (50). By identifying herself with and as this dark other, Anzaldúa employs her mestiza logic of both/and/neither/

nor to reject, accept, and transform the dominant culture's label. She is not only "a creature of darkness and a creature of light, but also a creature that questions the definitions of light and dark and gives them new meaning" (81). Indeed, she subverts the conventional definitions of all such dichotomous terms, for her submersion into the Coatlicue state has taught her "that down is up, and [she] rise[s] up from and into the deep" (74). Anzaldúa associates this alteration in consciousness with increased linguistic power. She can use words in new ways because she rejects the binary thinking that separates good from evil, light from dark, up from down, and subject from object by dissolving the boundaries between them.

Allen enacts a similar deconstructive process in *The Woman Who Owned the Shadows*. It is only at the point of death—when Ephanie has surrendered entirely to the dark and attempted to hang herself— that she recognizes her intense desire to live. By accepting her isolation, acknowledging her self-loathing, and immersing herself in the shadows, she can enter the "glossy, deeply gleaming blackness, . . . the door to the place of the Spider." Like Anzaldúa, Allen develops a spiritualized mythos to indicate that Ephanie's re(con)ceived otherness alters her self/worldview. As she begins recognizing the other in herself and herself in the other, Ephanie learns to draw parallels between the mythic story of the Iroquois Sky Woman and her own: to "fall" from the tree of light into darkness is to "rise" into a new world. And just as Anzaldúa encounters "[a] light . . . so intense it could be white or black" in her experiences of the Coatlicue state (*Borderlands*, 51), so Ephanie is visited by a spirit woman who is both numinous and dark, a woman with a "face of infinite, aching, powerful, beloved darkness, of midnight" (207–9).

III   Otherness becomes empowering critical difference when it is not given, but re-created. Defined with the Other's newly formed criteria.   TRINH MINH-HA

Both the transmutation of self/other dichotomies and the corresponding insight that extremes meet and "turn into their opposites"

(*Borderlands*, 51) are central to the transformational epistemologies developed by Allen, Anzaldúa, and Lorde. By positing the nonduality of self and other, they construct multilayered discourses recognizing both the diversities and similarities between and among apparently dissimilar people. Anzaldúa offers the most extensive justification for this desire to mediate between diverse cultures. As she explains in "*La conciencia de la mestiza*," she envisions a new race, "*la raza cosmica . . .* embracing the four major races of the world," and sees herself and other mestizas as the "officiating priestess[es]" in this cultural mestizaje (*Borderlands*, 77).

Throughout *Borderlands/La Frontera* Anzaldúa locates herself in the liminal spaces where these *razas* will converge; indeed, she celebrates her lesbian body as a crossroad—"*Su cuerpo es una bocacalle*"— for she believes homosexuals to be "the supreme crossers of cultures." She maintains that because they exist on the outskirts of all societies, lesbians and gay men can establish bonds with dissimilar peoples and create a transcultural, multiethnic tribe. By thus demonstrating that it is possible to form alliances that do not suppress difference, homosexuals represent a vital stage in the "(r)evolutionary" process, "a blending that proves all blood is intricately woven together" (80–84).[14] As the other in every nation, "the mirror reflecting the heterosexual tribe's fear," they challenge the dominant culture's concepts of selfhood. Thus Anzaldúa sees her same-sex desire as the ultimate denial of cross-cultural patriarchal standards. By rejecting the heterosexualism enforced by both Mexican American and U.S. Anglo mores, she separates herself from existing belief structures and acquires a radical freedom to rename herself according to her own (forbidden) desire (18–20).[15] And, by describing herself as "every woman's sister or potential lover" (80), she defies the cultural dictates that define "woman" exclusively in relation to "man" and reveals her willingness to establish bonds with women from diverse backgrounds. Significantly, Anzaldúa's desire to form cross-cultural sisterhoods functions simultaneously with her desire to create political alliances with gay men of all colors and other oppressed peoples. Thus she challenges lesbianfeminist separatists to recognize similarities between their experiences and those of gay men and people of color.

Although Allen and Lorde associate their sexuality with the spiritual, mythic, and communal traditions of Native American and West African cultures, they, too, believe their lesbianized desires challenge twentieth-century western concepts of sexuality and gender. In "Kochinnenako in Academe" and "*Hwame, Koshkalaka,* and the Rest: Lesbians in American Indian Cultures," for instance,[16] Allen rewrites Native American cultural history by depicting same-sex relationships as accepted forms of bonding among most precontact Native peoples. However, she does not simply transpose contemporary definitions of homosexual identity onto precolonial forms. She uses the differences between them both to critique twentieth-century concepts of gender and sexuality and to give readers new ways of living out same-sex desires. For example, Allen incorporates a spiritual component into her definition of precolonial lesbian desire. Thus she critiques the contemporary association of lesbianism with alienation and offers modern-day lesbians new, self-affirmative ways of perceiving themselves. Similarly, in *The Woman Who Owned the Shadows*, the myth of double woman—who Allen associates with Grandmother Spider and Naotsete—provides Ephanie with a model for adopting a positive lesbian identity. Her entry into myth enables her to make sense of her attraction to women, and at the novel's conclusion she takes up a new role combining this desire with the creation of new forms of female-centered community.

Like Anzaldúa, Allen uses her lesbian identity to foster bonds among apparently separate groups. Thus in "Some Like Indians Endure," she draws a number of parallels between "indians" and "dykes": Both "used to live as tribes"; both have survived despite massacres, forced removals, and other forms of erasure; and both forge communities in the face of despair. Perhaps most importantly, she defines both "indians" and "dykes" as collective identities based on self-determination and choice: They are an "idea" or self-image "some people have of themselves." This idea becomes a catalyst for new forms of connection and bonding:

> because the only home
> is each other
> they've occupied all
> the rest

colonized it; an
idea about ourselves is all
we own (301)

By creating a historical connection between these two sometimes overlapping groups, Allen generates new forms of bonding for "indians" and "dykes."

Lorde employs similar tactics as she uses analogies with history and myth to associate her lesbianism with precolonial West African communal traditions. Throughout *Zami* she connects her erotic love for women with the traditions of her mother's Caribbean homeland, and in several poems from *The Black Unicorn* she associates her sexual desire for women with West African orisha. In "Meet," for example, MawuLisa sanctions Lorde's intense, sexualized encounter with another woman: "Mawulisa foretells [their] bodies / as [their] hands touch and learn" (34). In other poems, such as "On a Night of the Full Moon" and "Love Poem," Lorde ritualizes her sexuality by drawing analogies between lovemaking and the earth's cycles. In the former poem, she likens herself to the moon and identifies her lover's body with sunlight, young birds, and limes; and in the latter poem, she uses metaphors of wind, mountains, and valleys to affirm her sensuous lovemaking. Similarly, in "Bridge Through My Window," landscape imagery underscores the naturalness of her attraction to other women. As she likens herself and her lover to shorelines that meet without merging, she depicts sexual desire between women as a self-empowering form of interdependence where individual and collective identities coexist, neither erasing the other. By thus naturalizing her lesbian identity, Lorde subtly challenges the homophobia in black communities and in dominant U.S. culture that condemns same-sex desire as unnatural. And, by associating her lesbian sexuality with West African precolonial traditions, she rejects the black-nationalist perspective that views homosexuality as cultural betrayal.

By publicly claiming the despised label, lesbian, Allen, Anzaldúa, and Lorde reject U.S. culture's heterosexualized, normative descriptions of woman.[17] They accept the label—lesbian as other—and use it to provoke change. Although lesbianism has generally been associated in Eurocentric thought with ultimate otherness, it plays a vital role in maintaining the existing social structure, for "[t]he sex/gender hierarchy functions smoothly only if sexual nonconformity is kept invisible" (Collins, 194). Public acknowledgment of women's same-sex relationships undermines the heterosexual matrix by demonstrating that it's possible to construct new female identities outside the male/female binary structure.

Allen, Anzaldúa, and Lorde disrupt this heterosexual matrix. However, by questioning—even as they repeatedly take up—lesbianism itself, all three writers take this disruptive process even further. Each writer incorporates what I describe as bisexual inflections—or doubled oscillations between homosexual/heterosexual desires and between male/female genders—into her poetry, fiction, and prose. These shifts destabilize the binary system structuring sex-gender categories. Thus in her discussion of precontact indigenous sexualities, Allen distinguishes between "lesbians" and "*koskalakas*," or "dykes," describing the former as women who established relationships with both women and men and the latter as women who bonded only with other women. Yet even this latter category has a bisexual, or doubly gendered, inflection because Allen translates "*koskalaka*"—a Lakota word she adopts to describe dykes—as both a "young man" and a "woman who doesn't want to marry" (*Sacred Hoop*, 258). By blurring the boundaries between "woman," "man," "lesbian," and "dyke," Allen compels readers to reexamine the labels we use to define ourselves.

Anzaldúa enacts similar shifts and provocatively crosses sexual, cultural, and gender boundaries. In *Prieta*, for example, her depiction of Prieta's heterosexual relationship with a Latino and her "impossible love" for a gay Anglo male challenge the apparent permanence and stability of the dichotomy between heterosexual and homosexual desire. Like her description of the *mita' y mita'* in *Borderlands/La Frontera*, this transgressive desire opens an ambivalent space where new definitions of sexuality and gender are played out.

Lorde uses similar oscillations in *Zami*. She declares in the Prologue:

> *I have always wanted to be both man and woman, to incorporate the strongest and richest parts of my mother and father within/into me—to share valleys and mountains upon my body the way the earth does in hills and peaks.*

I would like to enter a woman the way any man can, and to be entered—to leave and to be left—to be hot and hard and soft all at the same time in the cause of our loving. (7; her italics)

What does it mean when a self-identified lesbian—a writer praised for her erotic, woman-centered celebrations of female-female bonding—desires to be and to love *both* as a woman and as a man? Is she rejecting conventional definitions of lesbian identity? redefining what it means to be female or male? Although I return to this enigmatic passage in a later discussion of Lorde's lesbian phallus, I want point out that this bisexual inflection exposes the limitations in our conventional definitions of lesbian sexuality and desire.

By re(con)ceiving the lesbianized other, Allen, Anzaldúa, and Lorde both adopt the conventional idea of "lesbian" as "other" and rework it to generate new models of individual and collective identities for their readers. More specifically, these new models complicate and deconstruct the binary oppositions between categories such as male/female and heterosexual/homosexual. In the following section I will argue that this process of re(con)ceiving the other has important implications for developing a transformational politics of identity.

IV   She knows . . . that she is not an outsider like the foreign outsider. She knows she is different while at the same time being Him. Not quite the Same, not quite the Other, she stands in that undetermined threshold place where she constantly drifts in and out. Undercutting the inside/outside opposition, her intervention is necessarily that of both a deceptive insider and a deceptive outsider. She is this Inappropriate Other/Same who moves about with always at least two/four gestures: that of affirming "I am like you" while persisting in her difference; and that of reminding "I am different" while unsettling every definition of otherness arrived at. . . .
Whether she turns the inside out or the outside in, she is, like the two sides of a coin, the same impure, both-in-one insider/outsider. For there can hardly be such a thing as an essential inside that can be homogeneously represented by all

insiders; an authentic insider in there, an absolute reality
out there, or an incorrupted representative who cannot be
questioned by another incorrupted representative.

TRINH MINH-HA

Identity politics—or the development of political theories and strategies based on social actors' ethnic, gender, and sexual identities—has
played pivotal roles in contemporary feminist and ethnic movements.
By enabling oppressed peoples to unite across differences, identity
politics makes it possible to develop coalitions for social change. Too
often, however, this radical potential is greatly diminished. When personal identities become reified and defined as monolithic, coalitions
break apart from the inside as members begin focusing on the differences *between* what they perceive to be discrete gender/ethnic/sexual
categories. Thus they inadvertently reinscribe inflexible boundaries
between groups. This emphasis on mutually exclusive identities makes
it impossible to recognize commonalities among differently situated
social actors, preventing the establishment of effective alliances.

Pratibha Parmar makes a similar point in her assessment of self-
identified black British women's attempts to develop a cohesive feminist movement. Although she acknowledges the importance of identity politics, she emphasizes its limitations, explaining that "[w]hile
the articulation of self-identities has been a necessary and essential
process for collective organizing by black and migrant women, it also
resulted in political practices that became insular and often retro-
grade" (102). She, too, attributes these limitations to rigid exclusionary definitions of identity based on static conceptions of sexuality,
ethnicity, and class. She asserts that when British feminists relied on "a
language of 'authentic subjective experience'" derived from restrictive
self-definitions, they developed hierarchies of oppression that prevented the establishment of alliances across differences. This appeal to
authentic experience had other negative consequences as well. It led
to claims of epistemic privilege and to guilt-tripping, or the "self-
righteous assertion that if one inhabits a certain identity, this gives one
the legitimate and moral right to guilt-trip others into particular ways
of behaving" (107).

In short, it seems that conventional identity politics often base political strategies on humanist notions of stable, unitary identities that fragment groups from within. Yet the solution is not to abandon all references to personal experiences, but rather to take experientially based knowledge claims further by redefining identity. As Andrea Stuart states in her discussion of British feminists' identity politics:

> The problem was not, in a strange way, that we took the implications of organizing around identity too far, but that we didn't take it far enough. Had we really pushed this debate far enough, we would have come to appreciate that we are all oppressor *and* oppressed. . . . Instead of appreciating the interconnectedness of our oppressions we saw all our interests as mutually antagonistic, instead of making alliances we were in competition with one another. (39; her emphasis)

Stuart's critique applies to U.S. identity politics as well.[18] Racism, sexism, heterosexism, and classism are so deeply embedded in twentieth-century U.S. culture that people of all colors have been misshaped by these rigid forms of hierarchical thinking. We have all been trained to classify and judge people according to normative beliefs concerning appearance, economic status, and other evaluative standards. This training has been so thoroughly ingrained that it seems natural, and we must be jolted out of our complacency. However, until we begin to "actually *feel* what we have been forced to suppress each time we were a victim of, witness to, or perpetrator of racism" or other forms of discrimination, we remain unaware of our own complicity in these oppressive social structures (Yamato, 23; her emphasis). As in Anzaldúa's submersion into the Coatlicue state, this exploration of previously unacknowledged emotions involves suffering as people of all colors, genders, sexualities, and classes realize the various ways we've functioned as both the oppressor and the oppressed. Because our interconnections with others serve as potential triggers for such insights, it's less painful to deny the intricate interplay between commonalities and differences by creating generic models of identity. Yet these monolithic identities reinforce dominant/subordinate dualistic thinking, and it's this denial of the interplay that keeps us divided. To establish effective alliances, we must leave the safety of unitary, insular conceptions of identity by recognizing, expressing, and accepting both the differences *and* the similarities between ourselves and others.

Identity is always relational. Every time we distinguish ourselves from others, we begin with already established commonalities. In psychoanalytic terms, the recognition of differences cannot occur without the existence of a prior, though often erased, point of contact. Too often, however, differences are simplified and commonalities almost entirely ignored. As Homi Bhabha explains in his discussion of the ambivalent identification and slippage that occurs in the interactions between colonizer and colonized, "the disavowal of the Other always exacerbates the 'edge' of identification, reveals that dangerous place where identity and aggressivity are twinned. For denial is always a retroactive process; a *half*-acknowledgment of that Otherness that has left its traumatic mark" ("Remembering Fanon," 144; his emphasis).

But what if this disavowal of the other is only partially enacted? Or what if the other is first disavowed and then re(con)ceived, as it is in Anzaldúa's description of the Coatlicue state, Lorde's poetry, and Allen's description of Ephanie's "monstrous other"? I believe this emotionally charged re(con)ception of the other effects a shift in consciousness that opens a space where transformational identity politics can occur. If, as I argued previously, re(con)ceiving the other triggers the emotional commitment and the violent shattering of a unitary sense of self associated with differential consciousness, then this process makes it possible for social actors of whatever gender, sexuality, ethnicity, or class to develop politics based on shifting identifications with diverse groups of people.[19]

Although re(con)ceived otherness entails a period of intense psychic and emotional pain, I want to emphasize that the acknowledgment of previously suppressed emotions should not be equated with guilt. The point is not to encourage feelings of personal responsibility for slavery, decimation of indigenous peoples, land theft, and so on that occurred in the past. It is, rather, to enable social actors to more fully comprehend how these oppressive systems that began in the historical past continue misshaping contemporary conditions. Only then can we work to bring about a more equitable distribution of resources in the present. Guilt-tripping plays no role in this process. Indeed, I would argue that guilt functions as a useless, debilitating state of consciousness that reinforces boundaries between apparently separate groups.[20] When people feel guilty, they become paralyzed, deny any sense of agency, and assume that their privileged positions in the contemporary sociosymbolic system automatically compel them to act as 'the oppressor.' However, as I've been emphasizing throughout this chapter, there are no permanent, unitary identities. Even the notorious "white male" is far less monolithic than we often assume. But in order to recognize the otherness of every subject, we must deconstruct simplistic beliefs concerning our own self-identities. To again quote Anzaldúa, we must "leave the permanent boundaries of a fixed self . . . and see . . . through the eyes of the other" ("En Rapport," 145).

The work of Allen, Anzaldúa, and Lorde demonstrates that this "fixed self" only becomes fixed when we perceive it as such. When we define "difference" as "deviation" and "other" as "not-me," we rely on binary oppositions and create inflexible speaking subjects, pseudo-universal concepts of wo/manhood, that erect permanent barriers between mutually exclusive identities. Given such monolithic models of subjectivity it is, of course, impossible to see through the eyes of the other because the other has become entirely alien. However, by redefining difference as ever-changing fields of interplay occurring within, between, and among speaking or reading subjects, identity becomes pluralized, and we begin seeing through the eyes of the other. Like Allen, Anzaldúa, and Lorde, we can reject humanist models of self-identity and create multilayered discourses that replace unified subjects with fluid, shifting speakers.

Each writer exhibits what Trinh Min-ha describes as a "critical difference from myself"—the ability to perceive difference within, between, and among each speaking subject, which

> means that I am not i, am within and without i. I/i can be I or i, you and me both involved. We (with capital W) sometimes include(s), other times exclude(s) me. You and I are close, we intertwine.
> (*Woman*, 90)

As this proliferation of *I's*, *we's*, and *you's* suggests, Trinh uses a mestiza logic of both/and/neither/nor to deconstruct the notion of authentic identity as an essential core self buried beneath layers of false disguises. She claims that, because speaking subjects are always defined in relation to others (or "Not-I's"), each individual (or "I/i") is herself composed of "*infinite layers*" (her emphasis). Consequently, each conversation a speaker enters requires a new formulation, another variation of nonunitary plural subjecthood (or "*I/i's*"). It's this fluid speaker we hear when Lorde writes "I am blessed within my selves / who are come to make our shattered faces / whole" (*Black Unicorn*, 61–62); or when Allen claims that her "life is the pause. The space between. The not this, not that, not the other" ("Confluence," 151); or when Anzaldúa insists "I remain who I am, multiple / and one of the herd, yet not of it" (*Borderlands*, 173). In these passages each writer enacts her nonunitary identity differentially, based on the particular context in which she speaks.

Indeed, Allen, Anzaldúa, and Lorde take Trinh's deconstruction of "the line dividing *I* and *Not-I*, *us* and *them*" (*Woman*, 94) even further. In Lorde's words, they *become*

the sharpened edge
where day and night shall meet
and not be
one. (*Black Unicorn*, 7)

Not one, but not two either. Each writer locates herself on this ever-shifting marker separating *I* from *Not-I*, *us* from *them* and enacts new convers(at)ions—transformational dialogues—between and among nonunitary plural subjects. As they position themselves between *I/i*, *I/Not-I*, subject/object, self/other, and other binary pairs, they collapse the categories from within. Thus they replace binary thinking with nondual modes of perception that denaturalize the divisions between self and other.

Whereas social actors relying on conventional identity politics base their actions on static notions of an authentic engendered, racialized, and sexualized self, Allen, Anzaldúa, and Lorde do not. Instead, they create nonessentialized, constantly shifting locations where transformational identity politics can occur. Moreover, they destabilize the binary oppositions between oppressor and oppressed and locate the other(s) both within themselves and within their readers, opening new intersubjective spaces. These threshold locations function analogously to the "space of 'translation'" or "place of hybridity" Bhabha describes, "where the construction of a political object that is new, neither the one nor the Other," can take place ("Commitment," 117). Allen, Anzaldúa, and Lorde have begun constructing this new political object. In their dialogues between themselves and their readers, they create new subjectivities that are neither singular nor plural. Not one, but not two either. These convers(at)ions can play a significant role in the transformational identity politics I'm advocating. As we—whatever color, class, ethnicity, or sex 'we' are—see (ourselves) through the eyes of the other, we recognize the others in ourselves and ourselves in the others. We, too, enter threshold spaces where transcultural identifications—mestizaje connections—can occur.

Back to the Mother?
Paula Gunn Allen's Origin Myths

There is no arcane place for return. TRINH MINH-HA

The meanings of the past create the significance of the present.
PAULA GUNN ALLEN

Thus, "the feminine" wouldn't be the myths, etc. made by
men; it would be that which "I, woman" invent, enact, and
empower in "our" speech, our practice, our collective quest for
a redefinition of the status of all women. ROSI BRAIDOTTI

The "origin" of the tradition must be acknowledged, but
acknowledgment does not sanction simple repetition: each new
performer "signifies" upon that origin by transforming it, and
by allowing for infinite transmutations.

FRANÇOISE LIONNET

The title to this chapter reflects an ongoing debate in U.S. feminist movement: The political (in)effectiveness of "prepatriarchal" origin myths. Whereas some feminists see attempts to "recover" woman-centered creation stories as extremely misguided, others are firmly convinced that such attempts provide contemporary women with empowering models of identity formation. According to Mary Daly and Gloria Orenstein for example, accounts of a gynocentric prehistorical culture empower contemporary women in several inter-related ways. First, by positing a time *before* "patriarchy," feminist origin stories suggest the contingent nature of female oppression, motivating women to challenge restrictive social systems; in the words of Daly, women are inspired to "*transcend* the trickery of dogmatic deception," reject the "distorting mirror of Memory," and "recognize the Radiance of [their] own Origins" (*Pure Lust*, 113; my emphasis). Second, by depicting "nonpatriarchal" egalitarian communities of women, these stories offer a new teleological perspective, or what

Orenstein calls "the dream of a new feminist matristic Eden" (153). And third, by replacing the (male) "God" with the (female) "Goddess," feminist revisionary myths provide women with positive images of their own "biophilic" power.[1]

According to Donna Haraway, Judith Butler, and other poststructural theorists, however, feminists' use of subversive strategies that imply an "innocent and all-powerful Mother" and an "irrecoverable origin" in an imaginary, prehistorical past are far less effective than many revisionist mythmakers suggest.[2] They argue that mythic accounts of a maternal origin are exclusionary, divisive, and politically conservative, for they lead to simplistic identity politics—politics based on restrictive, ethnocentric notions of female identity that ignore the many differences among real-life women. Butler, for example, maintains that although feminist origin stories are employed to overthrow the dominant representational system, they generally replicate existing conditions:

> The postulation of the "before" within feminist theory becomes politically problematic when it constrains the future to materialize an idealized notion of the past or when it supports, even inadvertently, the reification of a precultural sphere of the authentic feminine. This recourse to an original or genuine femininity is a nostalgic and parochial ideal that refuses the contemporary demand to formulate an account of gender as a complex cultural construction. (*Gender Trouble*, 36)

In other words, feminists' attempts to recover or recreate 'prepatriarchal' forms of woman-centered communities inevitably rely on existing phallocentric definitions of Woman;[3] they reject conventional gender categories only to establish other equally restrictive male/female binary oppositions. Moreover, Butler maintains that focusing on a time supposedly prior to or *beyond* present socioeconomic and political conditions inhibits feminist analysis and action in the present.[4]

For Teresa de Lauretis as well, there is no "going back to the innocence of 'biology'" or to biologically based concepts of gender. As she explains in *Technologies of Gender*, because gender is produced by a wide range of discursive practices, including education, literature, cinema, television, and religion, it cannot be described as a "natural" attribute that all human beings are marked with at birth. Such descriptions reinforce normative, phallocratic definitions of "woman," as well as the hierarchical male/female binary system. Thus she rejects what she sees as

> some women's belief in a matriarchal past or a contemporary "matristic" realm presided over by the Goddess, a realm of female tradition, marginal and subterranean and yet all positive and good, peace-loving, ecologically correct, matrilineal, matrifocal, non—Indo-European, and so forth; in short, a world untouched by ideology, class and racial struggle, television—a world untroubled by the contradictory demands and oppressive rewards of gender as I and surely those women, too, have daily experienced. (20–21)[5]

Like these poststructuralist thinkers, I'm extremely suspicious of feminist identity politics founded on exclusionary accounts of "woman's experience." I, too, question the political effectiveness of rallying around normative, biologically based concepts of Woman, or mythic, monolithic images of "*the* Goddess." All too often these attempts at establishing commonalities among women have the opposite effect, inadvertently reinstating conservative descriptions of "Womanhood" and binary gender systems that exclude the experiences of many women. But to assume that we can—or even *should*—toss out *all* origin myths, along with *all* references to "Woman" or the "feminine," is too dismissive—not to mention highly unlikely. These categories have become so deeply ingrained in our personal and cultural meaning systems that we cannot simply reject them. Nor can we sort through the numerous images of women circulating in contemporary cultures and distinguish the truth from the lies. As Drucilla Cornell argues in *Beyond Accommodation*, "we can't just drop out of gender or sex roles" now that we recognize their oppressive, constructed nature (182); nor can we separate "Woman and women . . . from the fictions and metaphors in which she and they are presented, and through which we portray ourselves" (3).

As I see it, this debate over the (in)effectiveness of origin stories is part of a larger debate concerning the possibility of positing, from *within* the current representational system, new feminist—or perhaps even "feminine"—"beyonds": Can we affirm the "feminine" yet arrive at definitions of "Woman" that are *qualitatively* different from existing descriptions? Perhaps more importantly, can we do so without erasing the many material and cultural differences between real-life women? On the one hand, terms like Woman and the "feminine" can be extremely divisive when they prevent us from recognizing that because gender intersects with historical, ethnic, sexual, and other axes of difference in complex ways, gender is an unstable category with multiple meanings.[6] But on the other hand, to refuse all references to sexual difference, "the feminine," and Woman risks reinstating the pseudo-universal human subject defined exclusively by masculinist standards. Moreover, to ignore or actively deny the "feminine" perpetuates the current sociosymbolic system; as Cornell suggests, "the repudiation of the feminine is part of the very 'logic' of a patriarchal order" (*Beyond Accommodation*, 5).

In this chapter I want to suggest that *transculturally* contextualized metaphors of Woman and the "feminine" offer another alternative to these theoretical dilemmas. More specifically, I will argue that Allen's use of North American creatrix figures demonstrates the possibility of writing the "feminine" in open-ended, nonexclusionary ways. Rather than reject all references to "the Goddess," Woman, and prepatriarchal social systems Allen uses the terms differently. She locates herself in the present yet goes 'back' to a diverse set of non-Eurocentric mythic origins, developing metaphoric representations of Woman that neither erase her own self-defined cultural specificities nor erect permanent barriers between disparate groups. Instead, her writings affirm what I will call "feminine" mestizaje: "feminine" in its re-metaphorized images of Woman; "mestizaje" in its fluid, transformational, trans*cultural* forms. I borrow this latter term from Cuban literary and political movements where its usage indicates a profound challenge to existing racial categories. As Nancy Morejón explains, mestizaje transculturation defies static notions of cultural purity by emphasizing

> the constant interaction, the transmutation between two or more cultural components with the unconscious goal of creating a third cultural entity . . . that is new and independent even though rooted in the preceding elements. Reciprocal influence is the determining factor here, for no single element superimposes itself on another; on the

contrary, each one changes into the other so that both can be transformed into a third. Nothing seems immutable.[7]

Allen incorporates this ongoing cultural transmutation into her
mythic metaphors of Woman. By drawing on the dialogic elements of
verbal art, she utilizes metaphoric language's performative effects and
invites her readers to live out the "feminine" in new ways. As she does
so, she develops an interactive epistemological process—or what I
described in Chapter 2 as embodied mythic thinking—that challenges
feminists' conventional notions of identity politics.

As I will discuss in later chapters, Anzaldúa and Lorde engage in
similar transcultural affirmations of the "feminine." They, too, simultaneously intervene in existing systems of racialized and gendered
meaning and invent new definitions of the "feminine." However, I
have chosen to examine the poststructuralist debate concerning the
(in)effectiveness of woman-centered origin myths and their implications for feminists' representational politics exclusively in the context
of Allen's writings. I have several reasons. First, her origin myths play a
pivotal role in her creative and theoretical works. Second, Allen uses
her gynocentric mythic system to develop what could be interpreted
as a highly irrational, entirely nonacademic epistemology. Third, her
assertions concerning women's experience and the "feminine"—especially when read literally—are far more extreme than those made by
Anzaldúa and Lorde. Yet it's the radical nature of Allen's assertions I
find so intriguing. Why would a highly respected scholar of Native
American literature support her claims with references to "spirit
guides," "the Grandmothers," and other supernatural informants?
How can an epistemological process based on what seem to be conservative notions of women's biological functions support feminists' political projects?

Interestingly, Allen's feminist writings have received less critical
attention than Anzaldúa's and Lorde's. There is, I believe, an important parallel between this limited academic reception and the ex-
tremity of her claims. Rather than criticize what seem to be monolithic, essentializing views of spiritual forces and the "feminine" in
American Indian traditions, theorists generally avoid commenting on
these aspects of Allen's work. This avoidance is quite understandable.

Consider, for example, the following assertions in *The Sacred Hoop: Recovering the Feminine in American Indian Traditions*:

> The Mother, the Grandmother, recognized from earliest times into the present among those peoples of the Americas who kept to the eldest traditions, is celebrated in social structures, architecture, law, custom, and the oral tradition. To her we owe our lives, and from her comes our ability to endure, regardless of the concerted assaults on our, on Her, being. . . . She is the Old Woman Spider who weaves us together in a fabric of interconnection. She is the Eldest God, the one who Remembers and Re-members. (11)

> Among the tribes, the occult power of women, inextricably bound to our hormonal life, is thought to be very great. (47)

> Women are by the nature of feminine "vibration" graced with certain inclinations that make them powerful and capable in certain ways. (207)

> It is the nature of woman's existence to be and to create background. This fact, viewed with unhappiness by many feminists, is of ultimate importance in a tribal context. (243)

Coupled with her more recent references to "multitudinous Great Goddess(es)" in *Grandmothers of the Light*, it's difficult *not* to interpret these statements as indicating a concept of female identity rooted in biology and thus to conclude that the "feminine" Allen attempts to "recover" is an ahistorical, unchanging essence that supports conventional phallocratic definitions of Woman, as well as romanticized, nostalgic images of "Indians."

According to Allen herself, however, recovering the "feminine" in American Indian traditions does not imply a retreat into a mythical prehistorical past. Nor is it an attempt to apply conventional masculinist notions of femininity to Native American women. It is, rather, a political act situated in the material present. In "Who Is Your Mother? The Red Roots of White Feminism" she emphasizes that her interest in recovering the "red roots" of Euro-American feminism is not motivated by "nostalgia." As her title indicates, she argues that the principles guiding twentieth-century U.S. feminists have their source in

Native traditions. However, because they have forgotten "their history on this continent," feminists are unaware of the parallels between the forms of oppression experienced by contemporary women and those experienced by indigenous peoples and earlier European gynocentric cultures. Allen maintains that until mainstream and radical U.S. feminists recognize their efforts to establish egalitarian social structures represent the "continuance" of tribal gynocentric traditions, they restrict feminism to a gender-based movement and overlook important models for personal, political, economic, and cultural change (*Sacred Hoop*, 214).

Throughout "Who Is Your Mother?" Allen stresses that to alter current conditions, contemporary social actors must recognize their ties to the past. Origin stories play an important role in this process because they enable us to go 'back' to the 'past' to transform existing conditions. Thus she tells us

> traditionals say we must remember our origins, our cultures, our histories, our mothers and grandmothers, for without that memory, which implies continuance rather than nostalgia, we are doomed to engulfment by a paradigm that is fundamentally inimical to the quality, autonomy, and self-empowerment essential for satisfying, high-quality life. (*Sacred Hoop*, 214)

But what, exactly, is the difference between "continuance" and "nostalgia"? After all, both terms could be interpreted as the desire to recapture an earlier era. According to David Murray, for example, the two words are often used synonymously. As he explains in his discussion of contemporary writers' attempts to synthesize precolonial images of the past with present-day conditions, the "invocation of unity is a recurrent theme in American Indian writing."[8] He argues that although this holism could be politically motivated, generally it is not: "[I]n the existing body of American Indian writing, the idea of wholeness and unity are more usually an expression of a nostalgia without any political cutting edge—a nostalgia for a tribal unity, and for a simplicity which fits neatly into the patterns of literary Romanticism" (88).

Yet Allen's feminism, her theory of perpetual liminality, and her belief that time is nonlinear and human beings are "moving event[s] within a moving universe" make such interpretations untenable (*Sacred Hoop*, 149). In a dynamic, constantly changing world with no 'beginning' or 'end,' we cannot go *back* to an earlier point in time. Instead, we can use the so-called past to understand present conditions more fully and to direct future actions. For Allen, continuance implies the historical past's continuity, its constant *presence* and ongoing interaction with contemporary human life. Thus she distinguishes between the ritual-based "ceremonial time" found in Native American worldviews and the "chronological time" generally associated with history and daily life. As she explains in "The Ceremonial Motion of Indian Time: Long Ago, So Far," whereas western culture's exclusive emphasis on chronological time divides history into discrete segments and separates time itself from "the internal workings of human and other beings," Native American "ceremonial time" is achronological and mythic; events apparently located 'outside' the temporal present—whether or not we 'actually' experienced them—can have significant effects on our lives (*Sacred Hoop*, 149).

Continuance has additional implications for indigenous North American peoples. Given the specific types of oppression they have experienced for the past five hundred years—which include (but are not limited to) genocide, forced assimilation, sterilization, removal, Christianization, and reeducation—continuance, survival, and recovery are almost synonymous. Allen maintains that Native Americans' attempts to reclaim their non-European cultural traditions have played a central role in their struggle to resist assimilation into mainstream U.S. culture. Throughout *The Sacred Hoop* she emphasizes the feminist dimensions of this project by associating both the decimation of Native peoples and the widespread erasure of Woman-based ritual traditions with a shift from gynocentric to phallocratic social structures. She explains in "How the West Was Really Won" that "[t]he genocide practiced against the tribes . . . aimed systematically at the dissolution of ritual traditions . . . and the degradation of the status of women as central to the spiritual and ritual life of the tribes" (195). According to Allen, this cultural/spiritual/biological genocide continues today, often (but not always) in less obvious forms, like the highly romanticized stereotype of the "vanishing Indian" (*Sacred Hoop*, 151). Continuance, then, entails far more than a nostalgic desire for "tribal unity." Because she sees the ongoing systematic oppression of Native Americans as both gender- and culture-specific, she believes "[t]he central issue that confronts American Indian women throughout the hemisphere is survival, *literal survival*, both on a cultural and biological level" (*Sacred Hoop*, 189; her emphasis).

Allen's frequent references to the devastating effects of this ongoing material and ideological extermination make it difficult to dismiss either her origin myths or her desire to recover the "feminine" in American Indian traditions as an escapist retreat into an impossible, highly idealized past. It is, in fact, almost the reverse. Her emphasis on the sociopolitical and cultural implications of indigenous mythic systems attempts to reshape contemporary and future conceptions of American Indians, feminism, and U.S. culture. Indeed, Allen's feminized, Indianized "cosmogyny"[9] represents several significant alterations in current systems of meaning. First, by describing preconquest North American cultures as gynocentric, Allen revises previous academic interpretations of Native traditions and attempts to enlist all U.S. feminists—whatever their cultural backgrounds—in Native Americans' ongoing political struggles. Second, by attributing forms of oppression experienced by contemporary women to the "same materialistic, antispiritual forces . . . presently engaged in wiping out the same gynarchical values, along with the peoples who adhere to them, in Latin America" and other countries (*Sacred Hoop*, 214), Allen expands existing conceptions of feminist movement and challenges self-identified feminists to develop cross-cultural, cross-gendered alliances with other oppressed peoples. As she asserts in an interview,

> what I'm really attempting to do is affect feminist thinking. Because my white sisters—and they have influenced the Black and Asian and Chicano sisters—have given the impression that women have always been held down, have always been weak, and have always been persecuted by men, but I know that's not true. I come from a people that that is not true of. (quoted in Ballinger and Swann, 10)

Third, by associating a diverse set of Native American mythic creatrixes with a cosmic "feminine" intelligence, Allen develops an epistemological system that draws on the oral tradition's dialogical nature to redefine Enlightenment-based descriptions of the intellect.

11   Is it only the question of unearthing that which the colonial
      experience buried and overlaid, bringing to light the hid-
      den continuities it suppressed? Or is a quite different prac-
      tice entailed—not the rediscovery but the PRODUCTION of
      identity. Not an identity grounded in the archaeology, but
      in the RE-TELLING of the past?   STUART HALL

Allen's origin myths represent a significant departure from those described by earlier Native American literary scholars who relied on
male-centered stories from Christianized Native informants.[10] In *The
Woman Who Owned the Shadows* Allen synthesizes and alters the
Laguna Keres and Iroquois origin accounts to construct a gynocentric
mythic story reflecting her own experiences in twentieth-century U.S.
culture, as well as the experiences of her mixed-blood protagonist.[11]
More specifically, she replaces earlier masculinist interpretations of
Native American mythic systems with interpretations emphasizing the
centrality of "feminine" creative powers. As Elizabeth Hanson asserts,
"Allen redesigns her own creation myth and, in the process, . . . feminizes and personalizes the myth of Spider woman and her twin" (35).

Spider Woman and Allen's many other "personalized" mythic
creatrixes represent an equally significant departure from the goddesses found in traditional Graeco-Roman mythology, for she associates them with a cosmic intelligence that manifests itself through
language. She opens *The Sacred Hoop* by declaring: "In the beginning
was *thought*, and her name was *Woman*" (11; my emphasis). Similarly,
she begins *The Woman Who Owned the Shadows* with her version of
the story of Old Spider Woman, whose "*singing* made all the worlds.
The worlds of the spirits. The worlds of the people. The worlds of
the creatures. The worlds of the gods" (1; my emphasis). And again
in *Grandmothers of the Light* she attributes the creation of the entire cosmos—including nature, human beings, sociopolitical systems,
literature, and the sciences—to Grandmother Spider or "Thinking
Woman," who

   thought the earth, the sky, the galaxy, and all that is into being, and as
   she thinks, so we are. She *sang* the divine sisters Nau'ts'ity and Ic'sts'ity

... into being out of her medicine pouch or bundle, and they in turn sang the firmament, the land, the seas, the people, the katsina, the gods, the plants, animals, minerals, language, writing, mathematics, architecture, the Pueblo social system, and every other thing you can imagine in this our world. (28; my emphasis)

In these versions of Allen's woman-centered mythic stories, creation occurs through language and thought. These origin narratives have little in common with standard, phallocentric creation accounts that conflate "Woman" with "womb" and reduce the "feminine" to the highly sexualized yet passive bearer of (male) culture. Nor are they similar to those feminist origin myths that valorize women's previously denigrated maternal role by identifying goddess imagery and female power primarily with childbirth.[12] As a number of theorists have argued, feminist celebrations of motherhood can be problematic. Although they affirm traditionally devalued aspects of female identity, many revisionist accounts of mother goddesses or the maternal do not fully challenge the underlying, patriarchally defined gender roles. As Judith Butler points out, the reliance on existing systems of meaning inadvertently "engender, naturalize, and immobilize" binary gender relations and stereotypical notions of womanhood. She argues that by positing "the category of woman as a coherent and stable subject," feminists' representational politics inevitably reify conservative, heterosexist constructions of a normative female identity (*Gender Trouble*, 5).[13] It is this supposedly inevitable reification of exclusionary gender categories that leads her to question the political effectiveness of all revisionist accounts of Woman, "women's experience," and the "feminine."

However, Allen's "feminine" mestizaje indicates the possibility of rewriting the "feminine" in nonexclusionary ways. Rather than replace one coherent and stable female subject with another, her re-metaphorized Woman destabilizes both male and female gender-inflected subject positions. For example, in her discussion of the Laguna Keres creatrix Allen complicates the conventional relationship between women, the "feminine," and female gender roles. She refers to Thought Woman as "mother" and describes her power as "feminine" yet stipulates that this creatrix is "not limited to a female role in the total theology of the Keres people." By associating Thought Woman's creative power with a cosmic intelligence rather than with biologically based definitions of creation, Allen can insist that her role is not gender specific: "Since she is the supreme Spirit, she is both Mother and Father to all people and to all creatures. She is the only creator of thought, and thought precedes creation" (*Sacred Hoop*, 15). Similarly, Allen asserts that in many tribal cultures the terms "Mother" and "Matron" reveal the great respect paid to all women yet maintains that the titles themselves are not gender specific. They apply to both women and men, for they represent "the highest office to which a *man* or woman could aspire" (*Sacred Hoop*, 28–29; my emphasis).[14]

This insistence on nonbiological, "feminine" creative powers provides an important exception to Butler's belief that references to "women" or "women's experience" inevitably reinforce heterosexist concepts of female identity. According to Butler, "the category of women achieve[s] stability and coherence . . . in the context of the heterosexual matrix" (*Gender Trouble*, 5). She maintains that in contemporary, western sociosymbolic systems, Woman is always defined in relation to Man; consequently, representations of women automatically imply heterosexually defined gender roles. However, by incorporating nonwestern elements into her revisionist mythmaking, Allen retains the category of "Woman" yet detaches it from the "heterosexual matrix" underlying western images of gender identities. And indeed, she often describes her mythic figures in distinctly nonheterosexual terms. In her discussion of Keres theology she emphasizes that

> the creation does not take place through copulation. In the beginning existed Thought Woman and her dormant sisters, and Thought Woman thinks creation and sings her two sisters into life. . . . The sisters are not related by virtue of having parents in common; that is, they are not alive because anyone bore them. (*Sacred Hoop*, 16)

Similarly, when she retells the Navajo creation story of Hard Beings Woman she points out that creation did not occur through male/female sexual intercourse but rather through the merger of two "feminine" elements—the "meeting of woman and water" (*Sacred Hoop*, 14). In *Grandmothers of the Light* Allen again distinguishes between heterosexual, biological reproduction and other forms of creativity by associating her creatrixes with thought. She asserts that because the Mayan creators—Xmucané and Xpiyacoc, who she calls "the Grandmothers"—represent "the original measurers of time, or day keepers," their creative power goes beyond sexual reproduction to encompass a magical, nonbiological generative power (55). She maintains that scholars' references to heterosexually paired mythic figures as "(grand)mother" and "(grand)father" gods represent later patriarchal interpellations into earlier gynocentric texts. Thus she refers to both these Mayan creators (or "Grandmothers") in female-gendered terms and parenthetically notes that in twentieth-century accounts Xpiyacoc is generally referred to as "Grandfather" (29). Although Allen does not explicitly lesbianize her creatrix figures, her repeated emphasis on their nonbiological creative powers undermines readers' heterosexist assumptions.

Allen further discredits conventional, phallocentric gender categories by repeatedly insisting that the "feminine" creative power she describes cannot be interpreted according to contemporary Euro-American descriptions of maternal functions. In "Grandmother of the Sun: Ritual Gynocracy in Native America," she associates U.S. culture's sentimental notions of motherhood with the devaluation of contemporary women's socioeconomic status and asserts that gynocentric mythic traditions do not equate maternity and motherhood with biological functions.[15] She distinguishes between fertility cults, biological birth, and "sacred or ritual birth" and carefully associates North American creatrix figures exclusively with the latter. Thus she challenges the commonly held assumption that Thought Woman, Hard Beings Woman, Corn Woman, and other mythic mothers represent indigenous peoples' inadequate understanding of human conception. According to Allen, such assumptions are ethnocentric and sexist: In addition to trivializing both "the tribes . . . and the power of woman," they restrict "the power inherent in femininity" (*Sacred Hoop*, 14–15).

I want to emphasize that Allen does not disavow the importance of maternity itself. By positing a cosmic "feminine" intelligence her origin myths affirm the maternal—and, by extension, real-life women's experience—yet redefine it as "female ritual power" (*Sacred Hoop*, 27). In her discussion of Ixchel, the Yucatán Indian's "goddess of the moon, water, childbirth, weaving, and love," Allen explains that "female ritual power" encompasses far more than biological birth, for it contains all types of physical and nonphysical transformations, including "the power to end life or to take life away" and "the power of disruption" (*Sacred Hoop*, 27). Rather than *reducing* Woman to the maternal function, then, Allen expands conventional definitions of maternity to incorporate all forms of creativity and change, as well as all aspects of human existence. She associates Thought Woman's "power of Original Thinking or Creation Thinking" with "the power of mothering" yet depicts "mothering" in terms that include, but go beyond, biological reproduction: "'mothering' . . . is not so much power to give birth, . . . but the power to make, to create, to transform" (*Sacred Hoop*, 29). One form this creative mothering can take can be found in "Grandmother," Allen's poetic retelling of a Laguna Pueblo creation story about Grandmother Spider. In this short poem Allen alludes to biological birth yet reworks it to encompass other forms of creativity, such as weaving, storytelling, and writing. In the opening lines she describes creation in the following way: "Out of her own body she pushed / silver thread, light, air." This grandmother creator weaves "the strands / of her body, her pain, her vision / into creation."

By drawing connections between these mythic representations of Woman and historical Native women, Allen subtly underscores metaphoric language's performative effects, its influence on both psychic and material conditions. She maintains that this "feminine," all-inclusive, transformational force had significant implications for preconquest indigenous women's social status. Because "the power to make life" was seen as "the source of all power," women performed central functions in tribal ritual and political systems (*Sacred Hoop*, 27). According to Allen, "The blood of woman was in and of itself infused with the power of Supreme Mind, and so women were held in awe and respect" (*Sacred Hoop*, 28).

As these statements reveal, at times Allen seems to base her arguments concerning maternity and the "feminine" on women's reproductive capabilities. And in a sense, she does. However, by expanding conventional descriptions of reproduction to include imaginative and intellectual creativity, she downplays this biological aspect so significantly that she almost entirely discounts it. Consider the following description of "female ritual power":

[T]he power to make life is the source and model for all ritual magic and . . . no other power can gainsay it. Nor is that power really biological at base; it is the power of ritual magic, that power of Thought, of Mind, that gives rise to biological organisms as it gives rise to social organizations, material culture, and transformations of all kinds—including hunting, war, healing, spirit communication, rain-making, and all the rest. (*Sacred Hoop*, 28)

As in her equation of women's menstrual blood with "the power of Supreme Mind," Allen redefines both "femininity" and the mind, creating an epistemological process that simultaneously "feminizes" the intellect and spiritualizes the body.

I want to emphasize the innovative dimensions of Allen's "feminized" epistemology. By redefining the maternal as transformational thought, Allen unsettles the hierarchical, dichotomous worldview that equates "masculine" with transcendence, culture, and the mind, and "feminine" with immanence, nature, and the body.[16] Significantly, she does not replace one dualism with another: As "the necessary *precondition* for material creation," Allen's re-metaphorized Woman represents a dynamic, all-inclusive, intellectual, creative, maternal power that generates both "material and nonmaterial reality" (*Sacred Hoop*, 14–15; my emphasis). This "feminized" intelligence is both *supernatural* (Allen equates it with Old Spider Woman/Thought Woman) and *natural* (Thought Woman's intelligence encompasses human beings as well as the physical world: It "permeates the land—the mountains and clouds, the rains and lightning, the corn and deer" [*Grandmothers*, 34]). Unlike Athene, the Greek goddess of (patriarchal) wisdom whose divine intelligence entails the sacrifice of the mother,[17] Allen's mythic Woman represents a maternalized embodied intelligence, or what Luce Irigaray might describe as "a spirituality of the body, the flesh" ("Universal as Mediation," 135).[18]

III   One element of contemporary feminist reflection which I find particularly striking is the element of risk that these thinkers introduce into intellectual activity. Theirs is a more daring, risky form of intelligence; their approach to

**enunciation and to discursive practice is freer and more
disrespectful than the established norms.**

ROSI BRAIDOTTI

As her emphasis on the concrete, material dimensions of thought
implies, Allen develops an epistemological system that avoids the Cartesian mind/body dualism. By establishing a reciprocal relationship
between the intellectual, the physical, and the spiritual, she destabilizes classical western definitions of reason and rationality. Her embodied mythic thinking intervenes in western culture's "crisis of reason," a crisis related to the absence of certainty and secure foundations
in rationalist and empiricist theories of knowledge.[19] According to a
number of contemporary feminist philosophers, this crisis has its
source in the hidden masculinist bias in all supposedly universal
knowledge systems. As Elizabeth Grosz explains, because reason, rationality, and the mind have been symbolized as "masculine,"[20] this
previously unacknowledged bias has led to "the historical privileging
of the purely conceptual or mental over the corporeal" and the subsequent denial of the body. In western cultures the body has been traditionally associated with the "feminine," and this disavowal has important implications for real-life women:

> If the body is an unacknowledged or an inadequately acknowledged
> condition of knowledges, and if . . . [it] is always sexually specific,
> concretely "sexed," this implies that the hegemony over knowledges
> that masculinity has thus far accomplished can be subverted, upset, or
> transformed through women's assertion of "a right to know," inde-
> pendent of and autonomous from the methods and presumptions
> regulating the prevailing (patriarchal) forms of knowledge. ("Bodies
> and Knowledges," 187–88)

Allen's embodied mythic thinking, as well as her frequent references to Thought Woman and her use of North American creatrix
figures to "feminize" American Indian traditions, can be read as her
assertion of an independent and autonomous cognitive stance. Like
Hélène Cixous, Luce Irigaray, and the other autonomy-feminists
Grosz describes, Allen simultaneously critiques conventional western
knowledge systems and develops new ways of thinking that require

different intellectual standards. Her embodied mythic thinking exposes the phallocentric foundations of western culture's reliance on logical, rational thought and provides an alternative to analytical forms of thinking. As she explains in *Grandmothers of the Light*, she uses storytelling rather than logical proofs to unsettle contemporary readers' over-reliance on reason: "Many times the stories weave back and forth between the everyday and the supernatural without explanation, confusing the logical mind and compelling linear thought processes to chase their own tails, which of course is a major spiritual purpose behind the tradition's narrative form" (5).

But Allen's epistemic position departs more radically from Eurocentric masculinist conventions than the feminist epistemologies Grosz describes. Whereas autonomy-feminists generally support their alternate positions with arguments drawn from poststructuralist theory,[21] Allen relies extensively on information acquired from her "inner self" and "the supernaturals." She provides little "factual" scholarly evidence for her assertions. In the "Introduction" to *The Sacred Hoop*, for instance, she justifies her attempt to recover the "feminine" in American Indian traditions with the following highly unacademic statement:

> Whatever I read about Indians I check out with my inner self. Most of what I have read—and some things I have said based on that reading—is upside-down and backward. But *my inner self, the self who knows what is true about American Indians because it is one*, always warns me when something deceptive is going on. . . . Sometimes that confirmation comes about in miraculous ways; that's when I know *guidance from the nonphysicals and the supernaturals*, and that *the Grandmothers* have taken pity on me in my dilemma. (6–7; my emphasis)

She takes this open acknowledgment of supernatural guidance even further in *Grandmothers of the Light* and explains that she derived the information for her mythic stories "from a variety of ethnographic and literary sources, from the oral tradition, and from *direct communication with my own spirit guides*" (xiii; my emphasis).[22]

Similarly, in " 'Border' Studies" Allen replaces conventional epistemological methodologies and formalist theories of literary scholarship with her own highly idiosyncratic perspective on contemporary literary theory. This essay, published in the Modern Languages Association's *Introduction to Scholarship in Modern Languages and Literatures*, has little in common with the other, more conventional, scholarly essays collected in the anthology. Ostensibly a theoretical overview of literary production by contemporary self-identified U.S. women of color, " 'Border' Studies" could be more accurately described as Allen's own inventive literary origin myth, her personalized account of what she calls the "creative void," or the source of all original literary work (306). As in *The Sacred Hoop* and *Grandmothers of the Light*, Allen employs a variety of tactics that simultaneously critique and transform western academic literary conventions. She rejects margin/center discourse and all other oppositional theories as reactionary and maintains that many self-identified U.S. women of color writers, as well as other "*disappearadas*," position themselves in the "Void"—"the still, dark center of the heart of the gynocosmos where nothing at all exists and whence, paradoxically, all must emerge" (306).

Does this reliance on spirit guides, supernatural informants, and the "dark grandmother of human wisdom" (" 'Border' Studies," 305) discredit Allen's "feminine" mestizaje and the embodied mythic thinking it implies? I think it depends on your perspective. Viewed from within the academy, her truth claims are highly suspect, if not outright laughable. Indeed, most academic scholars avoid commenting on the feminist epistemological dimensions of Allen's recent work. According to Elizabeth Hanson, one of the few literary critics who has not simply ignored Allen's gynocentric origin myths, this conflation of Native American cultures with the "feminine" lacks sufficient explanation or proof: "Allen's vision of tribal life as gynocratic in nature, rather than simply mystical or psychic, reveals a remarkable contention, one that Allen herself recognizes as supported by limited verifiable evidence" (15–16). Hanson also notes that Allen's interpretation of the "feminine" in *The Sacred Hoop* cannot be supported by factual, historical information. Furthermore, it contradicts her own earlier view of Native cultures, as well as the perspectives of well-respected, "gifted and sensitive historians" (16).

It could be tempting to label Allen's inability or refusal to provide sufficient "factual" evidence, coupled with her references to supernatural informants, as New Ageish or "neo-Romantic"[23] and to dismiss her epistemological perspective entirely. But I want to suggest another possibility, one based on the limitations of contemporary academic discourse. In a Eurocentric patriarchal culture such as our own, an elite group of people defines what counts as scholarship and thus establishes the rules and definitions for knowledge claims, validation standards, and truth effects. But as Patricia Hill Collins explains, positivism and other conventional epistemological methods are inadequate for exploring the "subjugated knowledges" of black women and other subordinate groups, whose experiences and self-conceptions do not conform to the prevailing standards. Collins found her own academic "training as a social scientist inadequate to the task of studying the subjugated knowledge of a Black women's standpoint." Thus she relied on personal experience, the experiences of other black women, and "alternate sites" of knowledge production, like poetry, music, "daily conversations, and everyday behavior"[24] (202). Similarly, Allen's academic training as a literary scholar is inadequate to her undertaking. If, as Allen asserts, the decimation of Native peoples parallels the systematic erasure of gynocentric ritual and oral traditions,[25] how—relying on conventional positivist methodologies—could *anyone* examine the "feminine" in American Indian traditions? To borrow Luce Irigaray's term, both the "feminine" and the American Indian traditions Allen tries to recover are in a state of *déréliction*, or abandonment; they lack representation in the dominant cultural symbolic. There are no existing words or conceptual frameworks to convey the "feminized" Native traditions and beliefs Allen explores.

Allen does not provide readers with an authentic, gendered, ethnic-specific standpoint. Her epistemology is performative, not descriptive; and the effect is transcultural transformation. By writing her "feminine" mestizaje, she stages a fluid, transcultural self/worldview that she invites her readers—whatever their cultural backgrounds—to adopt. Instead of recovering a precolonial mythological system erased by patriarchal structures, Allen invents an ethical, *artificial* mythology—ethical, because her new Indianized metaphors of Woman provide imaginary alternatives to contemporary western definitions of the "feminine"; and artificial, because the "feminine" she affirms does not—yet—exist.

Thus Allen's inventive mythmaking embodies what Drucilla Cornell calls "ethical feminism," or what I would describe as an aspect of differential consciousness that employs performative speech acts to disrupt the prevailing phallocentric sociosymbolic order. Significantly, Cornell's ethical feminist does not attempt to replace contemporary definitions of the "feminine" with alternate definitions that more accurately reflect the truth of women's experience. Instead, her feminist speaks from "the utopian or redemptive perspective of the not yet" by using allegory and myth to *imaginatively* reconstruct the "feminine" (*Transformations*, 59). Thus, ethical feminism occurs in the subjunctive, in a liminal space between past, present, and future definitions. Or as Cornell explains, ethical feminism

> explicitly recognizes the "should be" in representations of the feminine. It emphasizes the role of the imagination, not description, in creating solidarity between women. Correspondingly, ethical feminism rests its claim for the intelligibility and coherence of "herstory" not on what women "are," but on the remembrance of the "not yet" which is recollected in both allegory and myth. (*Transformations*, 59)

In other words, ethical feminism reclaims and rereads already existing stories and myths of the "feminine" but interprets them in new ways.

At this point I want to adopt Cornell's ethical feminism and apply my own "redemptive perspective" to a reading of Allen's origin myths. Despite Allen's apparent comments to the contrary, I believe that her discussions of Thought Woman, Corn Woman, the Grandmothers, and other Native American creatrixes "should be" read performatively, as potentially transformational metaphors. In particular—and, quite possibly, *contra* Allen herself—I am suggesting that these mythic figures do not represent accurate descriptions of an authentic womanhood; nor do they indicate the recovery of an essential "feminine" nature. Such literal interpretations are far too limiting; they lead to restrictive definitions of the "feminine" and confine women's experiences to a predetermined set of characteristics. More importantly, if we read Allen's metaphoric language descriptively, we deny its performative effects and overlook the visionary, ethical dimensions of her work.

As Allen validates her claims with references to Thought Woman and other mythic figures, she draws on metaphoric language's performative effects to alter her readers' self/worldviews. In the revisionist myths she enacts, representation and creation become blurred. As Cornell explains, metaphoric language, "reality," and perception are inextricably related in complex ways:

> "Being" cannot be separated from "seeing," but it cannot be reduced to it either. We do not see what "is," directly. We see through the world presented in language. . . . [T]his world is never just presented as static, because the very language which allows us to "see" also allows us to see differently, because of the performative power of the metaphors that constitute reality. To reinterpret is to see differently. (*Beyond Accommodation*, 131)

Because language structures our perceptions of reality, new words and new concepts can provide us with new points of view, different perspectives enabling us to reinterpret existing social systems and forms of identity.

Allen's origin myths play a significant role in this reinterpretive process. Rather than entirely rejecting all references to Woman and the "feminine," as some poststructuralists suggest, Allen keeps the terms but redefines them *without* reinstating normative gender categories.[26] Just as her embodied mythic thinking destabilizes classical definitions of reason and rationality, her Indianized metaphors of Woman disrupt existing categories of identity and provide new alternatives. By associating her creatrix figures with a cosmic, divine, "feminine" intelligence, she intervenes in current systems of meaning and opens up possibilities for living out the "feminine" in new ways.

Paradoxically, then, Allen's "feminine" can be found neither within nor without the prevailing sociosymbolic structure. Yet it oscillates between the two. As Cornell argues in her discussion of Hélène Cixous's and Luce Irigaray's revisionist mythmaking, the "feminist reconstruction of myth" relies on a performative contradiction: Because the "feminine" system has been defined only in relation to the "masculine," the "feminine" *qua* "feminine" does not (yet) exist; consequently, the "feminine" Cixous, Irigaray, and other contemporary feminist writers—Allen, Anzaldúa, and Lorde among them—affirm "cannot be reduced or identified with the lives of actual women, nor adequately represented as the elsewhere to masculine discourse" (*Beyond Accommodation*, 150). But if this ethical affirmation of the "feminine" is neither fully inside nor entirely outside current meaning systems, how might we enact it?

IV   *Interviewer*: "Given your background and your culture and the way in which you straddle cultures or have incorporated a number of cultures, what makes an Indian?"
Allen: "I believe that it's a turn of mind."

Like Allen's theory of perpetual liminality, her ethical affirmation of the "feminine" indicates an ongoing creative process that occurs at the interface of inside and outside; as such, it involves the recovery of the "feminine" as an imaginative universal. According to Cornell, this recovery

> feeds the power of the feminine imagination and helps to avoid the depletion of the feminine imaginary in the name of the masculine symbolic. This use of the feminine as an imaginative universal does not, and should not, pretend to simply tell the "truth" of woman as she was, or is. This is why our mythology is self-consciously an artificial mythology; Woman is "discovered" as an ethical standard. And as she is "discovered," her meaning is also created.[27] (*Beyond Accommodation*, 178)

As Cornell's oscillation between creation and discovery indicates, this use of the "feminine" draws on the rhetoric of authenticity yet goes beyond existing definitions to emphasize the artificial, inventive nature of these mythologies.

I want to underscore the open-ended possibilities in this use of the "feminine" as an imaginative universal. Because the "discovery" of Woman as an ethical standard occurs within mythic metaphors, it defies literal, monologic interpretation, making possible a proliferation of meanings. Revisionist mythmaking plays an important role in this "discovery," for mythic images are open to multiple interpretations. As Cornell points out: "It is the potential variability of myth that allows us to work within myth, and the significance it offers, so as to reimagine our world and by so doing, to begin to dream of a new one" (*Beyond Accommodation*, 178).

Although Allen herself does not describe her gynocentric mythologies as artificial, they function analogously to the artificial mythologies Cornell describes. The rhetoric of discovery and authenticity Allen employs can be read as tactical maneuvers to bring about individual and collective transformation. When readers enter into Allen's origin narratives, they "discover" new definitions of the "feminine." By phrasing her new definitions in the language of discovery, she authorizes her words.

Significantly, Allen's use of the "feminine" as an imaginative universal serves an additional, related purpose, as well. By Indianizing her "feminine" mestizaje, she opens up a space for the construction of transcultural feminist social actors. If, as I suggested in the previous chapter, each subject is composed of multiple parts and located at the intersection of diverse—sometimes overlapping, sometimes conflicting—discourses, no identity is or ever can be stable and fixed. As Chantal Mouffe states, there is always "a certain degree of openness and ambiguity in the way the different subject-positions are articulated" (35). It's this potential openness to redefinition that makes personal and cultural change possible. To bring about radical social change, however, these subject positions cannot just be combined differently; they must be transformed:

> If the task of radical democracy is indeed to deepen the democratic revolution and to link together diverse democratic struggles, such a task requires the creation of new subject-positions that would allow the common articulation, for example, of antiracism, antisexism, and anticapitalism. These struggles do not spontaneously converge, and in order to establish democratic equivalences, a new "common sense" is necessary, which would transform the identity of different groups so that the demands of each group could be articulated with those of others according to the principle of democratic equivalence. (43)

In other words, in today's postmodern world political unities do not automatically arise; they must be consciously developed through a process of articulation.[28] Like the cultural translation Homi Bhabha describes, the creation of new political subjectivities occurs in an ambivalent, heterogeneous space that problematizes conventional assumptions concerning unitary identities based on shared histories or cultural traditions. Political subjects, priorities, and plans of action do not 'naturally exist; they must be constructed "through a process of translation and transference of meaning" ("Commitment," 119). Contemporary socialist democratic politics and policies must be invented, not discovered, "*because there is no given community or body of the people, whose inherent, radical historicity emits the right signs*" (119; his emphasis). We—no matter who 'we' are—do not automatically unite on the basis of shared 'natural' traits. Instead, shared identities must be created. Bhabha underscores the inventive nature of contemporary politics in an interview with Jonathan Rutherford, where he rejects the commonly held belief that politics entails mobilizing already existing social subjects:

> The concept of a people is not "given," as an essential, class-determined, unitary, homogeneous part of society *prior to a politics*; "the people" are there as a process of political articulation and political negotiation across a whole range of contradictory social sites. "The people" always exist as a multiple form of identification, waiting to be created and constructed. ("The Third Space," 220)

Allen's "feminine" mestizaje indicates one form this construction of "the people" can take. Because her "discovery" of Woman as an ethical standard occurs within metaphor, on an imaginary level, it potentially destabilizes readers' ego-ideal identifications, the master signifiers or symbols that shape our self-conceptions in pivotal ways. When we identify the "feminine" in ourselves with the "feminine" in Thought Woman, Hard Beings Woman, and Allen's other mythic figures, we experience a "metaphoric transference."[29] That is, we encounter a slippage within our current definitions of Woman and the "feminine" as we recognize a gap between what "is" and what "should be." It's this slippage between competing definitions that enables readers to act out the "feminine" differently. More specifically, because Woman and the "feminine" function as master signifiers in identity formation, this recognition produces a shift in our self-perceptions.[30] As Mark Bracher explains, "what happens to our sense of being or identity is determined to a large degree by what happens to those signifiers that represent us" (25).[31] By Indianizing the master signifiers that represent "us" women, Allen Indianizes her readers as well.

Allen's use of nonwestern North American "tribal" creatrix figures does not indicate a nostalgic desire to return to a prehistorical, utopian "Indian" community of women. By going back to previously erased indigenous conventions, she rewrites the past and invents new definitions. As Trinh Minh-ha asserts, "[T]he return to a denied heritage allows one to start again with different re-departures, different pauses, different arrivals" (*Moon*, 14). Allen's "returns" are performative, not descriptive. As she writes her "feminine" mestizaje, she engages in a to-and-fro movement that takes up yet disrupts conventional interpretations of Woman, "American Indians," women, and the "feminine." These disruptive oscillations enable readers to go beyond conventional feminist identity politics and open up new thresholds, textual and psychic locations, where transcultural identifications—mestizaje connections—can be made.

Writing the Body/Writing the Soul
Gloria Anzaldúa's Mestizaje Écriture

For silence to transform into speech, sounds and words, it must first traverse through our female bodies.

GLORIA ANZALDÚA

Women must write through their bodies, they must invent the impregnable language that will wreck partitions, classes, and rhetorics, regulations and codes, they must submerge, cut through, get beyond the ultimate reserve-discourse.

HÉLÈNE CIXOUS

This statement will not fail to arouse negative reactions. A woman's body? We don't want to hear any more about it! They talk about nothing but that! Both men and women do not hesitate to show their irritation or disgust as soon as the association body/feminine writing appears.

TRINH MINH-HA

As the first two epigraphs to this chapter indicate, Gloria Anzaldúa and Hélène Cixous associate women's access to language with their bodies. They maintain that western culture's masculinist bias has inhibited women's ability to develop self-affirmative forms of speaking and writing. Because Woman has been defined by male desire,[1] the female body has been objectified, appropriated, marginalized, and repressed in and by phallocentric language systems.[2] This representational bias has physical and psychic effects on women, who view themselves, their bodies, and their desires according to male-defined standards. As Linda Singer asserts,

> In the absence of a female-identified voïce, or for that matter recognition by women of this absence and the conditions that produce and normalize it, self-interested male dominated discourse is free to construct women's desires in their absence, and to construct us in ways

which both mark our subjugation and reproduce it, by investing us
with forms of desire that facilitate their domination, like the pleasures
of surrender, self-sacrifice, and service to others. (140)

This lack of autonomous, female-defined voices greatly restricts wom-
en's self-images and sense of agency, as well as their roles in contemporary social systems. It's this tie between women's subordinate status
and the absence of female-identified language that leads Anzaldúa and
Cixous to insist that voice, body, desire, and text are intimately related.
Both theorists believe that in order to develop revolutionary, self-
affirming forms of discourse women must reclaim their own bodies.
Anzaldúa asserts in her preface to *Making Face, Making Soul/Ha-
ciendo Caras*:

> For silence to transform into speech, sounds, and words, it must first
> traverse through our female bodies. For the body to give birth to ut-
> terance, the human entity must recognize itself as carnal—skin, mus-
> cles, entrails, brain, belly. Because our bodies have been stolen, brutal-
> ized or numbed it is difficult to speak from/through them. (xxii)

She maintains that women must learn to value, recognize, and express
their embodied experiences. Cixous makes a similar statement in
"Laugh of the Medusa." "Write your self," she tells her readers. "Your
body must be heard. Only then will the immense resources of the
unconscious spring forth" (250). In less metaphorical terms, Cixous
associates these immense resources with new forms of knowledge. The
hegemony of Cartesian knowledge claims requires the elevation of the
conceptual over the corporeal, as well as the corresponding denial
of the feminine. Thus the development of female-identified voices,
bodies, and texts breaks apart this gendered binary structure, providing a significant challenge to existing knowledge systems.

Yet as my third epigraph suggests, this connection between writing,
the feminine, and the body is generally regarded with great distrust. A
number of critics have observed that although writing the body seems
to affirm women's autonomy—their ability to defy phallocentric
meaning systems and define themselves—the emphasis on metaphoric
female anatomy relies on already existing, biologically based notions
of female identity. They maintain that because Woman in western

culture has been devalued through her symbolic association with the body and nature, "writing the body" reinforces this already existing hierarchical, gendered division. Ann Rosalind Jones summarizes many U.S. and British feminists' objections to this valorization of the feminine in "Writing the Body: Toward an Understanding of *l'Écriture Féminine.*" She argues that although Cixous uses body-writing to deconstruct male/female binary systems, she inadvertently reinstates the dualism she strives to negate: Because the French theorist does not interrogate the traditional western conception of Woman as Man's opposite, *écriture féminine* "reverses the values assigned to each side of the polarity, but it still leaves man as the determining referent, not departing from the male-female opposition, but participating in it" (369). According to Jones, then, Cixous fails because her celebration of *féminité* reinforces the male/female dichotomy she deplores.[3] Robert Con Davis makes a related point in "Woman as Oppositional Reader," where he argues that Cixous's work clearly demonstrates the political limitations of oppositional forms of thinking and writing. According to Davis, because Cixous has played a major role in attempting to alter western society by modifying the categories from within existing meaning systems, her inability to do so compels theorists to acknowledge the impossibility of "subvert[ing] and chang[ing] culture from within" (96–98).[4]

These objections to writing the body have troubling implications for feminists and other social actors interested in transforming the existing sociosymbolic system. First, body-writing offers the possibility of inventing new, nonphallic forms of knowledge. However, if writing the body draws on already existing stereotypes of Woman, how do we explore this potential without reinforcing these stereotypes even further? Is it impossible to write about women's gender-specific bodily experiences without slipping into essentialist concepts of identity, descriptions of "female" that reify existing masculinist, hierarchical discourse? Second, body-writing represents a visionary belief in writing's transformational power—its ability to bring about concrete material change. However, if as Davis and others suggest, the limitations in Cixous's argument demonstrate the political ineffectiveness of this visionary belief, must we reject Cixous's assertion that "writing is precisely *the very possibility of change*, . . . the precursory movement of a transformation of social and cultural structures"? ("Laugh," 249; her emphasis). Or, can writing the body be politically effective?

My argument in this chapter builds on these debates. In the following pages I set Anzaldúa and Cixous in conversation—both with each other and with critics of écriture féminine. The similarities between Anzaldúa's and Cixous's discussions of writing are, at times, quite striking. Yet scholars almost never explore these two women—one labeled "Chicana," the other "French"—in conjunction; instead, each is relegated to discrete categories of literary and feminist thought. By reading Anzaldúa and Cixous in dialogue, I hope to demonstrate the importance of developing transculturally contextualized theories enabling us to explore both the differences and the similarities among variously situated women.

Previous readings of écriture féminine provide a useful context for this exploration. By focusing almost exclusively on French theories of writing the body, Jones, Davis, and others overlook the possibility of inventing nonbinary oppositional tactics that would displace, rather than simply reverse, the hierarchical dualism suppressing women's power. Although Cixous's work illustrates this displacement of opposites, the French theorist's many decontextualized references to "woman," "women," and the "feminine" can obscure the radical implications of her work, as well as the liberating potential opened up by body-writing. However, by exploring Anzaldúa's theory of writing in conjunction with Cixous's, we see new versions of body-writing that disrupt without reversing western culture's hierarchical binarisms. Like Cixous, Anzaldúa employs embodied, metaphoric language to open up "space[s] that can serve as a springboard for subversive thought" ("Laugh," 249). Yet she expands her definition of "writing the body" to encompass "writing the soul" and develops a writing process that reflects the specific needs of self-identified women of color and other marginalized groups. Thus Anzaldúa generally evades the charges of essentialism and regressive political thinking often levelled at Cixous.[5] Unlike the French theorist's descriptions of écriture féminine, Anzaldúa's discussions of "making face, making soul" cannot be misinterpreted as a writing practice that inadvertently "reproduce[s] the dichotomy between male rationality and female materiality" (Stanton, 170). Nor can she be accused of "focus[ing] ... upon 'woman' as an eternal essence" (Wenzel, 272). Instead, she demonstrates that valorizing women's bodily experiences—especially when those bodies are "read" for their racialized, sexualized inscriptions—can be a tactical maneuver in feminists' ongoing efforts to transform male-defined sociolinguistic structures. Body-writing's visionary metaphoric language provides feminists with one way, among others, of disrupting the rationalist assumptions and binary systems structuring western thought.

As she translates her own (Chicana-tejana, dyke, working-class) body into words, Anzaldúa invents what I describe as mestizaje écriture, nonsymmetrical oppositional writing tactics that simultaneously deconstruct, reassemble, and transcend phallocentric categories of thought. By emphasizing the permeable, constantly shifting boundaries between "inner" and "outer" realities, she demonstrates—contra Jones, Davis and others—that oppositional forms of resistance *can* subvert culture from within. Like Allen's "feminine" mestizaje, which I described in the previous chapter, Anzaldúa's writing practice indicates the possibility of enacting the "feminine" in open-ended, nonexclusionary yet culture-specific ways. In short, her writings illustrate another form this "feminine" mestizaje can take.

II   First off, the basic theoretical question: Can the body be a source of self-knowledge?   ANN ROSALIND JONES

"The answer," according to Jones, "is no." She argues that because women cannot "experience their bodies purely, or essentially, *outside* the damaging acculturation" of phallocentric sociolinguistic systems, the female body cannot provide us with alternate ways of knowing or writing (365–67; her emphasis). By approaching the issue somewhat differently, however, we can arrive at another conclusion. Rather than ask if the *unmediated* female body can "be a direct source of female writing" and self-knowledge, we might rephrase the question: Can culturally inscribed bodies—despite, or perhaps because of, the ways they are marked by gender, class, ethnicity, and sexuality—provide us with alternate ways of knowing and writing? The answer, for Anzaldúa, would be yes. As she declares in her introduction to *Making Face, Making Soul/Haciendo Caras*, when self-identified U.S. women of color artists turn to their bodies, they acquire new tactics for political intervention and social change:

> Even when our bodies have been battered by life, these artistic "languages," spoken from the body, by the body, are still laden with aspirations, are still coded in hope and "*un desarme ensagretado*," a bloodied truce. By sending our voices, our visuals and visions outward into the world, we alter the walls and make them a framework for new windows and doors. We transform the *posos*, apertures, *barrancas, abismos* that we are forced to speak from. Only then can we make a home out of the cracks. (xxv)

By speaking or writing our bodies, we *can* change culture from within. But what, more precisely, is an artistic language spoken from and by the body? And how can these languages be "coded in hope"? As I'll explain in the following sections, by incorporating their bodily experiences into their creative and theoretical writings, Anzaldúa and the women she describes develop alternate forms of discourse. Thus they open up theoretical spaces that undermine existing systems of meaning; they are "visionaries, people with vision, with new things to say and new perspectives to say them from" (xxvi).

Anzaldúa associates writing's transformative potential with the body. In an early essay, "Speaking in Tongues: A Letter to Third World Women Writers," she urges her readers to rewrite the dominant culture's inscriptions and maintains, "It's not on paper that you create but in your innards, in your gut and out of living tissue—*organic writing*, I call it" (170). Like Cixous's "newly born woman," Anzaldúa's woman writer is a "*mujer magica*," a magical woman who invents new modes of perception and new forms of action. Because she believes that "a woman who writes has power, and a woman with power is feared," she exhorts her readers to "listen to the words chanting in your body" (170–72; her emphasis). But the female bodies she describes have specific ethnic, cultural, and economic markings rarely found in Cixous's écriture féminine. Although the French writer celebrates each woman's "infinite richness," her decision to explore what all women "have *in common*" has led some critics to question the validity of her theory and others to reject it as an elitist notion—a "classist, narcissistic, intellectualistic, ahistorical doctrine, irrelevant to the lives of black, poor, and third-world women."[6]

By investigating both the many forms women's "infinite richness" takes and the ways this diversity affects and often inhibits their access to language, Anzaldúa demonstrates that writing the body can be relevant to U.S. women of color. Throughout her work she examines the particular difficulties faced by Chicanas and women who identify as black, Asian, Native Indian, working class, poor, and/or lesbian as they attempt to translate their (colored) bodies' silences into words. Indeed, as coeditor of *This Bridge Called My Back* and as editor of *Making Face, Making Soul/Haciendo Caras*, Anzaldúa has played a vital role both in encouraging self-identified women and lesbians of color to write and in acquainting the "mainstream" U.S. feminist movement with the specific forms of oppression these women encounter.

In conjunction with the linguistic suppression all women experience in phallocentric cultures, the women Anzaldúa describes have been further silenced by skin color, sexual preference, economic status, education, and/or English language skills. In *Borderlands/La Frontera*, for example, she draws on her own experiences as a child born into a Spanish-speaking family to illustrate the additional forms of silencing these women might face. Punished in school for speaking Spanish—a language devalued by the dominant Texan culture—she explains that this externally imposed restriction led to self-shame and the belief she had nothing of significance to say. Not surprisingly then, Anzaldúa maintains that before she and other multiply oppressed women can even *begin* writing their bodies, they must recognize and reclaim their identities as embodied subjects. Yet she stipulates that to do so is not easy: "Because our bodies have been stolen, brutalized or numbed, it is difficult to speak from/through them" ("Haciendo caras, una entrada" xxii). Those Mexican American women who have been defined as "poor Chicanita[s] from the sticks," capable only of working in the fields, or black U.S. women stereotyped as "lumbering nann[ies] with twelve babies sucking [their] tits" must defy an oppressive set of external labels, as well as overwhelmingly negative internalized beliefs, before they acquire the self-confidence to write ("Speaking," 166–67; her emphasis).

This exploration of the specific difficulties experienced by women of color marks a significant difference between Anzaldúa's mestizaje écriture and Cixous's écriture féminine. Unlike the French theorist's highly celebratory version of writing the body, Anzaldúa's body-writing combines affirmation with the recognition of intense physical and psychic pain. Take, for example, the following passage near the opening of *Borderlands/La Frontera* where Anzaldúa describes the border dividing Mexico from the United States. It is a

> 1,950 mile-long open wound
> > dividing a *pueblo*, a culture,
> > running down the length of my body,
> > > staking fence rods in my flesh
> > > splits me   splits me
> > > > *me raja   me raja* (2)

By associating her body with the U.S./Mexico border and depicting both as an open wound—*una "herida abierta"* (3)—Anzaldúa extends her personal experience outward and graphically depicts the alienation, self-division, and pain played out on her own body as well as the bodies of other Mexican Americans. Similarly, in "*Del otro lado*" she draws analogies between geography and the body to express her experiences as a Chicana queer. Again, the alienation, division, and pain are expressed on and through the body: "She looks at the Border Park fence / posts are stuck into her throat, her navel" (2). As the fence posts piercing her throat imply, this politico-geographical division impairs her ability to speak. Although she "excelled in the Gringo's tongue," facility with the English language does not give her a sense of belonging; she is "a stranger, an 80,000 year old illegal alien" in the land of her birth. Nor can she celebrate the culturally specific elements of her Mexican Indian heritage. "The ancient dances [are] beaten back inside her, / the old song choked back into her throat." Alienated both from the dominant, English-speaking U.S. culture and from the indigenous past, the woman Anzaldúa describes is fragmented, almost entirely silenced, and alone:

> Her body torn in two, half a woman on the other side
> half a woman on this side, the right side.
> The half of her that's on the other side
> walks lost through the land
> dropping bits of herself, a hand,
> a shoulder, a chunk of hair.
> Her pieces scattered over the deserts,
> the mountains and valley.
> Her mute voice whispers through grass stems. (2)

Prevented from expressing herself, torn by physical and psychic pain, she has "[n]o right to sing, to rage, to explode" (3). As her family condemns her same-sex desire, her mother's scornful words inscribe themselves on her already battered body; they "are barbs digging into her flesh" (3). Cultural, ethnic, and sexual alienation converge, writing themselves on her body.

Anzaldúa's emphasis on the sociopolitical, economic, and cultural inscriptions that variously mark female bodies illustrates the deployment of nonbinary modes of consciousness; she uses oppositional tactics to break down, rather than simply reverse, western culture's hierarchical dualism. By depicting the specific circumstances that variously shape each particular woman, Anzaldúa prevents readers from visualizing a monolithic concept of female identity, a generic Woman in opposition to a generic Man. Like Cixous, she develops nonphallic modes of discourse, or what Morag Shiach describes as "*the feminine*, . . . forms of writing, and of thought, that exceed the binary oppositions which have structured western thought and . . . supported patriarchy." As Shiach asserts, readers who conflate the French theorist's vision of a feminine writing practice with essentialism overlook "the complexity of the project in which Cixous is involved, and . . . the extent to which she is, quite consciously, talking about representations and available strategies for their transformation, rather than about reality" ("symbolic," 155–57; her emphasis). But why do such misinterpretations occur?

Consider Cixous's declaration near the opening of "The Laugh of the Medusa," her "manifesto" of écriture féminine:

> I write this as a woman, toward women. When I say "woman," I'm speaking of woman in her inevitable struggle against conventional man; and of a universal woman subject who must bring women to their senses and to their meaning in history. But first it must be said that . . . there is, at this time, no general woman, no one typical woman. What they have *in common* I will say. But what strikes me is the infinite richness of their individual constitutions: you can't talk about *a* female sexuality, uniform, homogeneous, classifiable into codes—any more than you can talk about one unconscious resembling another. (245–46; her emphasis)

The feminine writing practice Cixous advocates in this essay and elsewhere must be distinguished both from Woman as a theoretical construct marginalized in western discourse and from "women" as historical, real-life beings. Yet these categories can be confusing, and often readers seem to interpret Cixous's description of the "inevitable struggle" between "woman" and "conventional man" as a binary opposition, a contest for mastery.[7] Again in "Sorties," Cixous's depiction of phallocentric discourse as a "universal battlefield" in which "I-woman am going to blow up the Law"—coupled with her metaphors of "war," "violence," "conflict," and "Death"—could suggest a binary opposition, a battle between two opposing parties (63–64). At times it seems even the most sympathetic readers cannot avoid using dualistic terminology to describe the French theorist's project. Verena Andermatt Conley, for example, claims Cixous adopts an "overt feminine militancy" in "Sorties": She "replaces the patriarchal 'know thyself' with a call to women to 'write themselves.' The call now addresses women, in the plural, as one of the terms in a binary configuration" (51). Although Cixous's goal is to break open the hierarchical dualism suppressing women, the militant tone she occasionally adopts can be misinterpreted as a struggle for dominance and control, rather than a tactic in her deconstruction of existing categories.

Anzaldúa, like Cixous, challenges oppressive sociolinguistic systems; yet her oppositional tactics cannot be misread as a monolithic conflict between a dominant male and a subordinate female group. Both theorists explore how phallocentric thought has "colonized" women's bodies, has "led them to hate women, to be their own enemies, to mobilize their immense power against themselves, to do the male's dirty work" (Cixous, "Sorties," 68). But Anzaldúa extends her analysis to encompass the many specific forms this "colonization" takes as it affects women of color and other marginalized people. She does not focus exclusively—or at times even primarily—on gender-based oppression. In *Borderlands/La Frontera*, for example, she combines autobiography with contemporary and historical accounts to describe diverse forms of oppression in twentieth-century U.S. culture. In addition to recounting how she was trained to despise her own Indian blood, her Spanish accent, and her female body, she examines the ways Anglo U.S. society oppresses Mexican American women, children, and men; the Chicano's internalized self-hatred; his sexist attitudes toward *la mujer*; and the ostracism encountered by "queers" of all nations. Similarly, in "La Prieta" and "En Rapport" Anzaldúa investigates the conflicts within and among self-identified U.S. women of color. As she explains in the latter essay, when oppressed people adopt the dominant U.S. culture's worldview—the "fixed oppositions, the duality of superiority and inferiority, of subject and object"—they project their internalized oppression outward and objectify each other. She destabilizes these fixed oppositions by encouraging her readers to acknowledge their "internalized whiteness,"—how Anglo culture has influenced their actions and beliefs. Only then can they "get out of the state of opposition and into *rapprochement*" (145–48).

According to Anzaldúa, there *are* no fixed oppositions, no permanent, clear-cut distinctions between subject/object, dominant/subordinate, or even male/female. Like Lorde, she underscores the specific ways U.S. third world peoples, women of all colors, and queers of every nation function as both oppressor and oppressed. The use of nondual modes of perception enables Anzaldúa to articulate diverse—sometimes conflicting—points of view. As Trinh Minh-ha explains:

When binaries no longer organize, the difficulty then becomes speaking from no clearly defined place. This shifting multi-place of resistance differs in that it no longer simply thrives on alternate, homogenized strategies of rejection, affirmation, confrontation, and opposition well-rooted in a tradition of contestation. (*Moon*, 229)

Whereas social actors engaged in binary oppositional movements generally employ monologic forms of discourse, those who position themselves on this shifting multi-place of resistance develop hybrid, multilayered discourses enabling them to "speak at least two different things at once" (*Moon*, 228). They transform conventional forms of oppositional consciousness into nondual forms of thinking. As they break open binary categories, they make it possible to develop flexible, apparently contradictory speaking positions.

Anzaldúa often locates herself at this shifting multi-place of resistance. Consider, for example, her discussion of sexuality in *Borderlands/La Frontera*, where she asserts that

> I *made the choice to be queer.* . . . It's an interesting path, one that continually slips in and out of the white, the Catholic, the Mexican, the indigenous, the instincts. In and out of my head. It makes for *loquería*, the crazies. It's a path of knowing—one of knowing (and of learning) the history of oppression of our *raza*. It is a way of balancing, of mitigating duality. (19; her emphasis)

Like Allen's theory of perpetual liminality and the threshold locations described in the first chapter, this constant slippage between and among white, Catholic, Mexican, indigenous, and instinctual perspectives enables Anzaldúa to transform these diverse worldviews into new forms of knowledge. She learns, for example, "to be an Indian in Mexican culture, to be Mexican from an Anglo point of view" (79). By positioning herself at this shifting multi-place of resistance, she develops the flexibility both to enter into dialogues with apparently dissimilar peoples and to challenge multiple forms of oppression simultaneously.

Similarly, in "*Cihuatlyotl*, Woman Alone," Anzaldúa oscillates between several speaking positions: By identifying herself as Cihuatlyotl, a precolonial representation of Coatlicue, and as a solitary individual, a "Woman Alone," she simultaneously accepts and rejects her cultural/ethnic heritage:

>   I refuse to be taken over   by
> things   people   who fear that hollow
> aloneness beckoning beckoning.   No self,
> only race *vecindad familia*.   My soul   has always
> been yours   one spark in the roar of your fire.
> We Mexicans are   collective animals.   This I
> accept   but my life's work   requires autonomy
> like oxygen.   This lifelong battle has ended,
> *Raza*.   I don't need to flail against you. (*Borderlands*, 173)

Even the style—the jarring line breaks and the unexpected, irregular spacing—indicates the difficulties Anzaldúa experiences in her efforts to negotiate between the personal autonomy she requires as a writer-activist and her membership in her ethnic community. However, she does not establish a clear-cut division between individual and communal identities. By locating her "soul" in the beckoning "hollow / aloneness" and in the collective Mexican *familia*, she disrupts the binary opposition between them.

In many ways Anzaldúa's nonbinary oppositional tactics illustrate Cixous's assertion that "[w]oman un-thinks the unifying, regulating history that homogenizes and channels forces, herding contradictions into a single battlefield" ("Laugh," 252). Yet Anzaldúa emphasizes the multiple, contradictory battles to be fought rather than the "single battlefield" where these many conflicts occur, thus indicating this single battlefield is really plural; it represents the political, metaphoric, and psychic Borderlands. People who position themselves in the Borderlands

> are neither *hispana india negra española*
> *ni gabacha, eres mestiza, mulata*, half-breed
> caught in the crossfire between camps
> while carrying all five races on your back
> not knowing which side to turn to, run from;

> To live in the Borderlands means knowing
> that the *india* in you, betrayed for 500 years,
> is no longer speaking to you,
> that mexicanas call you *rajetas*,

that denying the Anglo inside you
is as bad as having denied the Indian or black. (*Borderlands*, 194)

In Anzaldúa's Borderlands, there are no easy allegiances, no unified singular groups. By locating this complex battlefield both inside and outside herself and other social actors, she underscores the need for concurrent, multilayered, internal and external struggles.

III   Art is a sneak attack while the giant sleeps, a sleight of hands when the giant is awake, moving so quick they can do their deed before the giant swats them. Our survival depends on being creative.   GLORIA ANZALDÚA

What woman hasn't flown/stolen?   HÉLÈNE CIXOUS

In *Borderlands/La Frontera* Anzaldúa calls for "[a] massive uprooting of dualistic thinking" and maintains that mestiza consciousness enables the writer "to break down the subject-object duality that keeps her a prisoner and to show in the flesh and through the images in her work how duality is transcended" (80). This " 'alien' consciousness" is analogous to the process Cixous describes in "The Laugh of the Medusa." Just as the French theorist declares her undertaking "has at least two sides and two aims: to break up, to destroy; and to foresee the unforeseeable, to project" (245), Anzaldúa acknowledges the destructive and constructive measures necessary to alter oppressive sociolinguistic and cultural systems. The new mestiza "has a plural personality, she operates in a plural mode—nothing is thrust out, the good the bad and the ugly—nothing rejected, nothing abandoned. Not only does she sustain contradictions, she turns the ambivalence into something else" (*Borderlands*, 79). Not surprisingly, Anzaldúa's mestiza logic of both/and/neither/nor occasionally contradicts this assertion. Yet her ability to contain and transform contradictions enables her to begin altering oppressive social systems from within. Instead of entirely rejecting dominant U.S. culture, Anzaldúa's mestiza deconstructs it; she takes it apart, exposes its underlying tensions, and builds a new culture, *una cultura mestiza*.

Anzaldúa provides the fullest discussion of this flexible, multilayered oppositional consciousness in her preface to *Making Face, Making Soul/Haciendo Caras*. She describes writing as "*haciendo caras*," or "making faces," and adopts metaphors of masks, faces, and interfaces to illustrate the conflicting sets of discourse that misshape self-identified U.S. third world women. She explains that each person's face represents the point where inner and outer worlds converge; it is "the most naked, most vulnerable, exposed and significant topography of the body." For *las mestizas*—the "biologically and/or culturally mixed" women "inscribed by social structures, marked with instructions on how to be,"—faces also signify the convergence of overlapping external and internal oppressions. To meet demands made by the diverse cultures they inhabit, women of color have learned to "change faces"—to hide their psychic, emotional lives behind masks.

Anzaldúa's analysis of these self-imposed masks resembles Lorde's critique of double consciousness, which I will explain in the next chapter. Both theorists explore the ambivalent nature of these self-protective disguises. Anzaldúa asserts that although such tactics enable women to survive racism and sexism, double consciousness also leads to alienation and self-loathing as the "masked" women become "just a series of roles" ("Haciendo caras, una entrada," xv). Yet she emphasizes that these women are not passive victims; they are, rather, activists—agents of change who transform oppressive experiences into new forms of resistance, including mestiza consciousness itself. She insists that between the masks, hidden not only from society's hostile eyes but often from the women themselves, is the "interface . . . the space from which we can thrust out and crack the masks" ("Haciendo caras, una entrada," xv–xvi).

Anzaldúa associates the development of personal agency with these hidden interfaces. Because they represent unknown intervals—or spaces of unexplored potential between and within (self-)inscriptions—these hidden intervals enable las mestizas to reinvent themselves, to "remake anew both the inner and outer faces." She explains that by stripping away externally imposed social roles and exploring the "multilayered 'inner faces'" beneath the masks, mestiza writers have the power to deconstruct and reconstruct their own identities: "We begin to displace the white and colored male typographers and become, ourselves, typographers, printing our own words on the surfaces, the plates, of our bodies" when we recognize how gender, ethnicity, color, and class mark us as other (xvi).

Anzaldúa does not locate this body-writing entirely *outside* the dominant culture's inscriptions. To do so would participate in the dualistic thinking that subordinates women of color and other oppressed groups. By depicting herself and other self-identified artists-of-color as sites of plural and shifting identities, she dissolves conventional subject/object dualities and creates flexible speaking subjects capable of diverse interactions with numerous groups. The margins between "inside and "outside" break down as these writers construct collective identities partially inside and partially outside existing categories. Thus she refers to their creative works as the "inter-faces," or threshold locations where inner/outer, self/other realities converge. She explains that as these writers explore their own " 'inner' faces," they "are also uncovering the inter-faces, the very spaces and places where multiple-surfaced, colored, racially gendered bodies intersect and interconnect" (xvi).

To borrow the French theorist's words, Anzaldúa believes that "[w]omen must write through their bodies, they must invent the impregnable language that will wreck partitions, classes, and rhetorics, regulations and codes, they must submerge, cut through, get beyond the ultimate reserve-discourse" ("Laugh," 256). However, whereas Cixous associates this *"new insurgent writing"* with previously repressed psychosexual energies unleashed when women (and men) write their bodies, Anzaldúa associates it with the "soul." She describes writing as "making face, making soul" to underscore her belief that all creative endeavors include a "spiritual, psychic component" synthesizing "body, soul, mind, [and] spirit." As I explain in the following section, this correlation between the physical and the spiritual serves several interrelated purposes. First, it enables her to illuminate the continual displacement of opposites that generates alternate forms of knowledge and new models of collective identity formation. Second, by incorporating her body-soul-writing into her theory of invoked art, Anzaldúa challenges the ethnocentrism underlying western aesthetics. Third, by equating writing the body with writing the soul, she prevents readers from misinterpreting her writ-

ing practice as an impossible attempt to obtain a "precultural femininity," an unmediated relation to the biological female body.[8]

IV   Displacing is a way of surviving. It is an impossible, truthful story of living in-between regimens of truth. The responsibility involved in this motley in-between living is a
highly creative one: the displacer proceeds by unceasingly
introducing difference into repetition. By questioning over
and over again what is taken for granted as self-evident, by
reminding oneself and the others of the unchangeability of
change itself. Disturbing thereby one's own thinking habits, dissipating what has become familiar and clichéd, and
participating in the changing of received values—the transformation (with/out master) of other selves through one's
self. To displace so as not to evade through shortcuts by
suppressing or merely excluding.   TRINH MINH-HA

Like Trinh's description of displacement as ongoing, open-ended
thinking, Anzaldúa's theory of body-writing resists closure. Her writing practice is a dynamic, creative process involving multiple, concurrent outer and inner transformations: "[O]nly through the body,
through the pulling of flesh, can the human soul be transformed. And
for images, words, stories to have this transformative power, they must
arise from the human body—flesh and bone—and from the Earth's
body—stone, sky, liquid, soul" (*Borderlands*, 75). Matter and spirit
converge as Anzaldúa identifies writing the body with writing the soul:
Flesh melds with images, bones fuse with words, and the human
body-soul merges into the earth's. Similarly, she describes her own
writing practice as a perpetual, interconnected series of physical and
psychic rebirths. When she writes, she explains, "[her] soul remakes
itself through the creative act. It is constantly remaking and giving
birth to itself through [her] body" (73).

These highly metaphoric descriptions of writing indicate the development of deconstructive epistemological processes that under-

mine the binary oppositions structuring western knowledge systems. Anzaldúa's fluid movements between "body" and "soul" destabilize conventional meanings; the Cartesian mind/body dualism breaks down as consciousness circulates throughout the body. As Anzaldúa deconstructs her metaphorical body, she achieves what Trinh describes as "a constant displacement of . . . [analytical thinking's] two-by-two system of division." This continual displacement has important theoretical and political implications. It unsettles all notions of self-contained, unified identities and concepts. By "fragmenting so as to decentralize instead of dividing so as to conquer," body-writing disrupts western culture's "totalizing quest for meaning"—the Enlightenment-based, masculine association of rational thought with knowledge, mastery, and dominance (*Woman*, 40). Whereas analytical thinking's dualistic divisions facilitate control by putting people and things into rigid categories, Anzaldúa's body-soul-writing moves within, between, and among these categories, fragmenting them from within. In other words, Her mestizaje écriture subtly challenges the rationalism underlying western imperialism. In her epistemology, thought is fluid; to borrow Trinh's words, it is "an ongoing unsettling process" which demonstrates that, because knowledge does not reside in a single location, power is not hegemonic and cannot be possessed by any one group (*Woman*, 39–40).[9]

Anzaldúa further destabilizes the universalized value of Enlightenment-based knowledge claims by associating "making face, making soul" with what I describe as her theory of invoked art. She discusses invoked art in *Borderlands/La Frontera* and in "Metaphors in the Tradition of the Shaman," a brief essay written shortly after *Borderlands/La Frontera*'s publication. She reinterprets Aztec metaphysical beliefs from her contemporary perspective and incorporates them in her aesthetics. This synthesis of "western" and "nonwestern" practices allows her to expose the ethnocentric bias that dismisses Native peoples' belief systems as "mere pagan superstition."[10] She argues that tribal cultures' shamanic traditions represent the development of sophisticated, well-integrated aesthetic, religious, and political systems. As she explains in *Borderlands/La Frontera*, precolonial Mexican Indians believed art should be "metaphysical" yet communal, participatory, and intimately related to everyday life (67). Art played a vital role in the people's social and spiritual existence, for it validated their lives and empowered them to bring about collective and cosmic change.

Anzaldúa contrasts this tribal perspective with western aesthetics to emphasize invoked art's transformational function, its ability to revitalize individual and communal identities. She describes her own writings as

> acts encapsulated in time, "enacted" every time they are spoken aloud or read silently. I like to think of them as performances and not as inert and "dead" objects (as the aesthetics of Western culture think of art works). Instead, the work has an identity; it is a "who" or a "what" and contains the presences of persons, that is, incarnations of gods or ancestors or natural and cosmic powers. (67)

As "both a physical thing and the power that infuses it" (67), Anzaldúa's invoked art is a mixed breed; just as the mestiza mediates between diverse cultures, her art synthesizes past and present perspectives and mediates between political, personal, and spiritual dimensions of life. *Borderlands/La Frontera*, for example, is a living child "with a mind of its own": It "is alive, infused with spirit. I talk to it; it talks to me" (66–67).

Like Allen, Anzaldúa incorporates her interpretation of tribal cultures' dialogic, performative epistemologies in her work to underscore writing's transformational power. In her introduction to *Making Face, Making Soul/Haciendo Caras* she describes her writing process as a "constant dialogue" between her selves, her readers, and the words on the computer screen:

> Ultimately alone with only the hum of the computer, accompanied by all my faces (and often yours as well), the monitor's screen reflects back the dialogue among "us." I talk to myself. That's what writers do, we carry on a constant dialogue between language and hands and images, one or another of our identities trying desperately to get in a word, an image, a sound. (xxiv)

This conversation between writer, reader, and text resembles the highly political testimonials produced by self-identified third world women writers. Unlike the descriptive, personal nature of conventional western autobiographies that focus primarily on the development of a unified individual consciousness, Latin American narratives forcefully intervene in western readers' preconceived beliefs. As Chandra Mohanty explains, they emphasize the political implications of collective identities by constructing "relationships between the self and the reader in order to invite and precipitate change (revolution)" (37). Anzaldúa's "constant dialogue" serves a similar purpose: By depicting herself as the site of multiple identities (or "faces"), she challenges her reader's own self-conceptions and, by extension, western humanism's model of unitary selfhood.

Anzaldúa enacts a similar challenge to western concepts of selfhood when she draws on her embodied metaphysics to associate writing with spiritualized internal dialogues. In *"Tlilli, Tlapalli/*The Path of the Red and Black Ink" she likens her writing practice to

> [t]hought shifts, reality shifts, gender shifts: one person metamorphoses into another in a world where people fly through the air, heal from mortal wounds. I am playing with my Self, I am playing with the world's soul, I am in dialogue between my Self and *el espíritu mundo*. I change myself, I change the world. (*Borderlands*, 70)

These transitions between Self, world's soul, and *el espíritu mundo* break down conventional boundaries between individual and collective identities.

Similar transformations occur in Anzaldúa's description of writing as an ongoing event in which her "soul . . . is constantly remaking and giving birth to itself through [her] body" (*Borderlands*, 73). This equation of writing with continual physical-spiritual birth can be disruptive for readers. Trinh observes that "a subject who points to him/her/itself as a subject-in-process . . . is bound to upset one's sense of identity—the familiar distinction between the Same and the Other since the latter is no longer kept in a recognizable relation of dependence, deviation, or appropriation" (*Moon*, 48). This disruption illustrates the transformational, communal dimensions of Anzaldúa's invoked art. By deconstructing her own subjectivity, she deconstructs her readers' as well. She replaces western conceptions of isolated, self-contained identities with open-ended models of collective identity formation, making it possible to develop mestizaje connections—alliances between people from diverse sexualities, cultures, genders, and classes. If, as Homi Bhabha asserts, "the possibility of producing a culture which both articulates difference and lives with it could only be established on the basis of a non-sovereign notion of self" ("Third Space," 213), these mestizaje connections can lead to the construction of new forms of culture. By replacing western notions of self-autonomy with this model of identity formation open to external change, Anzaldúa illustrates the nonsovereign notion of selfhood Bhabha describes.

Anzaldúa's association of invoked art with indigenous shamanic traditions provides yet another challenge to U.S. ethnocentrism. Instead of validating her claims concerning writing's transformational potential with western philosophical discourse, she develops an argument based on embodied metaphysical power. In *Borderlands/La Frontera*, for instance, she employs metaphors of shape-shifters and shamanism to support her contention that writing and other forms of art can have concrete physical and psychic effects on both writers and readers. Like the Aztec shaman whose interaction with unseen forces enabled them to transform themselves and their people, the mestiza writer is "*nahual*, an agent of transformation, able to modify and shape primordial energy and therefore able to change herself and others into turkey, coyote, tree or human." She describes her own writing practice as "carving bone, . . . creating [her] own face, [her] own heart—a Nahuatl concept"—to emphasize how writing enables her to redefine herself and her interactions with others (74–75). Similarly, in "Haciendo caras, una entrada" she adopts a *Nahuatl* saying— " '[U]sted es el modeador de su carne tanto como el de su alma. You are the shaper of your flesh as well as of your soul' "—to emphasize her readers' ability to attain personal and collective agency (xxv).

Anzaldúa draws on the Aztec shamans' ability to negotiate the apparent boundaries between spiritual and material worlds, developing a theory of hybrid metaphors that unites visionary language with political intervention. She maintains that because "the spirit of the words moving in the body is as concrete as flesh and as palpable," metaphoric language can bridge the apparent gaps between writer and reader (*Borderlands*, 71). In "Metaphors in the Tradition of the Shaman," she describes writing as a fluid process between the writer's body and the reader's mind. She explains that writers "attempt to put, in words, the flow of some of [their] internal pictures, sounds, sensations, and feelings and hope that as the reader reads the pages these 'metaphors' would be 'activated' and live in her." As in "Haciendo caras, una entrada" and *Borderlands/La Frontera*, Anzaldúa defines herself as a "poet-shaman," a cultural healer or agent of change who uses metaphoric language to fight diverse forms of oppression existing in contemporary North American societies. She describes the negative images, destructive stereotypes, and false information concerning oppressed groups as "dead metaphors" that have concrete socioeconomic effects. People who see themselves continually referred to in derogatory terms internalize these negative images and begin acting them out. Anzaldúa insists that writers can replace such debilitating beliefs with "new metaphors":

> Because we use metaphors as well as *yierbitas* and curing stones to effect changes, we follow in the tradition of the shaman. Like the shaman, we transmit information from our consciousness to the physical body of another. If we're lucky we create, like the shaman, images that induce altered states of consciousness conducive to self-healing.
> ("Metaphors," 99–100)

Anzaldúa graphically illustrates, extends, and revises Cixous's description of the woman whose "flesh speaks true. . . . Really she makes what she thinks materialize carnally, she conveys meaning with her body. She *inscribes* what she is saying" ("Sorties," 92; her emphasis). Yet the poet-shaman Anzaldúa describes also makes what she thinks materialize in her readers. She "listen[s] to the words chanting" in her *own* body and attempts to inscribe them in the bodies of others (*Borderlands*, 68–71). According to Anzaldúa, metaphors can literally— physically and psychically—transform us; images communicate "with tissues, organs, and cells to effect change" ("Metaphors," 99). The borders between writer, reader, and text dissolve: Words have concrete physiological, ideological, and psychic effects and physical bodies are transformed into texts that the "poet-shaman" interprets and reinscribes. This theory of reading and writing has radical implications for personal and collective change. As I explain in the following chapter, if the words we read can inscribe themselves in our bodies as well as our minds, transformation potentially occurs on multiple levels.

In many ways, Anzaldúa's hybrid metaphors and her theory of invoked art function analogously to the "metaphorical thinking" Françoise Defromont locates in Cixous's body-writing. According to Defromont, Cixous combines poetical, philosophical, and political forms of thought to deconstruct masculinist categories; she creates "a new linguistic space," a way of writing and thinking that "anchor[s] thought into matter, embodying ideas, giving them something of a body—instead of just being ideas, they become thinkable" (117–19). In Cixous's writings the body functions metaphorically to subvert dualistic thinking. Language and thought become "a mobile and streaming continuity" that breaks apart and transforms subject/object and nature/culture dichotomies.[11]

Like Anzaldúa's "making face, making soul," Cixous's "writing the body" uses nonbinary oppositional tactics that simultaneously deconstruct, reassemble, and transform phallocentric linguistic systems. Both theorists demonstrate that visionary language, political intervention, and cultural change can be mutually *in*clusive. But Anzaldúa's assertions that writing the body and writing the soul are synonymous enables her to avoid the apparent reification of a biological female nature some readers find in Cixous's works. To be sure, the phrase "making soul" could imply that Anzaldúa has simply replaced one type of (gendered biological) essence with another (nongendered disembodied) type. I would argue, however, that the term functions differently. Like Cixous's description of writing as "questioning (in) the between" ("Sorties," 86), Anzaldúa's "soul" prevents closure by functioning as an unexpected variable, an ambiguous third term, in the writing process. Her theory and practice of "making face, making soul" allow us more fully to understand how visionary language can function within existing discourse yet move beyond it.

More specifically, Anzaldúa's revisionist use of the term "soul" problematizes matter/spirit, nature/mind, and feminine/masculine dichotomies. To begin with, "soul" is a slippery, enigmatic concept that defies concrete definition; yet by distinguishing between spirit and soul, Anzaldúa makes the concept even more elusive. Take, for example, her critique of conventional Judeo-Christian worldviews:

We're supposed to ignore, forget, kill those fleeting images of the soul's presence and of the spirit's presence. . . . We're supposed to forget that every cell in our bodies, every bone and bird and worm has spirit in it. . . . The Catholic and Protestant religions encourage fear and distrust of life and of the body; they encourage a split between the body and the spirit and totally ignore the soul; they encourage us to kill off parts of ourselves. We are taught that the body is an ignorant animal; intelligence dwells only in the head. (*Borderlands*, 37)

These religious teachings diminish people's sense of agency by compelling them to seek spiritual guidance in external authorities. But for Anzaldúa, the body is *not* an ignorant animal, and intelligence does *not* dwell only in the head. By locating both spirit and soul in human and natural worlds, she replaces the dualism between nature and spirit with a nondual metaphysics in which the body and nature function as alternate sources of knowledge. This nonbinary distinction between spirit, nature, and soul also enables Anzaldúa to provoke new relationships between apparently distinct categories. She incorporates these terms into her discussion of the patriarchal dimensions of Mexican culture. Drawing on Aztec mythic systems, she explains that

[t]he eagle symbolizes the spirit (as the sun, the father); the serpent symbolizes the soul (as the earth, the mother). Together, they symbolize the struggle between the spiritual/celestial/male and the underworld/earth/feminine. The symbolic sacrifice of the serpent to the "higher" masculine powers indicates that the patriarchal order had already vanquished the feminine and matriarchal order in pre-Columbian America. (*Borderlands*, 5)

This division between spirit and soul serves two purposes. First, it enables Anzaldúa to destabilize, without entirely reversing, western stereotypes that associate the feminine with nature and the body. She invents a spiritualized feminine psychic and material force that draws on yet expands conventional beliefs concerning female embodiedness. Second, by associating "spirit" with the masculine and "soul" with the feminine, she challenges the radical division between masculine and feminine categories. In her mythic system, both genders contain nonphysical components.

By writing her body-soul, Anzaldúa positions herself at what Trinh describes as a "non-binarist space of reflection," a liminal zone where new combinations of previously reified categories of thought can occur (*Moon*, 232–33). This nonbinary space intervenes in conventional politics of location by disrupting unitary (inside/outside, margin/center) subject positions; it opens up an interval between binary pairs. Neither "inside" nor "outside" the dominant cultural inscriptions, she stands on the thresholds between them and invents hybrid combinations. She uses familiar words like "body," "soul," "shaman," and "face," but uses them in new ways, expanding and transforming conventional meanings. Just as Allen's "feminine" mestizaje creates a transitional in-between-the-naming space that fluidly resists closure, body-writing cannot be contained within rigid binary categories of thought.

---

v   But we must make no mistake: men and women are caught up in a web of age-old cultural determinations that are almost unanalyzable in their complexity. One can no more speak of "woman" than of "man" without being trapped within an ideological theater where the proliferation of representations, images, reflections, myths, identifications, transform, deform, constantly change everyone's Imaginary and invalidate in advance any conceptualization.

HÉLÈNE CIXOUS

Given the many ways women's bodies—whether those bodies are coded "black," "white," "red," or "brown"—have been subjugated, repressed, and objectified, critics' apprehensive reactions to écriture féminine are understandable. As Janet Wolff observes, contemporary feminists' attempts to establish the body as a site of political intervention are always problematic: "Its pre-existing meanings, as sex object, as object of the male gaze, can always prevail and reappropriate the body, despite the intentions of the woman herself" (121). But can we simply ignore the female body and, by extension, the fact that women's bodily experiences have been controlled, defined, and marginalized by specific cultural ideologies? Or does this evasion, as Morag Shiach asserts, "reproduce a structure of oppression which has made of women's bodies their point of vulnerability and of guilt"? (*Hélène Cixous*, 20). Can we write (about) women's gender-specific bodily experiences without reinstating male/female dichotomies? Or should we reject writing the body entirely and, as Ann Rosalind Jones argues, "move outside that male-centered, binary logic altogether" (369)?

As I see it, there are at least two problems with Jones's suggestion. First, to dismiss écriture féminine and all other oppositional theories of resistance as ineffective replicates western culture's either/or thinking and overlooks the possibility of developing both/and/neither/nor forms of thought that displace—rather than reject—apparent dualisms. Furthermore, if, as I believe, Anzaldúa and Cixous open new theoretical spaces *within* existing structures, moving entirely "outside" masculinist binary systems becomes unnecessary; their body-writing demonstrates that phallocentric categories can be transformed from within the dominant culture. Although both theorists connect women's return to their bodies with the development of alternate, nonphallic ways of knowing and writing, neither Anzaldúa nor Cixous locates these bodies *outside* cultural inscriptions. Instead, by writing their own bodies into their works, they expose the ways female identities have been constructed in masculinist discourse.

More specifically, by deconstructing the radical dualism between "inside" and "outside," Cixous's "writing the body" and Anzaldúa's "making face, making soul" demonstrate that nonbinary oppositional tactics can be politically effective. Yet at times Cixous's metaphoric representations of Woman become so decontextualized that readers overlook body-writing's liberating potential and assume that the valorization of women's bodily experiences simply replicates already existing stereotypes. By enacting a dialogue between Anzaldúa and Cixous, I have tried to open up a new context where transcultural interconnections between these apparently separate feminist theories can be made. Viewed in light of Anzaldúa's theory and practice of "making face, making soul," the significance of writing the (female) body becomes more apparent, and the risks of misinterpretation, reappropriation, or essentialism diminish.

Anzaldúa's mestizaje écriture indicates there is no permanent division between inner and outer realities. Because she believes that "[n]othing happens in the 'real' world unless it happens in the image in our heads" (*Borderlands*, 75), Anzaldúa rewrites Mexican Indian shamanic beliefs and develops metaphoric configurations of psychic and political power such as the Borderlands, the Coatlicue state, and mestiza consciousness. Like Allen, she writes her own version of feminine mestizaje, inventing new metaphors that affirm the cultural specificities of her own heritage and open transcultural connections. When "invoked," or read, her graphic metaphors allow readers of all backgrounds to imaginatively reconstruct their worldviews and envision alternate ways of living. As William Doty explains, because mythical symbols contain "units of information that are not bound up by the immediate contours of what presently is being experienced, . . . [they] provide concrete conveyances for (abstract) thought. Alive in a world of metaphoric and symbolic meanings, they allow experimentation and play with images, ideas, and concepts that otherwise would remain too incorporeal to be engaged" (20).

Using mythic metaphors that "concretize the spirit and etherealize the body" (*Borderlands*, 75), Anzaldúa builds a new culture, *una cultura mestiza*. Her words incite readers to actively create a complex mixed-breed coalition of "queers"—outsiders who, because of ethnicity, gender, sexuality, class, position, or whatever, begin transforming dominant cultural inscriptions.

Inscribing "Black," Becoming . . .
Afrekete
Audre Lorde's Interactional Self-Naming

---

*Transformation is demanded of us precisely because there is no
self-enclosed subject who can truly cut herself off from the
Other.*   DRUCILLA CORNELL

*The identity question and the personal/political relationship is
a way of rewriting culture.*   TRINH MINH-HA

*The decision to "identify" as an African American or to "pass"
as white . . . is part of an ongoing performance of identity.*
PEGGY PHELAN

In Chapter 4, I proposed that Allen's origin myths
(need) not be interpreted as the recovery of monolithic, ahistorical
truths about "woman's nature," "American Indians," "female experience," or the "feminine." Allen employs memory, imagination, and
myth to reconfigure the past. Rather than accurately re-membering
historical facts or defining the essence of Woman, Allen synthesizes
"discovery" with "invention," reinterpreting the past from her present
perspective to alter contemporary conditions and establish new goals
for the future. This doubly enacted forward-and-backward movement
resembles what Drucilla Cornell describes as "conversion principles."
In the context of critical legal theory a "conversion both converts the
way we understand the past and converts our current practice of
interpretation as we attempt to realize it in the reconstruction of law"
(*Transformations*, 38). Thought Woman and Allen's other Native
American creatrix figures indicate mythic conversion principles. Her
revisionary myths offer feminist social actors ethical standards, new
meanings of Woman that disrupt current representations, making it
possible to develop mestizaje feminist connections.

This disruption corresponds to the transformational, communal dimensions of Anzaldúa's theory of invoked art. As I suggested in the previous chapter, by destabilizing the boundaries between writer, reader, and text, invoked art opens interstitial spaces where trans-cultural identifications and alterations in consciousness can occur. In my use of the term, invoked art indicates the possibility of developing a feminist theory and praxis of subjectivity that locates identity con-textually, always in relation to others. Trinh Minh-ha discusses a simi-lar process of individual and collective subject formation, which she associates with a specific type of feminist consciousness. She stipulates that this

> *[f]eminist consciousness is understood here not as a state of awareness arrived at after an accumulation of knowledge and experiences, but as the term of a process. It is a dialectical understanding and practice of identity and difference; a consciousness of identity not as the end point but rather the point of re-departure of the processes by which one has come to understand how the personal—the ethnic me, the female me—is political. Subjectivity cannot therefore be reduced to a mere expression of the self. The identity question and the personal/political relationship is a way of rewriting culture.* (*Moon*, 112–13; her italics)

In this chapter, I want to investigate the performative implications of this transpersonal theory of subjectivity through an analysis of Lorde's semiautobiographical fiction, poetry, and prose. More specifi-cally, I'm interested in exploring her use of imagination, language, and mythic conversion principles to invent new individual and collective gendered and ethnic identities. Like Trinh, Lorde depicts identity as an ongoing process where perceptions of similarity and difference serve as points of redeparture leading to further change. In *Zami*, for exam-ple, 'self'-transformation occurs only in the context of others, thus indicating an intersubjective construction of personal identity and an interactional self-naming process. Throughout her biomythography, Lorde equates other women's words with her growing sense of agency and ability to define herself. She implies that through both language and silence the women in her life—her mother, friends, and lovers—have shaped her and so enabled her to rename herself. By choosing the name "Zami," which she translates as "*women who work together as friends and lovers*" (255; her italics), Lorde redefines herself *as* the others and underscores the transformational, communal nature of self-definition and subject formation. Bonnie Zimmerman makes a related point when she describes Lorde's "auto-biography" as

> equally an other-biography. It answers the question—"who is the other woman?"—by showing that she is almost imperceptibly part of one's self. But this answer does not result in some inchoate merging of identities, but rather in "separation," a space in which new concepts of self, relationship, and community can be created. (*Safe Sea*, 202)[1]

What impact, if any, does this self/other interaction have on readers? If, as Anzaldúa suggests, invoked art can have concrete, interconnected physical and psychic effects on both writers and readers, how do Lorde's self-inscriptions inscribe themselves on her readers? Although I return to this question in the final chapter, I want to suggest that the alterations in consciousness Lorde enacts in *Zami* should not be confined to the text. As she reinvents her own gender/ethnic identity, Lorde reinvents her readers' as well.

---

11   My mother bore me into life as if etching an angry message into marble.

She never talked about color. . . . And she disarmed me with her silences.   AUDRE LORDE

Silence—the absence of language and the refusal to name—plays a significant role in Lorde's interactional self-naming. From her mother, who used silence to protect herself and her daughters from a racialist reality she was powerless to control, Lorde first learned the importance of speech. More precisely, her mother's strategic silences demonstrated language's double-edged power, both its restrictive and its liberating potential. According to Claudine Raynaud and Chinosole, Lorde's poetic voice has its roots in her mother's "special and secret relationship with words" (*Zami*, 31).[2] However, by focusing entirely on the special nature of her mother's language—on her euphemisms for unmentionable bodyparts and the puzzling phrases reminiscent of her island home—it becomes easy to overlook the ambivalent effects of her secrecy. Lorde does "use the written word to translate the oral poetry of her mother's language" (Raynaud, 225), but I would argue that Lorde also uses the written word to translate her mother's silences. As Anna Wilson notes, the desire to recuperate the family as a "model of development and structure for African-American women writers," coupled with Lorde's own construction of a matrilineal heritage, has led critics to downplay or overlook the ambivalence in Lorde's relationship with her mother (95). Yet an analysis of the distinctions Lorde makes between herself and her mother—especially as they influence the personal and collective ethnic identities she invents—yields important insights concerning the ways maternal secretiveness shaped the daughter's theory of transformational language, as well as her creation of a racialist "blackness."[3]

Throughout the early sections of *Zami* Lorde associates her mother's silence both with the linguistic distortions surrounding U.S. racial discourse and with the Eurocentric, masculinist standards that structure racialist divisions. During her childhood, her father and mother spoke as "one unfragmentable and unappealable voice" (15). Together, they chose to withhold "vital pieces of information" concerning the realities of racism in everyday life (69). Perhaps most importantly, it was "from the white man's tongue, from out of the mouth of her father" that her mother learned to use language defensively (58), to ignore or misname the racism and discrimination she was unable to change. In order to deny the prejudice that threatened her family, she would not openly acknowledge her own "blackness"; nor would she discuss the differences in skin tone between herself, her husband, and her three daughters.[4]

These strategic silences served an important but highly ambivalent purpose. Lorde writes that by refusing to name those aspects of racist U.S. culture she was powerless to alter, her mother attempted to deny their existence (69). For instance, she did not tell her young daughter that the "nasty glob of grey spittle" that often landed on her coat or her shoe was motivated by irrational racialist hatred; she attributed it instead to the lack of manners in ignorant "low-class people" who spit into the wind (17–18). Similarly, young Audre's desire to become class president of the predominantly "white" sixth grade was met with maternal scorn—not because the "white" children would never vote for a "black" girl, but because it was " 'foolishness' " and " 'nonsense' " to run (61–65).

This selective use of language restricted her ability to define herself and prevented her from understanding how her skin color and ethnicity positioned her in the racialist structure of twentieth-century U.S. social systems. Because she "had no words for racism," she was unable to comprehend its implications or its effects in her life. She didn't know why the children in grade school called her names (60). Nor could she understand why her "white" high school friends didn't invite her to their parties, houses, or summer homes. She blamed herself rather than other people's racist beliefs for the "invisible barrier" isolating her from the rest of the world (81). Because racism went unacknowledged in her family, Audre's feelings—her sense of injustice when she lost the grade school election, her anger when her family was refused service at a drugstore in the nation's capitol—were either ignored or condemned. Not surprisingly, then, Lorde writes that as a child she was unaware of what it meant to be "*Colored*" (58).

The personal and cultural confusion Lorde describes in *Zami* illustrates an important component of her theory of transformational language, as well as a recurring pattern in her work: The erasure of differences—even when motivated by the desire to establish bonds among differently situated subjects—inadvertently widens the gap between disparate groups. By exploring the inadequacy of her mother's silence, Lorde exposes the limitations in well-meaning attempts to establish generic, pseudo-universal definitions of identity. In *Zami*, the absence of a racialized discourse leads to an assumed commonality that, paradoxically, creates further divisions.

Lacking the words to articulate the differences between herself and her family and friends, she felt alienated, and Lorde writes that during her adolescence she sensed an absence in her life and longed for something she "could not name" (85). This silence and alienation play important roles in Lorde's construction of a racialized "blackness." The unnameable absence Lorde refers to indicates what Michael Fischer describes as the "ethnic anxiety" depicted in many recent U.S. autobiographies. He explains that "[b]y attempting to spare children knowledge of painful past experiences, parents often create an obsessive void in the child that must be explored and filled in" (204). This void leads to the seemingly paradoxical situation in which ethnic identity is neither innate nor constructed—or, perhaps, it's both, for it requires self-invention yet appears to exist prior to the individual subject. As Fischer observes, this ambiguous oscillation between invented and discovered identities challenges commonly held theories of ethnicity: "Ethnicity in its contemporary form is thus neither, as the sociological literature would have it, simply a matter of group process (support systems), nor a matter of transition (assimilation), nor a matter of straightforward transmission from generation to generation (socialization)" (197).

In other words, U.S. ethnic identities do not represent authentic, preexisting categories of meaning automatically conferred on social subjects by virtue of birth. They are, rather, dynamic creative processes—the complex outcome of intense external and internal struggles in which the subject negotiates between the desire for continuity with past cultural traditions and the desire to establish an ethical vision for the future. The result, according to Fischer, is a new type of identity, "a (re-)invention and discovery of a vision, both ethical and future-oriented" (196). He explains that "what is discovered and reinvented in the new works about ethnicity is, perhaps increasingly, something new: to be Chinese-American is not the same thing as being Chinese in America. In this sense there is no role model for becoming Chinese-American" (196). Like Allen's embodied mythic conversion principles, this paradoxical process of ethnic identity formation synthesizes invention with discovery. By going 'back' to an invented ethnic past, Lorde and many other contemporary U.S. writers develop new ethnic identities that shape present conditions and establish alternate directions for future growth.

Lorde enacts ethnic anxiety and the concurrent oscillation between invention and discovery in her poetry. Significantly, her depiction of the interplay between "blackness" and "whiteness" complicates the "black" Africanized identity she seems to discover, for Lorde demonstrates—perhaps inadvertently—that these two apparently distinct ethnic identities are mutually constituted. In "Prologue," for example, she dismisses "the accusations / that I am too much or too little woman / that I am too black or too white" and affirms her own authentically dark voice:

through my lips come the voices
of the ghosts of our ancestors
living and moving among us
Here my heart's voice as it darkens
pulling old rhythms out of the earth (*Chosen Poems*, 58)

Yet Lorde invents the authenticity that she celebrates. By associating her darkening voice with her ancestors, her heart, and the earth's core, she employs metaphors of temporal and spatial depth that heighten the contrast between "blackness" and "whiteness"; more specifically, she naturalizes and internalizes her "blackness" while locating her "whiteness" on the surface. Lorde disrupts easy distinctions between "white" and "black" identities, however, by implying that her voice darkens in the context of an oppressive maternal "whiteness"—a "mother beating me / as white as snow melts in the sunlight" (*Chosen Poems*, 59). As in *Zami*, she associates this maternally imposed "whiteness" with the ability to survive U.S. racism yet emphasizes its destructive effects:

when I was a child
whatever my mother thought would mean survival
made her try to beat me whiter every day
and even now the color of her bleached ambition
still forks throughout my words (*Chosen Poems*, 59)

Although whiteness might be externally imposed, it has become so deeply ingrained that it leaves its mark on Lorde's work. Similarly, in "Pathways: From Mother to Mother" Lorde thinks back through the "nightmares / of . . . early learning" and explores the ways maternal "whiteness" has marked the daughter: "Wherever she wore ivory / I wear pain" (*Black Unicorn*, 71).

In these poems and others, Lorde underscores the interconnections between "blackness" and "whiteness" by repeatedly contrasting a "pale," "bleached," and "ivory" mother with the development of her own dark voice. Again in "From the House of Yemanjá" she describes an ambiguous, doubly marked mother. As in "Pathways" and "Prologue," this mother leaves an ambivalent mark on the daughter, and Lorde writes

I bear two women upon my back
one dark and rich and hidden
in the ivory hungers of the other
mother
pale as a witch. (*Black Unicorn*, 6)

This pale mother cannot meet the speaker's needs; her own "ivory hungers" leave the daughter "forever hungry," and the poem concludes with an expression of insatiable longing, an inner emptiness similar to the obsessive void Fischer describes:

Mother I need
Mother I need
mother I need your blackness now
as the august earth needs rain.

I am
the sun and moon and forever hungry
the sharpened edge
where day and night shall meet
and not be
one (*Black Unicorn*, 6–7)

There are at least two ways of interpreting these lines. First, they can be read in a very literal, autobiographical fashion. According to Joan Martin, for example, "From the House of Yemanjá" "ends, as do the others about Lorde's childhood relationship with her mother, in frustration that is total and complete. The poet is girl-child—hopeless, confused, loving, and not being loved in return" (283). I would suggest, however, that the title indicates another, less literal (but perhaps equally autobiographical) interpretation. By drawing from West African myth, Lorde reconstructs another mother, a mythic maternal figure whose darkness enables her simultaneously to discover and invent her own "black" ethnic identity. As Chinosole explains, this poem illustrates the juxtaposition and creative synthesis of two apparently contrasting cultures: "As a Black woman, the speaker must accept both aspects of herself and recognize the conflict that cannot be resolved; that is creative irreconcilability" (389). By doubly inscribing a West African "blackness" and a U.S. "whiteness" onto her body/text,

Lorde creates a mestizaje cultural identity. Thus Chinosole reads the final lines, with their allusion to MawuLisa, as an indication of self-transformation: "The speaker emerges in the end as the principle of difference, and Mawulisa is the implied *orisha* of the sun and moon or nonpolar duality" (390). This alteration does not indicate the rejection of the "white" mother but rather an acknowledgment of the ambivalent interplay between "black" and "white" in Lorde's own ethnic identity.

III   My mother taught me to survive at the same time as she
          taught me to fear my own Blackness. "Don't trust white
          people because they mean us no good and don't trust any-
          one darker than you because their hearts are as Black as
          their faces." (And where did that leave me, the darkest
          one?) It is painful even now to write it down.

          I grew Black as my need for life, for affirmation, for love,
          for sharing—copying from my mother what was in her, un-
          fulfilled. I grew Black as Seboulisa, who I was to find in the
          cool mud halls of Abomey several lifetimes later—and, as
          alone.   AUDRE LORDE

In an early section of her biomythography entitled "How I Became a Poet," Lorde sharply distinguishes her own voice from her mother's by declaring that when her "*strongest words*" remind her of those she heard as a child, she must reevaluate everything she wishes to say (31; her italics). Similarly, in an interview with Adrienne Rich, Lorde contrasts her speech with that of her mother's and explains that although her mother's selective silences taught her necessary survival skills, while she was growing up she wanted nothing to do with her mother's use of language (*Sister Outsider*, 83). And in "Eye to Eye" she again associates her mother's silences with her ability to survive racism yet maintains that the same "silences also taught [her] isolation, fury, mistrust, self-rejection, and sadness" (*Sister Outsider*, 149).

Lorde maintains that the absence of intersubjective, woman-to-woman speech opens up a void in each woman's life, a self-consuming absence: "Black women eating our own hearts out for nourishment in an empty house empty compound empty city in an empty season, and for each of us one year the spring will not return—we learned to savor the taste of our own flesh before any other because that was all that was allowed us" (*Sister Outsider*, 157). She locates the possibility of change at an interface—the space between identity and difference—and asserts that in order to act on the many commonalities "black" women in U.S. culture share, each woman must overcome her self-imposed silences and explore both the differences and the similarities between herself and other "black" women. Thus she urges her readers to acknowledge the ambivalent effects of this "secret isolation" and begin speaking out (*Sister Outsider*, 164).

Lorde's interrogation of self-protective silence indicates a provocative intervention into the double consciousness and "culture of dissemblance" employed by African American women. As I mentioned in Chapter 2, a vital oppositional strategy in "black" U.S. women's ability to resist the dominant ideology's debilitating stereotypes has been the development of self-protective masks. Citing Lorde's description of how members of subjugated groups must learn to observe the actions of those in positions of socioeconomic power, Patricia Hill Collins asserts,

> This "watching" generates a dual consciousness in African-American women, one in which Black women "become familiar with the language and manners of the oppressor, even sometimes adopting them for some illusion of protection" ([*Sister Outsider*,] 114), while hiding a self-defined standpoint from the prying eyes of dominant groups. (91)

The women Collins and Lorde describe take up dominant culture's standards by putting on self-protective "white" masks. Darlene Clark Hines describes a similar strategy, which she calls the culture of dissemblance. She explains that African American women developed an external persona to protect themselves from the highly demeaning, sexualized stereotypes of "black" women circulating in nineteenth-century U.S. culture:

> The dynamics of dissemblance involved creating the appearance of disclosure, or openness about themselves and their feelings, while ac-

tually remaining an enigma. Only with secrecy, thus achieving a self-imposed invisibility, could ordinary Black women accrue the psychic space and harness the resources needed to hold their own in the often one-sided and mismatched resistance struggle. (294)

Both theorists stress the importance of this self-imposed secrecy. According to Hines, dissemblance enabled African American women to maintain a sense of agency: "A secret, undisclosed persona allowed the individual Black woman to function . . . all while living within a clearly hostile white, patriarchal, middle-class America" (294). Similarly, Collins stipulates that the outward silence often accompanying these behavioral masks "is not to be interpreted as submission" but rather as an assertion of autonomy. She sees "black" women's selective silences as acts of resistance enabling them to construct a psychic space of freedom, a "private, hidden space of Black women's consciousness" (92–93).

Yet Lorde delves into this private hidden space and finds the internalized effects of racism and sexism—intense anger, isolation, self-loathing, and fear.[5] This emphasis on the destructiveness that so often accompanies "black" women's self-imposed secrecy could be read as a negative critique, but I prefer to read it as Lorde's attempt to expand her own agency, as well as that of other "black" women. Like Anzaldúa, she underscores her audience's sense of personal power by challenging them to recognize the ambivalent nature of these self-protective "white" masks. As Hortense Spillers implies, to be effective double consciousness must be recognized and deployed tactically: "The fact of domination *is* alterable only to the extent that the dominated subject recognizes the potential power of its own 'double-consciousness.' The subject is certainly seen, but she or he certainly sees. It is this latter seeing that negotiates at every point a space for living" ("Interstices," 84; her emphasis). Lorde turns this double consciousness back on itself to negotiate an even wider space for living. By exposing the "white" nature of "black" women's self-protective masks, she indicates that, as an oppositional strategy, double consciousness is limited by the racialist context in which it developed. Like the two sides of a single coin, double consciousness is both "black" and "white." As Gina Dent notes, "double consciousness has always implied the articulation of two *identifiable* and *opposing* modes of consciousness—blackness and whiteness. In other words, it has remained inside the sphere of its invention, the twentieth-century American color line" (18; her emphasis).

Lorde takes this oppositional strategy outside the sphere of its invention. She expands her interrogation of double consciousness to incorporate an analysis of the detrimental effects these "white" masks have on social actors of all colors. In essays like "The Transformation of Silence into Language and Action" and "Uses of the Erotic," she seems to suggest that the "white" mask and the "white" standards we adopt when we prevent ourselves from speaking out affect people of all ethnicities. She equates "the tyrannies of silence" with Eurocentric, masculinist language systems and insists that self-imposed silences and misnaming give women of all colors a false sense of agency. She maintains that when oppressed peoples accept the dominant culture's language without examining its harmful effects, they lack self-definition and remain invisible—even to themselves. They "swallow" the words of the father until they "sicken and die . . . still in silence" (*Sister Outsider*, 41). As in "Eye to Eye," Lorde locates the possibility of change at the interface between identity and difference. She associates women's self-imposed silences with their fear of acknowledging their differences—both from the dominant culture and from each other—and maintains that ignoring ethnic, sexual, or class differences creates a false assumption of commonalities that reifies arbitrary divisions between women.

Although it sounds paradoxical, the denial of differences prevents the recognition of commonalities. To become visible—first to themselves, then to others—Lorde implies that people (of all colors) must take off their "white" masks by stripping away externally imposed labels and internalized negative beliefs. They must speak out, despite their fears of rejection.[6] Drawing on her own experience, she insists that "for every real word spoken, for every attempt I had ever made *to speak those truths for which I am still seeking*, I had made contact with other women while we examined the words to fit a world in which we all believed, bridging our differences" (*Sister Outsider*, 41; my emphasis).

Lorde's assertion illustrates the apparently paradoxical, circular nature of performative language use, or what I described in Chapter 4 as the "performative contradiction." Lorde attempts to speak "truths" that do not—yet—exist. But by speaking out, she begins constructing the world she envisions; that is, she creates a new discourse enabling her to invent a world in which those truths can materialize. Similarly, in "The Master's Tools" she associates her belief in the mutually creative use of differences with the invention of "a world in which we can all flourish": "Within the interdependence of mutual (nondominant) differences lies that security which enables us to descend into the chaos of knowledge and return with true visions of our future, along with the concomitant power *to effect those changes which can bring that future into being*" (*Sister Outsider*, 111–12; my emphasis). This future world does not yet exist; however, by defining differences as mutually enriching, women acquire the confidence to create the future they envision.[7]

Lorde also illustrates this performative use of language in *Zami*. By acknowledging the differences between herself and her mother, she begins acquiring her own voice, a voice that enables her to create new commonalities between herself and her mother.[8] Indeed, her mother's silence serves as the first step in Lorde's self-definition. As she states in "Black Mother Woman," "I learned from you / to define myself / through your denials" (*Chosen Poems*, 53). From her mother's self-destructive denial of racism and direct speech, the daughter learns the importance of self-affirmative language and action. In "The Women of Dan Dance With Swords in Their Hands to Mark the Time When They Were Warriors," Lorde declines the self-destructive, self-sacrificing silence of "a secret warrior" who hides her sword in her mouth and refuses to speak. Instead of "slicing [her] throat to ribbons / of service with a smile," she boldly announces her presence: She "come[s] as a woman / dark and open"; her words will nurture the living and destroy the dead (*Black Unicorn*, 14–15).

Like her mother, who dealt with those aspects of reality she was unable to change either by refusing to name them or by dissembling, Lorde recognizes the power of language. She, however, rejects her mother's selective silence and names the differences between herself and others. The expression of differences serves as a catalyst for change, enabling her to construct a collective identity. Thus in the

Epilogue to *Zami* Lorde connects her relationships with other women to her own self-development when she implies that the women she has loved represent parts of herself: "Every woman I have ever loved has left her print upon me, where I loved some invaluable piece of myself apart from me—so different that I had to stretch and grow in order to recognize her. And in that growing, we came to separation, that place where work begins. Another meeting" (255).

I find Lorde's description intriguing. What can it mean to love an "invaluable piece" of oneself if this piece is so different that it cannot be recognized without significant growth? Does this recognition indicate self-discovery or self-invention? Do the women she has loved *change* her as they imprint themselves upon her? Or does she love them because they remind her of herself? And what role does agency play in this process?

This passage illustrates a process of interactional identity formation where self-change occurs only in the context of others. Because the self, or what we call *I*, is a nonunitary plural subject composed of *not-I*'s, self-change is almost inevitable; or as Drucilla Cornell puts it in *Transformations*: "Who 'we' are is the intersection with otherness. As a result, we are constantly pulled to modify our habits" (44). This constant pull arises from the intersubjective nature of desire, which is embedded in contextual social situations. Cornell describes these constant modifications as natality, or interactional self-change: "[T]he possibility of re-generative interactions that actually do innovate in the sense of effecting change in self-definition" (41). In other words, Cornell associates self-transformation with the shifts in self-perception and desire stimulated by our interactions with others. Drawing on the Lacanian theory of subjectivity, she explains that because we know ourselves—or our *I*'s—only in relation to others, or *not-I*'s, self-definition is contextual, always open to reinterpretation and change. Cornell emphasizes the necessity of self-transformation in all social exchange, insisting that

> [t]ransformation is demanded of us precisely because there is no self-enclosed subject who can truly cut herself off from the Other. We are constantly being challenged by otherness, including the otherness that marks the boundaries of the self "within," such as the unconscious.

The "I" repeats itself through its iterability, but only in a field of otherness in which the "I" is given significance. . . . What we think of as
agency is precisely the engagement of the self with its own iterability,
which is never just given but always confirmed or disconfirmed in the
process of signing for oneself. (41)

According to Cornell, then, the iterability of language—the repetition
implying both sameness and difference that occurs even when we use
the same word(s)[9]—makes personal agency and self-definition communal and always open to additional reinterpretation. Because subjectivity is constituted in language, we redefine ourselves each time we
speak or write "I."

Agency plays an important role in this intersubjective, transformational process. We shape this repetition of sameness and difference by
employing memory and imagination. Cornell explains,

The recollection of oneself is always an act which imagines through
the remembrance of its own claims of selfhood what can never be
fully recollected but only forever reimagined and re-told. The iterability of language allows us to regenerate ourselves through the continuing process of re-definition. In psychoanalytic terms, the self re-
collects itself through a series of hypothetical fantasies that allow for
ever-changing self-definitions. (42)

That is, who we mean when we refer to ourselves as "I" depends on
how we remember ourselves. In each situation we enter, we bring this
"I" forward, redefining ourselves as we go. Moreover, our redefini-
tions are themselves influenced by intersubjective desires.

Lorde illustrates this process of continual redefinition in *Zami*. Her
desire to name the apparent differences between herself and the various others in her life enables her to also name commonalities; the
recognition and expression of difference expands her self-perception,
eventually enabling her to recognize each other as an "invaluable
piece" of herself (255). This interactional identity formation entails
the simultaneous invention and discovery of subjectivity analogous to
the process of hybrid ethnic identity formation Fischer describes. By
defining Audre with words she does not recognize as her own, the
women she interacts with transform her; they enable her to recognize

additional aspects of herself—dimensions that had to be called into existence. Take, for example, Audre's interactions with Ginger, her first woman lover. Ginger's term for the sexually inexperienced Audre seems inaccurate, for she is not a "slick kitty from the city" (129), an experienced lover of women; and Audre wonders, "What was it about me that I would now have to pretend to fulfill?" (135). But the name is performative. Motivated by the fear of "los[ing] some face [she] never had," Audre responds to Ginger's challenge (137–39).

Again we see the apparently paradoxical nature of performative language use. It's impossible to lose a "face" or persona that you've never possessed. However, by deciding to act out the role "that Ginger had *discovered* or *invented* in her own mind" (137; my emphasis), Audre *becomes* a "slick kitty from the city." In bed with Ginger, she simultaneously discovers and invents new dimensions of herself: "Uncertainty and doubt rolled away from the mouth of my wanting like a great stone, and my unsureness dissolved in the directing heat of my own frank and finally open desire" (139).

Audre's relationship with Ginger gives her the confidence to acknowledge her attraction to women more openly, and in Mexico she risks rejection to tell Eudora she desires her sexually. When Eudora expresses concern that her radical mastectomy will repel her, Lorde writes that she experienced an unexpected transformation as she assures Eudora of her attraction: She watched as her own words "touch[ed] and [gave] life to a new reality within . . . some half-known self come of age" (167). Just as Ginger's speech opened the way for new actions, so Eudora's leads to self-change: Audre learns new "things about loving women" and new things about being loved; for the first time, she surrenders control and allows a woman to make love to her.

When the complications in Eudora's life compel her to send Audre away, she does not ignore Audre or treat her as though she were "invisible," and Lorde states that although she was hurt, she was not lost. Rather, in parting from Eudora she sees herself differently and finds or invents new dimensions of herself. No longer isolated, she's willing to adopt an openly lesbian identity by positioning herself in a community of women: She has become "a woman connecting with other women in an intricate, complex, and ever-widening network of exchanging strengths" (175).[10]

This ever-widening network illustrates Lorde's assertions in "Eye to Eye" and "Transformation of Silence into Language and Action": When women overcome their fear of difference and speak, their words create bonds uniting them in new ways, making possible further acts of mutual self-creation. The perceptions of similarity and difference Audre acquires in her relationships with Ginger and Eudora reflect and shape her own self-transformations. From Eudora, Audre learns the importance of transforming her experience into language. Because Eudora taught her "how to love and live to tell the story, and with flair" (209), Audre found the strength to survive the break-up with Muriel. More specifically, Eudora's injunction to "*[w]aste nothing, Chica, not even pain. Particularly not pain*" encouraged her to openly express her sorrow (236; her italics).

Once again, language triggers self-change, but unlike her previous discoveries the insight Audre obtains while boarding a bus shortly after her separation from Muriel is not directly stimulated by another woman's words. This enigmatic passage is worth discussing at length, for it illustrates the performative, transformational nature of Lorde's self-naming process:

> The bus door opened and I placed my foot upon the step. Quite suddenly, there was music swelling up into my head, as if a choir of angels had boarded the Second Avenue bus directly in front of me. They were singing the last chorus of an old spiritual of hope:

> Gonna die this death
> on Cal-va-ryyyyy
> BUT AIN'T GONNA
> DIE
> NO MORE . . . ! (239)

The "angelic orchestration" that seems to fill the bus is so real that Audre looks at the other passengers to assure herself that the gospel song exists only in her own head. Lorde emphasizes that the words come from within. As Claudine Raynaud points out, this old spiritual is "a song of hope, of death and resurrection, a parallel to her own progress," and the vision accompanying this song reveals the extent of Audre's growth. Yet this scene represents more than Lorde's attempt to "graphically . . . bring to the reader's mind the power of the melody" (232). More significant than the song itself is the surrealistic experience it initiates: As the outer world of Seventh Avenue disappears, Audre is suddenly transported to "a hill in the center of an unknown country, hearing the sky fill with a new spelling of [her] own name" (239).

But what can it mean to discover a "new spelling" of one's name? Like the description of her life in the Epilogue as "new living the old in a new way" (255), or like Allen's origin myths, Lorde's phrase suggests both continuity and change. She is not transformed into a new person; rather, she sees herself differently. In *Diving Deep and Surfacing*, Carol P. Christ defines such transitions in consciousness as "awakenings." She contrasts the epiphanies described by women with those depicted by their male counterparts and explains that unlike traditional religious conversions that entail the seeker's self-abandonment, the spiritual awakenings in woman-authored texts imply the reverse. Rather than lose herself, the protagonist finds herself as she strips away the false labels and acquires a sense of agency. Christ emphasizes that an important part of this process is the protagonist's "new naming," her ability to translate this experience into words she can share with others, thus making possible collective transformations (17–26). She associates this linguistic power with social change: "As women begin to name the world for themselves not only will they create new life possibilities for women, they will also upset the world order that has been taken for granted for centuries" (24).

This naming process has additional, historically specific implications for women of the African diaspora. As Hortense Spillers asserts in "Mama's Baby, Papa's Maybe," naming has functioned as "one of the key sources of a bitter Americanizing for African persons" (73). Indeed, the "dehumanized naming" (69) that occurred during the enslavement of African peoples could be more accurately described as a violent *dis*naming because it entailed an incredible cultural severance encompassing "the destruction of the African name, of kin, of linguistic, and ritual connections" (73). This "Americanization" stripped away gender roles, severed body from flesh, and converted human offspring into property. Spillers associates this material and linguistic disjuncture with the production of an "American grammar book," her ironic term for the sociopolitical symbolic order that "be-gan"[11] with the Middle Passage and continues today. She contrasts this symbolic order with conventional psychoanalytic inscriptions of gen-der roles, sexuality, and kinship relations, contending that

> under conditions of captivity, the offspring of the female does not "belong" to the Mother, nor is s/he "related" to the "owner," though the latter "possesses" it. . . . In the context of the United States, we could not say that the enslaved offspring was "orphaned," but the child does become, under the press of a patronymic, patrifocal, patri-lineal, and patriarchal order, the man/woman on the boundary, whose human and familial status, by the very nature of the case, has yet to be defined. (74)

By locating this captive African body on the boundary of conventional gender roles, Spillers points to a liminal zone, a "vestibular cultural formation" (74) that is, in effect, a cross-cultural vacuum. Although this ambiguously nongendered threshold could lead to the develop-ment of liberating subject positions, the extreme cultural dislocation has been highly disabling. As Spillers explains in a later essay,

> the African name is not only "lost" to cultural memory, but on that single ground the captive African is symbolically broken in two—ruptured along the fault of a "double consciousness" in which the break with an indigenous African situation is complete, but one's cul-tural membership in the American one remains inchoate. A social subject in abeyance, in an absolute deferral that becomes itself a new synthesis, is born—the African-American, whose last name, for all in-tents and purposes, becomes historically X, the mark of his/her bor-rowed culture's profound "illiteracy." ("Permanent Obliquity," 130)

Given this violent disjuncture, it is extremely significant that Au-dre's "new naming" directly precedes her encounter with Kitty/ Afrekete, Lorde's personalized version of a West African linguist/trick-ster figure.[12] Indeed, Lorde's use of revisionist myth to respell her "own name" indicates a provocative inscription onto the void Spillers reads in the "American Grammar Book." Lorde's self-inscription oc-curs in the ambivalent space opened by the interplay between lan-guage and silence, between "blackness" and "whiteness." By rewriting

Yoruban/Fon myth, she invents a discovered connection between the irrevocably lost indigenous African past and her life in twentieth-century U.S. culture. Put differently, Afrekete serves as a conversion principle enabling Lorde to develop an Africanized "blackness" that collapses conventional distinctions between invention and discovery. Her body becomes text as she emerges, "blackened and whole. . . . *Becoming. Afrekete*" (5; her italics).[13]

IV   This problematizing of gender takes her . . . out of the traditional symbolics of female gender, and it is our task to make a place for this different social subject. In so doing, we are less interested in joining the ranks of gendered femaleness than gaining the insurgent ground as female social subject. Actually claiming the monstrosity (of a female with the potential to "name"), which her culture imposes in blindness, "Sapphire" might rewrite after all a radically different text for a female empowerment.   HORTENSE SPILLERS

Not "masculine," not completely "feminine" either.

TRINH MINH-HA

But who is Afrekete? From a pantheon of almost six hundred orisha, Lorde has selected a figure never mentioned in scholarly works on the subject. Indeed, in *The Black Unicorn* Lorde herself does not refer to Afrekete by name. And although in *Zami* she describes Afrekete as MawuLisa's "*youngest daughter, the mischievous linguist, trickster, best-beloved, whom we must all become*" (255; her emphasis), in Dahomean and Fon mythic narratives MawuLisa's youngest child is generally portrayed as a highly masculinized figure named Eshu/Legba.[14] Like Afrekete, this orisha is the divine linguist and trickster. Lorde explains in *The Black Unicorn* that Eshu/Legba is

the youngest and most clever son of Yemanjá (or of Mawulisa). The mischievous messenger between all the other *Orisha-Vodu* and humans, he knows their different languages and is an accomplished linguist who both transmits and interprets. This function is of paramount importance because the *Orisha* do not understand each other's language, nor the language of humans. Eshu is a prankster, also, a personification of all the unpredictable elements in life. He is often identified with the masculine principle, and his primary symbol is frequently a huge erect phallus. But Eshu-Elegba has no priests, and in many Dahomean religious rituals, his part is danced by a woman with an attached phallus. (119–20)

Eshu/Legba is a perpetually liminal figure, a mediator symbolizing the disruption of boundaries that bring about personal, social, and cosmic change. In Fon metaphysics Legba's mediational role is highly disruptive yet viewed in a positive light, for Legba's ability to generate conflict is closely associated with magic and transformations of all kinds. As Robert Pelton states, Legba defies rigid structures and "draws into the open the power of all boundaries, opens passageways to new life, and makes transformation possible even as he stimulates conflict" (84). Similarly, in Yoruban cosmology Eshu represents the boundary transgression leading to new combinations in a never-ending process of transmutation and change. Pelton explains that Eshu's transformational power illustrates both the liminal possibilities contained within all margins and the Yorubans' belief that "the internal and external boundaries of their lives are charged with power, that these must be explored carefully to overcome stagnation and to deal with explosions, and that they must be constantly transformed to heal division and renew life" (142).

By identifying herself with this orisha, Lorde underscores the transformational power of language, as well as her own linguistic authority. Like Eshu/Legba, she is a liminal figure, a language-maker who uses words to disrupt boundaries, making individual and collective change possible. Henry Louis Gates's use of Eshu/Legba as a central trope in *The Signifying Monkey* reveals this figure's importance to contemporary literary theory. As Gates notes, Eshu/Legba's mediational role provides us with a cross-cultural metaphor depicting "an unbroken arc of metaphysical presupposition and a pattern of figuration shared through time and space among certain black cultures in West Africa, South America, the Caribbean, and the United States" (6). Indeed, Gates implicitly identifies himself with this West African orisha by redefining Eshu/Legba as "the indigenous black metaphor for the literary critic" (9). Gates's description is worth quoting at length because it indicates Eshu/Legba's mediational and linguistic roles:

> Esu is the sole messenger of the gods, . . . he who interprets the will of the gods to man; he who carries the desires of man to the gods. Esu is the guardian of the crossroads, master of style and of stylus, the phallic god of generation and fecundity, master of that elusive, mystical barrier that separates the divine world from the profane. Frequently characterized as an inveterate copulator possessed by his enormous penis, linguistically Esu is the ultimate copula, connecting truth with understanding, the sacred with the profane, text with interpretation, the word (as a form of the verb to be) that links a subject with its predicate. In Yoruba mythology, Esu is said to limp as he walks precisely because of his mediating function: his legs are of different lengths because he keeps one anchored in the realm of the gods while the other rests in this, our human world. (6)

Eshu/Legba's hypermasculinity is far more complex than Gates here implies, for this trickster figure is not "really" masculine. Or, rather, s/he is no more masculine than s/he is feminine. As Gates himself points out, although he consistently refers to this orisha "in the masculine, Esu is also genderless, or of dual gender, as recorded Yoruba and Fon myths suggest, despite his remarkable penis feats. . . . Each time I have used the masculine pronoun for the referent *Esu*, then, I could just have properly used the feminine" (29).[15]

Before I explore the radical implications of Afrekete/Legba's ambiguously gendered status, I want to discuss the twofold transformational process reflected in Lorde's revisionary use of this liminal figure. First, by replacing the Judeo-Christian religio-mythic system with the Yoruban/Fon, she simultaneously discovers and invents the cultural dimensions of her identity; and second, by emphasizing Eshu/Legba's feminine components, she appropriates for herself the linguistic authority generally associated with masculinity. In so doing, Lorde challenges conventional western imagery of the divine as exclusively male.

This latter move is similar to those made by a number of contemporary "theologians" who reject patriarchal Judeo-Christian religious terminology for earlier woman-identified metaphors of the divine.

Daly, Christ, and other twentieth-century writers and thinkers depict God as a woman, denouncing the hierarchical worldview that elevates men (who are made in God's image) over women (who are not). In *Beyond God the Father* Daly argues that genuine selfhood—which entails each individual's ability to name the self, God, and the world—has been "stolen" from women. By defining God as "the Father" and human beings as "mankind," conventional language has effectively silenced women; it has denied their existence (6–11). She maintains that to move from silence and "nonbeing" to self-affirmation and speech, women must establish a new relationship to language, one acknowledging their presence by recognizing their "Female/Elemental divinity" within. Christ makes a similar point in *Diving Deep and Surfacing*: "To name God in oneself, or to speak the word 'Goddess' again after many centuries of silence is to reverse age-old patterns of thinking in which male power and female subordination are viewed as the norm" (128). She asserts that this shift in thought signals a new model for female subject formation: Women see themselves differently; they identify with the divine and recognize the sacredness of their own being. No longer silenced by feelings of inferiority, they reject masculinist definitions and begin "a new naming of women's power, women's bodies, . . . and women's bonds with each other" (128).

Other theorists, however, are far less sanguine about the effectiveness of these attempts to move beyond God the father. As I explained in my discussion of Allen's origin myths, often such calls for feminist spiritualities and a female divine are dismissed as regressive, essentializing strategies that inadvertently reinstate normative gender roles and exclusionary practices.[16] But I want to explore the psycholinguistic implications of these attempts in greater detail. I believe that the Eurocentrism in existing accounts prevents feminists on both sides of this debate from utilizing the liberating potential found in non-European mythic systems and thus inventing new forms of "feminine" agency, or what Hortense Spillers describes as "a female with the potential to 'name'" ("Mama's Baby," 80).

One of the key difficulties with the new naming process Daly, Christ, and other feminist theologians describe is the ease with which this linguistic shift seems to take place. Daly, for example, implies that transformation occurs simply by redefining isolated words and reversing their current patriarchal meanings. Yet, reversals remain locked in binary oppositional struggles. To be effective, women's revisionist myths cannot simply overturn existing hierarchical structures by replacing "God the Father" with "God the Mother." As Rosi Braidotti asserts in *Patterns of Dissonance*, when renaming operates only "at the level of lexicon, of the vocabulary," it inadvertently reinforces the underlying phallocentric discursive system, or the "syntax of representation" (207). That is, when feminists attempting to reject patriarchal religions simply reverse the existing gender structure, they cannot effectively challenge current ontological, epistemological, and ethical systems. Rather than develop new concepts of subjectivity, Daly feminizes well-known humanist beliefs concerning a universal subject. This reactionary strategy simply perpetuates existing hierarchical systems and provides further support for conventional gender categories.[17] Luce Irigaray raises a similar objection to what she describes as Daly's "notion of the divine . . . defined as the result of a narcissistic and imperialistic inflation of sameness" ("Equal to Whom?" 73–74). She, too, maintains that reversal is inadequate and cannot bring about lasting change.

"New naming" cannot be effective unless it operates on multiple levels to transform the prevailing sociosymbolic system. Thus Irigaray attempts to invent a more sophisticated female-feminist theology. She calls for representations of a "feminine" divine that would exist in addition to, rather than in replacement of, the "masculine." She maintains that to construct feminine subjectivities *qualitatively* different from the "masculine," contemporary western cultures must reinvent[18] images of independent female gods: "Divinity is what we need to become free, autonomous, sovereign. No human subjectivity, no human society has ever been established without the help of the divine" ("Divine Women," 62).

In conventional western religious systems, representations of a divine "masculine" gender play a pivotal role in constructing male subjectivities by providing men with an ideal to measure themselves against. As Irigaray explains, "Man is able to exist because God helps him to define his gender (*genre*), helps him orient his finiteness by reference to infinity" ("Divine Women," 61). But this system leaves women stranded. Because phallocentric religions contain no models of an autonomous "feminine" divine and, consequently, no maternal genealogy, many contemporary western women are left in a state of "dérélection,"[19] or abandonment; they lack adequate representation in the existing sociosymbolic system and thus have no "artistic, iconic, religious mediation that might allow them to look at and admire themselves in some ideal her" ("Limits of Transference," 111). Consequently, they cannot define themselves as autonomous subjects[20] but must measure themselves against an ideal corresponding only to "masculine" standards.[21]

This absence of a divine "feminine" ideal inhibits women's ability to establish a female sociality or woman-to-woman relations. Irigaray maintains that because the present symbolic system does not contain images of female gods providing women with diverse models of identity formation, women cannot relate to each other as independent subjects. Reduced to a single subject position in the existing sociosymbolic system, they exist in a state of rivalry and confusion, or nonindividuation, in which it is impossible to differentiate between themselves:

> If women have no God, they are unable either to communicate or commune with one another. They need, we need, an infinite if they are to share *a little*. Otherwise sharing implies fusion-confusion, division, and dislocation within themselves, among themselves. If I am unable to form a relationship with some horizon of accomplishment for my gender, I am unable to share while protecting my becoming. ("Divine Women," 62; her emphasis)

According to Irigaray, a primary step in creating a "feminine" divine entails establishing a female genealogy and mother/daughter couples to symbolize intersubjective relationships between women. As she asserts in "Women-Mothers," women in western societies should reject images of maternal omnipotence and develop "a woman-to-woman relationship of reciprocity with our mothers, in which they might possibly also feel themselves to be our daughters" (50). These mother/daughter relationships would enable women to begin expressing their own desires, rather than those of the father (52). Similarly, in "A Chance for Life" she suggests the strategic placement of mother/daughter images in public spaces could "begin to heal a loss of individual and collective identity for women" (189).[22]

Although I am sympathetic to Irigaray's feminist reconstruction of myth and know from personal experience that the recognition of female gods can be empowering, I am not fully persuaded that Irigaray escapes the binary logic structuring phallocentric discourse. While it's true she does not fall into Daly's trap of simply reversing already existing categories, she, too, remains locked into dualistic structures. At best, her call for a female genealogy and an autonomous feminine divine represents the possibility of shifting from male/nonmale to male/female dichotomies. But this transition from hierarchical to nonhierarchical duality cannot effectively transform the existing gender system. As I'll explain in the following section, Lorde's revisionary use of Legba/Afrekete demonstrates that this exclusive focus on European-based models greatly restricts the liberating potential of a "feminine" divine.

---

v   I grew Black as my need for life, for affirmation, for love, for sharing—copying from my mother what was in her, unfulfilled. I grew Black as Seboulisa, who I was to find in the cool mud halls of Abomey several lifetimes later—and, as alone.   **AUDRE LORDE**

Like Irigaray, Lorde associates hostility between women with the absence of positive representations of female gods and implies that new configurations of identity could significantly affect women's ability to construct intersubjective relationships, or what she calls "interdependency."[23] There are, however, at least two significant differences between each theorist's tactics. First, Irigaray posits an irreducible distinction between the "masculine" and the "feminine"—a distinction that Lorde irrevocably blurs with her use of Yoruban/Fon mythic systems. Second, and closely related to the first, Irigaray focuses almost entirely on European-based images of "feminine" specificity, whereas Lorde does not. Lorde maintains that ignoring non-European mythic and cultural systems inhibits the establishment of woman-to-woman bonds. As she implies in her well-known letter to Mary Daly, when feminists create alternate models of female identity based exclusively on Eurocentric traditions, they replace the Judeo-Christian myths that silenced all women by denying their subjecthood with new myths of a generic woman. Yet these new myths can be almost as detrimental as the old, for they silence those women whose specific historic, cultural, or ethnic backgrounds are erased by the dominant western paradigm. Lorde maintains that by focusing entirely on Graeco-Roman mythology and ignoring "black" women's cultural roots, Daly inadvertently creates divisions between women and diminishes the effectiveness of her work:

> Mary, I ask that you be aware of how this serves the destructive forces
> of racism and separation between women—the assumption that the
> herstory and myth of white women is the legitimate and sole herstory
> and myth of all women to call upon for power and background, and
> that nonwhite women and our herstories are noteworthy only as dec-
> orations, or examples of female victimization. (*Sister Outsider*, 69)

As in *Zami*, Lorde attributes the establishment of genuine connections to the acknowledgment of both differences and commonalities. She asserts that by ignoring ethnic and cultural diversity and focusing solely on women's similarities, Daly "denied the real connections that exist between all of us" (*Sister Outsider*, 68). Although Daly's European-based models of female identity can be at least partially attributed to a desire to unify women, her inability or reluctance to recognize and express the differences between women parallels the maternal silence and subsequent alienation Lorde describes in the opening sections of her biomythography.

Lorde's concepts of interdependency and self-mothering illustrate an open-ended acceptance of difference. She explains in "The Master's Tools Will Never Dismantle the Master's House" that interdependency is a "redemptive," nonpatriarchal mode of woman-to-woman nurturing based on the creative use of nondominant differences. She urges her audience to incorporate a more sophisticated, complex analysis of the differences among women into their work, asserting that

[d]ifference must not be merely tolerated, but seen as a fund of necessary polarities between which our creativity can spark like a dialectic.
Only then does the necessity for interdependency become unthreaten-
ing. Only within that interdependency of different strengths, acknowledged and equal, can the power to seek new ways of being in the
world generate, as well as the courage and sustenance to act where
there are no charters. (*Sister Outsider*, 111)

Similarly, in "Eye to Eye" Lorde underscores the importance of
using differences creatively. She associates interdependency with the
production of collective maternal bonds, or what she describes as
"mothering ourselves." Like Cornell's concept of natality, Lorde's self-
mothering indicates interactional self-transformations. More specifically, self-mothering entails self-acceptance and an empowered use of
language that leads to the construction of positive individual and
collective identities. Lorde explains that for "black" women, self-
mothering

means we must establish authority over our own definition, provide
an attentive concern and expectation of growth which is the beginning of that acceptance we came to expect only from our mothers. It
means that I affirm my own worth by committing myself to my survival, in my own self and in the self of other Black women. (*Sister
Outsider*, 173)

The self-mothering Lorde advocates is performative. Just as the expectation of growth makes individual and collective growth possible, the
affirmation of one's self in the other leads to the development of
intersubjective relationships.[24]

Lorde illustrates this performative self-mothering in the final episode of *Zami* as she describes Audre's brief love affair with Kitty, a
mysterious, semimythical "black" southern woman whose birth name
is Afrekete. Lorde underscores her connection with Afrekete by emphasizing this orisha's power over language; like Eshu/Legba, Afrekete
is "the rhyme god, . . . [the] communicator, linguist, and poet"
(quoted in Grahn, 125). Lorde further stresses the similarities between
herself and this "black" god/dess by giving Afrekete the nickname

Audre received from Ginger; both women are the "slick kitty from the city."[25] Thus, she does not exaggerate when writes that "[s]omething about Kitty made me feel like a rollercoaster, rocketing from idiot to goddess" (*Zami*, 248), for in their erotic lovemaking she redefines herself and becomes Afrekete.

Although scholars have identified Kitty/Afrekete with Lorde, they have not explored the full implications of this doubling. They focus their attention on Lorde's use of this mythical figure to establish her ties to a specific ethnic, gender, and/or sexual identity, and so overlook the transcultural, transgendered, transexualized dimensions of her revisionist myth. Julia Watson and Yvonne Klein, for example, associate Kitty/Afrekete with Lorde's affirmation of her own identity as a "black" lesbian. According to Watson, "In finally creating a satisfactory relationship with a lover, mythicized as the black lesbian goddess Afrekete, who can both move within and laugh at white patriarchy, Lorde uses autobiography to undermine its socially integrative purpose and to stage an alternative birthing of herself through writing her life as a movement toward an origin 'elsewhere'" (153). And Klein maintains that Lorde's lovemaking with Kitty enables her both to recover "the latitudes of Carriacou, the lost lesbian paradise and source of her own mother's power," and to begin "incarnat[ing] herself as Afrekete" (335).[26] Other critics, like Claudine Raynaud and Anna Wilson, emphasize the collective ethnic identity Lorde constructs. According to Raynaud, Kitty/Afrekete embodies "the black woman of the future" (238); and Wilson claims Kitty/Afrekete enables Audre to establish a connection with the "black" community of Harlem (84). In a much earlier version of this chapter, I extended these interpretations by arguing that *Zami*'s final episode could be read as Lorde's construction of a multiethnic, gender-specific collective identity, a universalized woman:

> As she describes her sensual lovemaking with Kitty, Lorde celebrates both her own sexuality and that of all women. As she depicts the sacredness of women's loving relationships with each other, she validates the importance of each woman's self-love. She relays the lessons she has learned from the women in her life to her female readers and

offers them a new way of perceiving themselves and their world. . . .
By naming the Black goddess in herself, Lorde empowers other
women to do so as well. (30)

Now, however, I'm less persuaded by these interpretations. If, as
Gates and other scholars assert, Eshu/Legba represents a highly phallic yet ambiguously gendered "third principle—neither male nor female, neither this nor that, but both, a compound morphology" (*Signifying Monkey*, 29), as well as a perpetually liminal, transformational
figure, it seems too restrictive to define Afrekete in an ethnic-, gender-,
or sexually-specific fashion. Instead, I want to suggest that Lorde's
revisionary use of this liminal trickster figure destabilizes any self-
contained, purified configuration of identity.

Consider the ways gender and sexual boundaries blur in scholars'
discussions of Eshu/Legba's ritual enactments. Lorde, for example,
maintains that in many Dahomean rituals, "his" role "is danced by a
woman with an attached phallus" (*Black Unicorn*, 120). Even more
intriguing is the unacknowledged deconstruction of gender and sexuality in Pelton's description of Fon initiations in the "Mawu-Lisa
cult." To begin with, MawuLisa is also ambiguously gendered; s/he "is
an androgynous god or, more accurately perhaps, a male-female High
God" (103). Mawu is associated with the feminine and the moon,
while Lisa is associated with the masculine and the sun. At the rite of
emergence, the heterosexual matrix breaks down as both male and
female initiates become "wives of Mawu," the *feminine* aspect of this
androgynous/male-female orisha. These male and female wives of a
female god "appear wearing the folded cloth about their waists which
is the mark of a married woman." In the following passage, Pelton
combines Melville Herskovits's description of this ritual with his own.
Note the gender shifts occurring in the two scholars' references to
Legba:

> On the next day "Legba" makes *his* first appearance. *He* is represented
> by a young girl . . . and on the final days of the emergence ritual this
> "Legba" leads the dancing of the novitiates. When Herskovits ob-
> served the ceremony, the girl dressed as Legba came forward, "danc-
> ing toward the drums. When *she* reached the drummer, *she* put *her*
> hand under the fringe of raffia about *her* waist." Herskovits says that

Legba continued to dance in "exaggerated mimicry of sexual connection," and then seized one of the younger girls, with whom *he* mimed intercourse. When Legba moved back to the initiates . . . *he* led them in a dance. (101; my emphasis)

Lorde indicates a similar defiance of conventional categories in the Prologue to *Zami*:

> *I have always wanted to be both man and woman, to incorporate the strongest and richest parts of my mother and father within/into me—to share valleys and mountains upon my body the way the earth does in hills and peaks.*
>
> *I would like to enter a woman the way any man can, and to be entered—to leave and to be left—to be hot and hard and soft all at the same time in the cause of our loving.* (7; her italics)

In a sense, by renaming herself Afrekete, Lorde enacts these desires. Like the sex/gender confusion that occurs when western scholars describe Eshu/Legba's ritual enactments, her revisionary myth transgresses heterosexual and homosexual norms, as well as binary systems of gendered meaning. Her desire to be both man and woman, to penetrate and to be penetrated, destabilizes the masculinist bias and the "heterosexist logic"[27] structuring the Lacanian Symbolic. To borrow Judith Butler's phrase, Lorde makes "gender trouble." As Butler persuasively argues, gender and sex are performative effects, not natural states of existence: "The univocity of sex, the internal coherence of gender, and the binary framework for both sex and gender are . . . regulatory fictions that consolidate and naturalize the convergent power regimes of masculine and heterosexist oppression" (*Gender Trouble*, 33). In other words, western culture's belief in a heterosexually dual gendered system, where the masculine is elevated over the feminine, is not a natural fact but rather a constantly repeated act— naturalized by these constant repetitions. The apparent naturalness functions as a "regulatory fiction," a normative way of being, that compels us to be either a woman or a man. This binary system relies on and reinforces a belief in impermeable physical boundaries where anatomical bodies are marked—and, simultaneously mark us—as either male or female. But as Butler points out, these boundaries are themselves produced through the complex interplay between the psychic and the material.

Lorde's revisionary myth exposes the fictional nature of this binary gendered system, as well as the interconnections between the psychic and the material components of identity. As she renames Eshu/Legba "Afrekete," Lorde feminizes this highly phallic yet ambiguously gendered orisha. She denaturalizes the belief in two mutually exclusive genders by disrupting the boundary between them. In psychoanalytic terms, Kitty/Afrekete functions analogously to what Butler calls the "lesbian phallus." By identifying lesbian desire with the phallus—generally viewed as the signifier of male desire—this theoretical fiction calls into question our perceptions concerning the naturalness of sexed bodies. As Butler explains in "The Lesbian Phallus and the Morphological Imaginary," by displacing the Lacanian phallus from its position as privileged signifier of the existing masculine symbolic, the lesbian phallus unfixes male/female anatomical references. The lesbian phallus exposes a transgressive masculine—and, perhaps, even a heterosexual—desire *within* lesbian sexuality, thus challenging two important beliefs. First, it unsettles attempts to envision alternative forms of purely masculine and purely feminine desire. Second, the lesbian phallus crosses the division between hetero- and homosexual desire. By challenging the assumption that only certain bodies with a specific body part can symbolize the phallus, the lesbian phallus blurs the boundaries between binary gender and sexual systems. In this schema, a woman's lesbian desire for another woman becomes somewhat masculinized.

This theoretical fiction serves a similar purpose in Lorde's revisionary myth. Her use of Afrekete and other Yoruban/Fon orisha, such as the ambiguously gendered Eshu/Legba and the male-female Mawu-Lisa and Seboulisa, can be read as provocative interventions into the heterosexist feminine Imaginary theorized by Irigaray and other female feminists of difference. As in Yoruban/Fon metaphysics where Eshu/Legba's constant to-and-fro movement makes possible a proliferation of genders and sexualities that destabilizes binary systems, Butler's concept of the lesbian phallus and Lorde's Afrekete/Legba open up "anatomy—and sexual difference itself—as a site of proliferative resignifications" (Butler, 162–63).

But Lorde's lesbian phallus is "black." Or is it? If, as Uzo Esonwanne suggests, Eshu/Legba takes on "blackness" only in the context of racialist categories of meaning, then Lorde's lesbian phallus only *becomes* "black" in the context of her interactional self-naming. As Esonwanne points out in his discussion of Gates's reference to Eshu/Legba as "the indigenous *black* metaphor for the literary critic" (*Signifying Monkey*, 9; my emphasis), the notion of an indigenously "black" African orisha is senseless:

> To prove that Ésú is black, it is necessary to identify for whom blackness is of some relevance. Surely neither Ésú nor his/her yoruba devotees would be self-motivated to delineate a racial identity for the divinity. The need for racial identification arises in situations where race is at issue; where it is not, as among the Yoruba, the identification of Ésú as the figure of a black hermeneutic indicates that its blackness is a blackness *for*, an extraverted blackness. Further, if blackness also indicates racial self-awareness, then it is unlikely that Ésú, as a divinity straddling the abyss separating humans from deity, is necessarily black, for the consciousness of the divine self as being a racial self is far from being demonstrated in Gates's work. (576; his emphasis)

Esonwanne's description of a nonessential, extraverted "blackness" parallels the relational nature of "black" and "white" identities in psychoanalytic theories of subjectivity. As Drucilla Cornell explains, "[i]n the Lacanian understanding of the constitution of identity through difference, what 'black' signifies can only be understood through its asymmetrical, differential articulation against whiteness" (*Transformations*, 190). In other words, the delineation of "black" as a racialist identity is context-specific and occurs only in situations where "race" is created and used to construct differences by marking people differentially.

Indeed, "race" itself is a context-specific category, an ambiguous, constantly changing concept that has little—if anything—to do with biology or scientific descriptions. As Michael Omi and Howard Winant persuasively demonstrate: "The meaning of race is defined and contested throughout society, in both collective action and personal practice. In the process, racial categories themselves are formed, transformed, destroyed, and re-formed" (61). Though people in the United

States generally think of "black" and "white" as permanent, trans-historical racial markers indicating distinct groups of people, they are not. The Puritans and other early European colonizers didn't consider themselves "white"; they identified as "Christian," "English," or "free," for at that time the word "white" had nothing to do with "race." Not surprisingly, racialization was economically and politically motivated. It was not until around 1680, when the slave trade was restricted to people of African lineage, that the term "white" was used to describe a specific group of people. As Yehudi Webster explains, "The idea of a homogeneous white race was adopted as a means of generating cohesion among explorers, migrants, and settlers in eighteenth-century America. Its opposite was the black race, whose nature was said to be radically different from that of the white race" (9). Significantly, then, the "white" and "black" "races" evolved simultaneously; each half of this notorious binary acquired meaning only in relation to the other. As people whose specific ethnic identities were Yoruban, Ashanti, Fon, and Dahomean were forcibly removed from their homes in Africa and taken to the North American colonies, they became "black" as the Europeans became "white."

I see a similar process in *Zami* where Lorde's interactional self-naming simultaneously enacts and displaces this binary opposition between "black" and "white." Audre *becomes* "black" in the context of a maternal "whiteness," itself a response to the importance placed on racialized categories of meaning.[28] The "black" self-inscription initiated when Audre/Lorde began defining herself through her mother's denials culminates in the episode with Kitty/Afrekete. Through revisionist mythmaking and other oppositional strategies, she inscribes her particularized, Afrocentric "blackness" into her texts. Viewed in light of Cornell's conversion principles, Eshu/Legba can be read as a doubly enacted forward-and-backward movement enabling Lorde to develop an Africanized "blackness" that collapses conventional distinctions between invention and discovery.

If, as Gates and others suggest, "race is a text, . . . not an essence," a text that "must be *read* with painstaking care and suspicion,"[29] then how do we read the ways Lorde's flesh becomes text as she inscribes herself "black"? In "The Winds of Orisha" for example, she lets "[i]m-patient legends speak through [her] flesh." Indeed, flesh becomes text:

She is "[her]self / an incantation / dark raucous many-shaped characters / leaping back and forth across bland pages." Lorde's words are performative, disruptive, and transformational. By invoking "Mother Yemanja," Eshu, Oya, and other orisha, she will unsettle the land, stir the sea, and speak in the "roaring winds." Her self-inscription unites writer, reader, and text: She defiantly promises to "swell up from the pages" and incite readers to action (*Chosen Poems*, 48–49).

But why de-essentialize "black" and "white" racialist categories? Given the extremely empowering effects of Lorde's "black" self-inscription—effects enabling me and many other readers to read and inscribe our own "blackness" in new ways—why deconstruct the binary between "black" and "white"?

Crossing Over
Toward a Womanist Genealogy

---

*This myth-making impulse . . . seems to be an impulse that
leads us in the direction of an imagining of identity, a
realization of who we are.*   N. SCOTT MOMADAY

*This is good, AnaLouise, but you need to include more of
yourself in the writing.*   GLORIA ANZALDÚA

If you were to ask what drew me to Allen, Anzaldúa,
and Lorde, I might tell you it was their use of precolonial spiritual and
mythic beliefs to reinvent themselves, their readers, and their worlds.
They create dynamic models of individual and collective identity formation that begin with multiple returns to previously erased cultural
traditions. I would, of course, emphasize that these returns are performative, not descriptive: By going "back" to Laguna, Mexican Indian,
and Yoruban/Fon belief systems, they go forward; they redefine the
past from their present perspectives to alter contemporary social conditions and create new modes of living and thinking. If I felt really
comfortable with you, I might admit that, even more than this ambivalent oscillation, it was their ability to transform alienation into new
types of connection that attracted me to them. I'd tell you how their
words spoke to me, empowered me in new ways, and I might even
read to you from my journal:

> In Allen's poetry and fiction, I've found echoes of my own desires re-
> flected back to me. I'm struck by the intense longing & the attempt to
> describe, to draw words around, absence itself. In *Shadow Country*,
> the quest for roots—or perhaps for connection or meaning—is almost

overwhelming. It knocks me over. Yet meaning itself seems ungrasp-able. Intangible, elusive, but not—quite—impossible. It's a partially recognized, partially erased feeling or belief or desire. . . . These terms are inadequate. But the emotion triggered in me as I read Allen's words is so very, very familiar! The intense desire to connect—or to make a space for belonging, to create something new. I know that de-sire! And the belief—desperate at times—that what seems to be gaping absence can be transformed. Maybe Allen takes this absence and re-defines it as the void—a creative chaotic space of potential meaning she describes in *Grandmothers* as self-aware, thinking energy. Or maybe I'm just rewriting Allen's words, letting my own imagination and desires guide my interpretation? Maybe I'm like Ephanie. She, too, feels fragmented, alienated, and unable to make sense of her life yet persists in believing that meaning exists—somewhere: "Inside and outside must meet, she knew, desperately. Must cohere. Equilibrate. No one mentioned it. They said it was all within. They said it was all outside. But she was the place where the inside and the outside came together. An open doorway." Or a threshold, a space where connec-tions can occur. Yes, Ephanie makes herself into a threshold. And al-though Allen implies that Ephanie *discovers* this liminal space, this meaning for her life, I'd say she invents it. Just like she transforms her alienated location into a threshold, so she uses the stories of Grand-mother Spider and double woman to create spiritual meaning for her life.

But to be honest, I hate talking—or writing—about myself. The impersonal, supposedly objective nature of academic life, coupled with my love of reading, played a pivotal role in my decision to go to graduate school, study Emerson and other canonical U.S. writers, and become a professor: I could hide behind books, computer screens, lecture podiums, the canon, and the other paraphernalia of academic life. The fact that I've openly inserted myself into *Women Reading Women Writing* demonstrates the power of Allen, Anzaldúa, and Lorde. Because I can't leave myself out. (Believe me—I'd like to.) Their words have transformed me so extensively that I feel compelled to chart this transformation. But as I do so, I shift between more and less "scholarly" prose, between first-, second-, and third-person voices. I have not—yet—reached the point of self-exposure and willing vulnerability I find in the words of Allen, Anzaldúa, and Lorde; I still need to hide.

Also, I believe theory provides a useful vehicle for extending the personal outward and making new connections between apparently divergent perspectives. Because it seems to hide personal desires behind rational, objective discourse and abstract thought, theory can be more persuasive for some readers. And I desperately want to persuade readers—to persuade *you*—that the writings I've examined in *Women Reading Women Writing* are transformational.

II   The moment of "fiction" or "literary" in the act of interpretation is what allows us to tell a "new" story and to project the stories we read into the tradition as constitutive of that tradition, as well as regulative of who we might become.

DRUCILLA CORNELL

At this point, I want to continue my forays into ethical feminism by applying my own "redemptive perspective" to a reading of Allen, Anzaldúa, and Lorde. More specifically, I want to propose an interactional, performative theory of reading and suggest that we should read their texts according to Anzaldúa's practice of invoked art. If, as Anzaldúa implies, metaphoric writing can literally—psychically and physically—transform us, then Allen's, Anzaldúa's, and Lorde's mythic self-inscriptions can inscribe themselves on their readers. The reading practice I want to enact is dialogic and begins with the assumption that the texts we read are not inert dead objects but instead come alive as we read them. To borrow Anzaldúa's words, each piece of poetry, fiction, or prose "has an identity; is a 'who' or a 'what' and contains the presences of persons, that is, incarnations of gods or ancestors or natural and cosmic powers" (*Borderlands*, 67). As I explained in Chapter 5, Anzaldúa reinterprets Aztec beliefs and invents a transformational, communal theory of art; she describes writing as a fluid process between writer and reader, a "constant dialogue" between her selves, her readers, and the words she writes. These words have the potential to transform us; the images we read communicate "with tissues, organs, and cells to effect change" ("Metaphors," 99). We re-enact these dialogues in new ways each time we read her words. In only slightly less metaphorical and more personal terms, Anzaldúa writes her desires on the pages I read. I internalize these desires and they change me; that is, they either reflect or become *my* desires. In this transformational, performative reading practice the borders be-tween writer, reader, and text dissolve: Words have concrete phys-iological, ideological, and psychic effects.

Let me illustrate this process with an interactional reading of *Zami*. If, as Lorde asserts in the opening pages of her biomythography, she became "black," is it possible that readers (can) grow "black" in the process of reading her work? That they, too, can emerge "blackened and whole"? (5)

Performative reading is not as far-fetched as it might sound. Be-cause "race" is an ideological, psychic inscription and not a biological fact, it's quite possible that Lorde's text interpellates readers—whatever the color of our skin—into alternate ideologies of "blackness." Con-sider the following excerpt from *Zami*:

> *Afrekete Afrekete ride me to the crossroads where we shall sleep, coated in the woman's power. The sound of our bodies meeting is the prayer of all strangers and sisters, that the discarded evils, abandoned at all crossroads, will not follow us upon our journeys.* (252; her italics)

Who is the "me," the "us," and the "we" in this passage? Whose bodies meet at the crossroads? Although I can't articulate the powerful im-pact these words have on me, I can tell you they change me. No matter how many times I read it, this erotic invocation to Afrekete pulls me in, carries me to this threshold, this place of new beginnings. Lorde enacts a similar open-ended invitation several pages later: "MawuLisa, thunder, sky, sun, the great mother of us all; and Afrekete, her young-est daughter, the mischievous linguist, trickster, best-beloved, whom we must all become" (255).

What happens when other readers identify themselves with the "us," the "we," and the "all" in Lorde's words? Do they, too, meet at the crossroads, the liminal space where transformation occurs? Do they begin becoming Afrekete? After all, there is no preexisting group that constitutes the "us" or the "we" Lorde refers to. As Judith Butler asserts, the pronoun "we" is performative, not descriptive:

> Every description of the "we" will always do more than describe; it will constitute and construct an imaginary unity and contrived total-ity, a phantasmatic ideal, which makes the "representability" of the we into a permanent impossibility. This might be understood lin-guistically as the inevitable performativity of the representational claim: the categories of identity instate or bring into "the real" the very phenomenon that they claim to name only after the fact. This is not a simple performative, but one which operates through exclusion-ary operations that come back to haunt the very claim of represent-ability that it seeks to make. ("Force," 121)

Read from the perspective of representational accuracy, the performa-tive implications of "we" are, as Butler suggests, problematic. In the context of readers' interaction with *Zami*, however, Lorde's "we" func-tions in an inclusionary, rather than exclusionary, fashion. Indeed, I would argue that the very "slipperiness" of all such inscriptions can play a vital role in redefining fixed categories of meaning. This ambig-uous "we" is potentially transformational and highly political. Bar-bara Johnson makes a similar point:

> The pronoun "we" has historically proven to be the most empowering and shiftiest shifter of them all. It is through "we" that discourses of false universality are created. With its cognitive indeterminacy and its performative authority, it is both problematic and unavoidable for discourses of political opposition. For this structure of the stressed subject with an indeterminate predicate may well be the structure necessary for empowerment without essentialism. At the same time, it is an empowerment always in danger of presuming too much. But, then, can there be empowerment without presumption? (43)

On the one hand, "we" can imply a false sense of unity that ignores the many differences among us—whoever this "us" might be. On the other hand, this "we" can speak to our personal sense of difference—or, as I suggested in the previous chapter, the intersection with other-ness that defines "us." In such instances, readers willingly adopt the empowering "we" they've been invited to enter.

But to return to my interactional reading of *Zami*: What would this empowerment entail? What transformations (would) occur in the process of becoming Afrekete? Let me fictionalize my own experience as an answer to these questions.

Say, for instance, a woman—not "white," but not "black" either; not "straight," but not quite "lesbian"—spends almost her entire life reading, searching for an explanation to account for her sense of difference, her feeling of not—ever—fitting in. She doesn't know what, exactly, she's looking for. A sense of belonging, perhaps? An intellectual or spiritual space where differences generate commonalities? After years of education, a dissertation on Emerson's epistemology, and thousands of books, she reads *Zami: A New Spelling of My Name*. Lorde's biomythography literally transforms her. She recognizes Audre's otherness in herself, and her otherness in Audre. The boundaries between reader, text, and writer break down, and she experiences what I described in the third chapter as re(con)ceived otherness. She acquires a new self/worldview, becomes a black feminist, and adopts a new spelling of her name.

As she continues reading—*The Black Unicorn*, *Sister Outsider*, *Borderlands/La Frontera*, *Prieta*, *The Sacred Hoop*, and *The Woman Who Owned the Shadows*,—she begins piecing together her own female genealogy, similar to but most definitely not identical to Irigaray's. To distinguish her genealogy from the French theorist's, she mixes her words with Alice Walker's and names it "womanist":

> Womanist : *Also*: A woman who loves other women, sexually and/or nonsexually. Appreciates and prefers women's culture, women's emotional flexibility . . . and women's strength. Sometimes loves men, sexually and/or nonsexually. Committed to survival and wholeness of entire people, male *and* female. Not a separatist, except periodically, for health. Traditionally universalist, as in: "Mama, why are we brown, pink, and yellow, and our cousins are white, beige, and black?" Answer: "Well, you know the colored race is just like a flower garden, with every color represented."

Unlike the more conventional female genealogy Irigaray describes— which is far too Europeanized, too stereotypically "white" feminine to be useful—her womanist genealogy is "universalist" and encompasses both male and female. But it does so with a difference: Thought Woman, Coatlicue, Legba/Afrekete, and the other mythic figures she's encountered open new thresholds, providing her with transgressive models that blur boundaries between supposedly distinct categories based on gender, sexuality, "race," or other systems of difference. Drawing on these mythic figures, she incorporates a bisexual inflection—an oscillation between "masculine"/"feminine" representations, between homosexual and heterosexual desires—into the womanist genealogy she invents. These bisexual inflections destabilize the binary system structuring self/other categories, enabling her—enabling me—to act out "blackness," the "feminine," and other stereotyped categories in new ways.

Her womanist genealogy de-centers the Eurocentric perspective that's stifled her for years. As she inscribes Thought Woman, Coatlicue, and Legba/Afrekete in her mind, on her body/text, and incorporates them into her teaching, she begins scrambling the labels that simultaneously define and confine us (whoever this "us" might be).

She seeks a new discourse—terms that fragment and decenter "black"/"white," male/female, hetero/homo, self/other binary pairs. Who knows what this new discourse might look like? *She* certainly doesn't (not yet), but she attempts to enact it in her teaching. She assigns *Borderlands/La Frontera*, *Zami*, *The Sacred Hoop*, *This Bridge*, *Making Face, Making Soul/Haciendo Caras* and invites students (whatever the color of their skin, her students think in "white" ways) to begin seeing themselves differently, to recognize and deconstruct their "whiteness," to divest themselves of the "white" ideology they've been taught for years. As they read, they too experience subtle shifts in perception. Rigid categories break down, and they begin recognizing the similarities and differences between self and other.

I'm positing a dialogic reading practice where the texts we read (can) open new thresholds, providing us with alternate ways of perceiving ourselves and our world. These shifts in self/worldview can transform us. If, as Anzaldúa asserts in "To(o) Queer the Writer," "[r]eading is one way of constructing identity" (257), her self-inscriptions, as well as those by Allen and Lorde, enable readers—enable "us"—to reconstruct our own self-identities. Each time we read, we engage in new convers(at)ions—transformational dialogues between writer, reader, and text. As we recognize ourselves in the various others we encounter as we read, and these others in ourselves, we define ourselves differently. Binary oppositions between self and other break down. We cross over, rewriting culture, rewriting self, as we go.

Notes

Chapter 1 / Threshold Identities

1. I use the term "self-identified" to indicate the volitional dimension of contemporary feminist identity politics. Also, throughout *Women Reading Women Writing* I will use the term "U.S.," rather than "American," when referring to the United States. As I see it, the word American is too general, for it incorporates Canada, Mexico, and all of Central and South America. I borrow the phrase "U.S. third world feminists" from Chela Sandoval; in my work, as in Sandoval's, it denotes a constructed category: "the political alliance made during the 1960s and 1970s between a generation of U.S. feminists of color who were separated by race, class, or gender identifications but united through similar responses to the experience of race oppression" ("U.S. Third World Feminism," 17).

2. This self-description appears in Anzaldúa's 1992 *vita*.

3. The phrase "betwixt and between" is Victor Turner's. See, for example, his discussion of liminality and "liminal *personae*" in *The Ritual Process* (95–97).

4. Braidotti cites Teresa de Lauretis's assertion in "The Essence of the

Triangle": "feminist theory is all about an essential difference, an irreducible difference, though not a difference between man and woman, nor a difference inherent in 'woman's nature' (in woman as nature), but a difference in the feminist conception of woman, women, and the world" (quoted in *Patterns of Dissonance,* 209). To my mind, however, this difference is less "irreducible" than de Lauretis suggests. As I explain in the following discussion of Norma Alarcón, this "female-feminist" difference relies on an underlying (heterosexist) binary male/female structure.

5. "Whether it goes under the heading of 'gender,' or of 'sexual difference,' the common project that is emerging is the radical redefinition of female subjectivity from a feminist standpoint" (Braidotti, *Patterns of Dissonance*, 264).

6. Elizabeth Grosz makes a similar point in "The In(ter)vention of Feminist Knowledges," where she underscores the new possibilities she finds in these female-feminist epistemologies. Like Braidotti, she associates this potential with a new, nonsymmetrical understanding of sexualized difference. Whereas phallocentric representational systems define the "feminine" exclusively in relation to the "masculine," Irigaray, de Lauretis, and other autonomy feminists attempt to break open these hierarchically structured binary categories by defining the former as qualitatively—rather than quantitatively—different from the latter. According to Grosz, this nonbinary exploration of sexual difference leads to the invention of new forms of thinking: "Feminist knowledges, on this model, are *not* competing intellectual paradigms, vying with patriarchal knowledges for primacy. They are *different*, possibly even incommensurable knowledges, knowledges which make contrary claims about truth, objectivity, confirmation, neutrality. They are knowledges which constitute not only Truth, but also autonomy and political effectivity" (103; her emphasis).

7. According to Alarcón, "There is a tendency in more sophisticated and elaborate gender standpoint epistemologists to affirm 'an identity made up of heterogeneous and heteronomous representations of gender, race, and class, and often indeed across languages and cultures,' with one breath, and with the next to refuse to explore how that identity may be theorized or analyzed, by reconfirming a unified subjectivity or 'shared consciousness' through gender" (364). The

quotations are from Teresa de Lauretis's "Feminist Studies/Critical Studies."

8. Chela Sandoval makes a similar point in "U.S. Third World Feminism." She suggests that writings by many self-identified U.S. third world feminists indicate the "existence of at least one other category of gender," a liminal gender, as it were: "This in-between space, this third gender category is also explored in the writings of such well-known authors as Maxine Hong Kingston, Gloria Anzaldúa, Alice Walker, and Cherríe Moraga, all of whom argue that U.S. third world feminists represent a different kind of human—new 'mestizas,' 'Woman Warriors' who live and are gendered 'between and among' the lines, 'Sister Outsiders' who inhabit a new psychic terrain which Anzaldúa calls 'the Borderlands,' la nueva Frontera" (4–5). See also Jane Flax's discussion of the interventional role played by women of color in her appropriately entitled essay, "The End of Innocence." She asserts that "[a]s much if not more than postmodernism, the writings of women of color have compelled white feminists to confront problems of difference and the relations of domination that are the conditions of possibility of our own theorizing and category formation" (459). This essay also provides a useful discussion of the masculinist bias in conventional western knowledge systems.

9. I follow Anzaldúa in using the upper case "B" when referring to what she describes as the "psychic and emotional" Borderlands. As she explained in a recent interview, "the little 'b' is the actual Southwest borderlands or any borderlands between two cultures, but when I use the capital 'B' it's like a mestiza with a capital M. It's a metaphor, not an actuality."

Chapter 2 / Mythic Ways of Knowing?

1. See DuPlessis, Joanne Frye, Rubenstein, Walker, and Greene.

2. For discussions of women's revisionary myths see DuPlessis (105–41), Ostriker (210–40), and Walker (49).

3. In *Beyond Accommodation*, Drucilla Cornell provides a lucid discussion of cultural myths' positive and negative effects on our beliefs concerning human nature.

4. Anzaldúa and Allen make similar points. See, for example,

Borderlands/La Frontera (36–37) and *The Sacred Hoop* (103–17). See also Bruce Lincoln on Barthe's description of myth as "mystification" (5–8) and David Murray's discussion of reactions to analyses of Native American myths. According to Murray, "Myth has generally been seen in Western societies as the area of the irrational, a way of thinking superseded by rational and scientific thought. As such, it can either be a privileged enclave (it does not have to be true in scientific terms to be meaningful) or, almost indistinguishable from this, dismissively marginalized (it does not have to be true because its claims are irrelevant)" (99).

5. William Doty provides a useful overview of the distinctions scholars make between myth and science (2–40).

6. Quoted in Houston Baker's *Blues, Ideology, and Afro-American Literature* (115; my emphasis).

7. Laura Mulvey makes a similar point: "The literal representation of transition as movement through a threshold, from one space to another, has a very different mythic connotation from that of a binary opposition. Here it is the possibility of change that is celebrated, and the alteration of status implies movement on a linear model, rather than opposition on a polar model" (171).

8. I am, of course, referring to the subtitle of Allen's book, *The Sacred Hoop: The Recovery of the Feminine in American Indian Traditions*. I discuss Allen's revisionary use of the term "feminine" at length in Chapter 4.

9. For another example of the ways Allen's perspective impacts readers who do not identify as Native American, see Renae Bredin's "Becoming Minor."

10. Similarly, in an earlier, possibly prefeminist essay entitled "Something Sacred Going on Out There," Allen defines myth as "a language construct that contains the power to transform something (or someone) from one state or condition to another.... [I]t is at base a vehicle, a means of transmitting paranormal power" (*Sacred Hoop*, 103). Although the differences between the two versions are subtle, Allen's references in the more recent description to "*shaping* paranormal power and *using* it to effect desired ends" place additional emphasis on agency (*Grandmothers*, 7; my emphasis).

11. According to Braidotti, "In the radical feminist philosophies of

sexual difference, the strategy of repossessing the body aims at elaborating alternative forms of knowledge and representation of the subject" (*Patterns of Dissonance*, 219). That is, embodied subjectivities destabilize the Cartesian mind/body dualism.

12. "The basic nature of the universe of power is magic"; Allen associates this "magic" with her interpretation of the "feminine," claiming that "the name given to the practice of a mage *Ma* (the *m*-syllable again) comes in variants. . . . All are versions of the same morpheme . . . and refer in one way or another to the Great Mother or Great Goddess of the Indo-Germanic tradition" (*Grandmothers*, 15). Not surprisingly, Allen maintains that "magic, as the word itself implies . . . is primarily a womanly enterprise" (*Grandmothers*, 24).

13. For Allen, participation entails fully entering the mythic tales. She explains that any reader who enters the stories "as a room is entered . . . moves into mythic space and becomes a voyager in the universe of power" (*Grandmothers*, 109). Similarly, in *The Sacred Hoop* she states that "entry into the narrative tradition. . . . lets people realize that individual experience is not isolate but is part of a coherent and timeless whole, providing them with a means of personal empowerment and giving shape and direction to their lives" (100).

14. Annette Van Dyke notes, "Ephanie is told to pass the story—the information—on to the Euro-American woman, Teresa . . . and presumably on to us, the readers" (351).

15. I discuss the role of the shaman in Anzaldúa's writing in greater detail in Chapter 5. But see, for example, her assertion that "[t]he ability of story (prose and poetry) to transform the storyteller and the listener into something or someone else is shamanistic. The writer, as shape-changer, is a *nahual*, a shaman" (*Borderlands*, 66).

16. See *Borderlands/La Frontera* (66) and "Haciendo caras, una entrada" (xvi).

17. For examples of Anzaldúa's shifts between first- and third-person narration see *Borderlands/La Frontera* (42–43 and 140–41). For her description of code-switching see the preface to *Borderlands/La Frontera*.

18. I use the term "god/dess" to indicate the inclusionary nature of this mythic figure, which encompasses what we generally consider feminine and masculine attributes.

19. In the previous chapter, "Entering into the Serpent," Anzaldúa describes these two modes of perception as "la facultad" and "the rational, reasoning mode which is connected to external reality, the upper world, and is considered the most developed consciousness—the consciousness of duality" (36–37).

20. Lorde employs this mestiza logic in "A Woman Speaks": "I am / woman / and not white" (*Black Unicorn*, 5).

21. The term "heterosexual matrix" is Judith Butler's. She defines it as "that grid of cultural intelligibility through which bodies, genders, and desires are naturalized, . . . a hegemonic discursive/epistemic model of gender intelligibility that assumes that for bodies to cohere and make sense there must be a stable sex expressed through a stable gender (masculine expresses male, feminine expresses female) that is oppositionally and hierarchically defined through the compulsory practice of heterosexuality" (*Gender Trouble*, 151).

22. Sandoval explains that differential consciousness is a "learned intellectual and emotional skill" rather than an inborn biological trait ("U.S. Third World Feminism," 23).

23. Jeanne Perreault makes a similar point that Lorde's self-inscription in these journals "entails an ethical commitment. This writing of self participates in the communal development of feminism" (14).

24. For additional discussions of this erasure see Lorde's "Open Letter to Mary Daly" in *Sister Outsider*, Sabrina Sojourner, and Dierdre Bádéjó.

25. As Vicki Kirby points out: "Given the continued instability of the culture/nature division, maintaining anti-essentialism versus essentialism as the respectively good and bad sides of any argument can install a dubious moral agenda" (7). I discuss feminists' debates concerning essentialism in Chapter 5.

26. Lorde first presented "Uses of the Erotic" in 1978, at the Fourth Berkshire Conference on the History of Women.

27. For a discussion of women in the academy, see Joan Hartman's "Telling Stories: The Construction of Women's Agency." The separation of intellectual inquiry and social activism that occurred when feminism became institutionalized is a recurring theme throughout Hartman and Messer-Davidow's *(En)Gendering Knowledge*.

28. See "Poetry Is Not a Luxury" and her discussion of the interconnected roles reason and intuition play in her interview with Adrienne Rich (*Sister Outsider*, 100–101).

29. See, for example, Rosi Braidotti's comments on Gilles Deleuze in *Nomadic Subjects*.

30. While I agree with Holloway that often there are significant differences between depictions of Afrocentric and Eurocentric goddesses, I think she overstates her case.

31. See also Allen's "Who Is Your Mother? The Red Roots of White Feminism" in *The Sacred Hoop* and Anzaldúa's discussion of transcultural alliances in Keating, "Writing, Politics, and *las Lesberadas*: *Platicando con* Gloria Anzaldúa."

Chapter 3 / Transformational Identity Politics

1. I follow bell hooks in using the phrase "feminist movement," rather than *the* feminist movement. To my mind, the former term is less monolithic than the latter; also, it more fully captures both the unity and the diversity among contemporary feminists. See her *Feminist Theory: From Margin to Center*.

2. See also Elizabeth Spelman's assertion that "[t]here are multitudes of persons all correctly referred to as 'women,' but it doesn't follow that there *must* be something we all have in common that explains what 'women in general' means" (*Inessential Woman*, 110–11; her emphasis).

3. I borrow this phrase from the subtitle to Moraga and Anzaldúa's anthology, *This Bridge Called My Back*.

4. Chela Sandoval makes a similar point in "Feminism and Racism," where she summarizes U.S. third world feminists' response to racism in the "mainstream" U.S. women's movement: Determined "to end the destructive 'othering' from which we have all suffered," these feminists called for a more sophisticated analysis of the many differences among U.S. women. Significantly, Sandoval emphasizes that the phrase "U.S. third world feminism" does not represent a natural group of women but rather a "mutant unity" composed of racially and ethnically diverse people: "This unity has coalesced across differences in

race, class, language, ideology, culture, and color. These differences are painfully manifest: materially marked physiologically or in language, socially value laden, and shot through with power. They confront each feminist of color in any gathering where they serve as constant reminders of their undeniability" (67–68). And in "U.S. Third World Feminism: The Theory and Method of Oppositional Consciousness in the Postmodern World" she again emphasizes that "this unity does not occur in the name of all 'women,' nor in the name of race, class, culture, or 'humanity' in general" (17–18). For additional accounts of self-identified U.S. third world feminists' reactions to this "destructive othering," see Moraga's "La Guëra," Lynet Uttal's "Inclusion without Influence," and Michelle Cliff's "Object into Subject."

5. For additional comments on the problematic state of contemporary feminism, see Marianne Hirsch and Evelyn Fox Keller's "Introduction" and "Conclusion" in *Conflicts in Feminism*.

6. For useful analyses of this humanist self see Paul Smith's *Discerning the Subject* and the first chapter of Sidonie Smith's *Subjectivity, Identity, and the Body*.

7. Although the identities they deploy occasionally resemble what Gayatri Spivak terms "strategic essentialism," I describe their renaming process as tactical, rather than strategic, to underscore the temporary, inventive nature of their maneuvers. Spivak discusses strategic essentialism in *In Other Worlds* (197–221) and *Outside in the Teaching Machine* (3–8). For a useful explanation of the differences between strategies and tactics see Michel de Certeau's *The Practice of Everyday Life*.

8. Allen's self-description is worth quoting at length. In her review of *This Bridge Called My Back* she defines herself as a "multicultural event who was raised in a Chicano village in New Mexico by a half-breed mother and a Lebanese American father, surrounded by people who spoke Laguna, English, Spanish, Arabic, German, Navajo and everything in between; related to people who were Protestants, Jews, Roman Catholics, traditional American Indians, atheists and all imaginable combinations of the above" (127).

9. Allen refers to herself as a "confluence" in the "Autobiography of a Confluence."

10. Anzaldúa discusses the new *mestiza* throughout *Borderlands/La Frontera*, but see especially chapter 7, "*La concienca de la mestiza*: Towards a New Consciousness."

11. For critiques of the male bias in Chicano literature and theory, see Ramón Saldívar and Anzaldúa in "To(o) Queer the Writer."

12. Patricia Hill Collins explains this othering process in *Black Feminist Thought*. Gail Pheterson offers a useful analysis of racism and the effects of internalized oppression in "Alliances Between Women." For additional accounts see Aletícia Tijerina, "Notes on Oppression and Violence"; Gloria Yamato, "Something about the Subject Makes It Hard to Name"; and Virginia R. Harris and Trinity A. Ordoña, "Developing Unity among Women of Color."

13. The term "Female/Elemental divinity" is Daly's. See *Pure Lust* (89).

14. Judy Grahn also discusses lesbians and gay men's role as "mediator between worlds" in *Another Mother Tongue*.

15. For additional accounts of Chicana lesbians' "betrayal" of cultural values, see Carla Trujillo's introduction to *Chicana Lesbians* and Marta A. Navarro's "Interview with Ana Castillo."

16. These essays are found in *The Sacred Hoop*.

17. For additional accounts of the ways lesbians exist "outside" the dominant culture, see Judy Grahn's *Another Mother Tongue* (179–80); Monique Wittig's "One is Not Born a Woman"; and Marilyn Frye's "To Be and Be Seen" in *The Politics of Reality*.

18. Henry Giroux provides a useful analysis of the correlations between U.S. and British identity politics in *Living Dangerously*, especially chapters 3 and 4. For additional critiques of the limitations in U.S. feminists' identity politics, see Jenny Bourne; Judith Butler's *Gender Trouble*; Kathy Ferguson; June Jordan's *Civil Wars* and *Technical Difficulties*; and Sara Suleri.

19. Patricia Hill Collins makes a related point in her discussion of the interconnection between emotional repression, externalized oppression, and social change: "Recognizing that the corrupting and distorting basic feelings human beings have for one another lies at the heart of multiple systems of oppression opens up new possibilities for transformation and change" (197–98).

20. As Nancie Caraway suggests, "guilt depoliticizes us by instilling a sense of fatalism" (16).

Chapter 4 / Back to the Mother?

1. The term "biophilic" is Daly's.

2. The phrase "innocent and all-powerful Mother" is Haraway's ("Manifesto," 218), and the reference to an "irrecoverable origin" is Butler's (*Gender Trouble*, 78).

3. Throughout this chapter I will capitalize "Woman" when indicating the term's metaphoric character, including both the oppressive and the potentially liberating aspects of the term. Also, in this chapter I will put "feminine" in scare quotes to emphasize the provisional, speculative, and potentially transformative dimensions of Allen's use of the term.

4. According to Butler, "If . . . it is a life of the body beyond the law or a recovery of the body before the law which then emerges as the normative goal of feminist theory, such a norm effectively takes the focus of feminist theory away from the concrete terms of contemporary cultural struggle" (*Gender Trouble*, 42).

5. Donna Haraway makes a similar point in "Manifesto for Cyborgs" when she claims that in today's fragmented, postmodern world, "[i]t's not just that 'god' is dead; so is the 'goddess'" (81). She maintains that references to gods, goddesses, or other "transcendental authorizations" lead to restrictive political agendas based on totalizing and imperialistic identity politics that prevent feminists from constructing effective coalitions in the sociopolitical, historical present. According to Haraway, "There is nothing about being 'female' that naturally binds women." Indeed, "There is not even such a state as 'being' female, itself a highly complex category constructed in contested sexual, scientific discourses and other practices" (72). Thus she challenges feminists to reject all such naturalized identities and develop temporary strategic alliances based on situational choices.

6. Butler summarizes this view in *Gender Trouble* (3–6).

7. Nancy Morejón is quoted in Lionnet (15–16). As Lionnet notes, mestizaje is incompatible with conventional notions of a singular origin: "In this constant and balanced form of interaction, recipro-

cal relations prevent the ossification of culture and encourage system- atic change and exchange. By responding to such mutations, language reinforces a phenomenon of creative instability in which no 'pure' or unitary origin can ever be posited" (16).

8. David Murray describes this commonly invoked holistic world- view: "Rather than seeing the world as made up of different realms of experience to which we apply different methods of understanding and evaluation (religious, scientific, and so on), there is a sense of a funda- mental unity underlying the facets of experience, which is regularly characterized in traditional images of circles or living organisms" (88).

9. "Cosmogyny" is Allen's neologism. She explains that "[f]or my purposes, 'cosmogyny' is more accurate [than 'cosmology']. It con- notes an ordered universe arranged in harmony with gynocratic prin- ciples" (*Grandmothers*, xiii–xiv).

10. For a discussion of how Christianized informants de-feminized Native myths, see Linda Danielson's "Storyteller: *Grandmother Spi- der's Web*."

11. Renae Bredin discusses Allen's appropriation of Iroquois stories in " 'Becoming Minor.' "

12. For examples of feminist celebrations of motherhood, see Elinor Gadon's *The Once and Future Goddess* and Kathryn Rabuzzi's *Motherself*.

13. Drucilla Cornell points out that another potential danger in mythic images of Woman is the possibility that "[t]he counter- valorization of Woman associated with the re-metaphorization would risk the danger of essentialism and of claiming a special status of one vision of Woman" (*Beyond Accommodation* 167). To my mind, femi- nists' re-metaphorized Mother Goddesses often fall into these traps.

14. Allen later reiterates her point: "At Laguna, all entities, human or supernatural, who are functioning in a ritual manner at a high level are called Mother" (*Sacred Hoop*, 28).

15. In her discussion of Thought Woman, Allen again distinguishes between Thought Woman's creative power and biological reproduc- tion by emphasizing that this creatrix figure's power is not "simply of biology, as modernists tendentiously believe. When Thought Woman brought to life the twin sisters, she did not give birth to them in

the biological sense. She sang over the medicine bundles" (*Sacred Hoop*, 27).

16. As Margaret Whitford notes, in western philosophical traditions "reason, conceptualized as transcendence in practice came to mean transcendence of the feminine, because of the symbolism used" ("Luce Irigaray's Critique," 111).

17. Athene represents a highly masculinized version of femininity. As Irigaray rather poetically remarks, "A woman—the other—will be asked to set the seal of necessity upon this/her burial. A woman, in truth: of divine reality. A divinity conceived in the head of the God of gods. Well born—without a mother" (*Marine Lover*, 94). Irigaray discusses Athene and other Greek goddesses in "Veiled Lips" (*Marine Lover*, 77–119).

18. I explore Irigaray's "spirituality of the body" in greater detail in Chapter 6.

19. Elizabeth Grosz provides a useful overview of western culture's "crisis of reason" in "Bodies and Knowledges." This "crisis" began in its modern form with Descartes. Today, it manifests itself in a variety of ways in a diverse group of thinkers, including Heidegger, Habermas, Lyotard, Rorty, Jameson, Foucault, Derrida, and Deleuze. According to Grosz, "This crisis has been variously described as a crisis of identity, of modernity, of capitalism, of morality, and even of science. It is a crisis of self-validation and methodological self-justification, formulated in different terms within different disciplines and periods; a crisis of reason's *inability to rationally* know itself; a crisis posed as reason's inability to come outside of itself, to enclose and know itself from the outside: the inadequation of the subject and its other" (189; her emphasis). For other contemporary feminist critiques of traditional masculinist epistemologies see Braidotti's *Patterns of Dissonance*; Gatens's "Towards a Feminist Philosophy of the Body"; Hodge's "Subject, Body and the Exclusion of Women from Philosophy"; Moi's "Patriarchal Thought and the Drive for Knowledge"; and Whitford's "Luce Irigaray's Critique of Rationality."

20. It is important to note that this equation of rationality with the masculine occurs on a symbolic level; as Whitford asserts in "Luce Irigaray's Critique of Rationality," "To describe rationality as male is not to restrict rationality to men" (124).

21. Luce Irigaray, for example, holds doctorates in both linguistics and philosophy. She frequently uses poststructural theory to expose the masculinist bias in conventional systems of knowledge. See, for instance, *Speculum of the Other Woman*.

22. For another remarkable example of Allen's unconventional research methods, see her assertion that she "was honored to have channeled information" about the Crystal Skull (*Grandmothers*, 195).

23. The term "neo-Romantic" is Bat-Ami Bar On's. See her brief discussion of "neo-Romantic subjectivity" in "Marginality and Epistemic Privilege."

24. *Muchas gracias a* Debra Miller for reminding me about this chapter in *Black Feminist Thought*.

25. In several essays collected in *The Sacred Hoop* Allen associates tribal genocide with a shift from matricentric to phallocratic belief systems. See, for example, her assertion in "How the West Was Really Won": "The genocide practiced against the [North American] tribes . . . aimed systematically at the dissolution of ritual traditions . . . and the degradation of the status of women as central to the spiritual and ritual life of the tribes" (195).

26. As Cornell points out, "We cannot escape the hold of the feminine on the unconscious, which is precisely why we work within myth to reinterpret and transform, rather than merely reject. Theoretically, identity may be deconstructed as pure form or structure, as *de-sistance* of *mimesis*; but gender identity is, practically, very much in place and enforced by the law" (*Beyond Accommodation*, 182; her italics).

27. Cornell further asserts that "[w]e re-collect the mythic figures of the past, but as we do so we reimagine them. It is the potential variability of myth that allows us to work within myth, and the significance it offers, so as to reimagine our world and by so doing, to begin to dream of a new one. In myth we do find Woman with a capital letter. These myths, as Lacan indicates, may be rooted in male fantasy, but they cannot, as he would sometimes suggest, be reduced to it" (*Beyond Accommodation*, 178).

28. Ernesto Laclau and Chantal Mouffe describe this process of articulation in *Hegemony and Socialist Strategy*.

29. I borrow the term "metaphoric transference" from Cornell: "The metaphors of Woman, in and through which she is performed,

are enacted signifiers which, as such, act on us as genderized subjects. But this performance keeps us from 'getting to the Other' of the prediscursive 'reality' of gender or of sex. Metaphoric transference, in other words, recognizes the constitutive powers of metaphor, but only as metaphor" (*Beyond Accommodation*, 100).

30. As was already mentioned, Cornell explains that "metaphors of Woman, in and through which she is performed, are enacted signifiers which, as such, act on us as genderized subjects" (*Beyond Accommodation*, 100).

31. Both Bracher and Cornell maintain that alterations in the social system entail psychic change as well. Bracher, for example, insists that "any real social change must involve not just changes in laws and public policy but alterations in the ideals, desires, and jouissances of a significant number of individual subjects" (73). See also Ross Chambers's *Room for Maneuver*.

Chapter 5 / Writing the Body/Writing the Soul

1. As in the previous chapter, I will capitalize "Woman" when indicating the term's metaphoric character.

2. Elizabeth Grosz makes a similar point in "Bodies and Knowledges." She explains that because women have been constructed as men's other—"as the bodily counterparts to men's conceptual supremacy, women's bodies, pleasures, and desires are reduced to versions or variants of men's bodies and desires" (204).

3. Domna Stanton makes a similar claim: "Irigaray, Cixous, and Kristeva countervalorize the traditional antithesis that identifies man with culture and confines woman to instinctual nature. . . . And they reproduce the dichotomy between male rationality and female materiality, corporeality, and sexuality" (170). See also Toril Moi's *Sexual/ Textual Politics* (123).

4. For additional analyses of how oppositional readings of culture can be co-opted by the dominant ideology, see Frederic Jameson's *Postmodernism, Or, The Cultural Logic of Late Capitalism*; Andrew Ross's "New Age Technoculture"; and Alice Jardine's *Gynesis*.

5. According to Hélène Vivienne Wenzel, for example, "Cixous's *pratique* and theory of *écriture féminine* have little interest in address-

ing themselves to social change, the women's movement, political feminism, or lesbianism. They focus instead upon 'woman' as an eternal essence" (272). See also Jones's "Writing the Body" (367); Stanton; and Moi's *Sexual/Textual Politics*. However, as Morag Shiach demonstrates through close readings of the French theorist's works, Cixous's references to female anatomy are metaphorical and indicate her belief that, because " 'the body' . . . [is] profoundly embedded in the cultural, it is always already inscribed by sociohistorical discourse" (*Hélène Cixous*, 20–21). See also Arleen B. Dallery, "The Politics of Writing (the) Body"; and Verena Andermatt Conley (56–57). For Cixous's own disavowal of a biological "destiny" and a precultural, prediscursive "essence" or "nature," see "Sorties" (83).

6. From Arlene Dallery's "The Politics of Writing (the) Body," (60). Dallery herself does not reject écriture féminine, but she provides a useful summary of the arguments made by those who do. See also Jones's doubt that "one libidinal voice, however nonphallocentrically defined, can speak to the economic and cultural problems of all women" ("Writing the Body," 371); and Moi's assertion that "[i]t is just this absence of any specific analysis of the material factors preventing women from writing that constitutes a major weakness of Cixous's utopia" (*Sexual/Textual Politics*, 123). For more ambivalent reactions to this French theorist's visionary project, see Gilbert's Introduction to *The Newly Born Woman* and Larsen's "Text and Matrix."

7. As Morag Shiach notes in *Hélène Cixous*, "The Laugh of the Medusa" "has undoubtedly provoked strong reactions, and has been the focus of many of the frequent charges of 'essentialism': the claim that Cixous reduces women to an essence, specifically an anatomical essence, and thus negates the possibility of the very change which she seeks to promote." However, Shiach also points out that Cixous's "tentativeness is an important part of her argument, despite its polemic" (17).

8. Jones (368). According to Jones, Cixous "is convinced that women's unconscious is totally different from men's, and that it is their psychosexual specificity that will empower women to overthrow masculinist ideologies and to create new female discourses" (365). But as Shiach argues in *Hélène Cixous*, Cixous's attempt "to locate sexual pleasure at the level of sexual pleasure . . . [is] clearly a strategic move.

It removes any possibility of identifying femininity and masculinity with the certainties of anatomical differences. It also places sexual difference in the realm of the unknowable" (18). See also Dallery's "The Politics of Writing (the) Body" (59), and Cixous's assertion: "I do not believe in sexual opposition nor in a sexuality that would be strictly feminine or strictly masculine, since there are always traces of originary bisexuality" (quoted in Conley, 136).

9. For Trinh's discussion of the "territorialized knowledge" that accompanies this quest, see "The Totalizing Quest of Meaning" in *When the Moon Waxes Red* (29–50).

10. See, for example, "*Tlilli, Tlapalli*, The Path of the Red and Black Ink" in *Borderlands/La Frontera* where Anzaldúa contrasts the Aztec's "ethno-poetics" with western culture's "white sterility." She urges North American readers of all racial and ethnic backgrounds to reexamine rationalist assumptions and free themselves from "the tyranny of Western aesthetics": "Let's all stop importing Greek myths and the Western Cartesian split point of view and root ourselves in the mythological soil and soul of this continent" (*Borderlands*, 68).

11. As Defromont explains, in Cixous's body-writing, "The body is then simultaneously the beloved object to be written about, and the writing subject which supports the rising of the feminine identity. Access to the symbolic order of language—that is, to culture—occurs through the body—that is, nature—thus bringing about a continuity of a new kind" (119–20).

Chapter 6 / Inscribing "Black," Becoming . . . Afrekete

1. See also Erin Carlston's suggestion that Lorde's biomythography depicts "identity as a product of the dialectic between social inter-(re)action and self-(re)creation" (229).

2. Chinosole, 386; Raynaud, 223–27.

3. Throughout this chapter, I will put "black," "white," "blackness," and "whiteness" in scare quotes to emphasize the problematic, constructed nature of these terms.

4. As Lorde informs us early in the biomythography, her mother

was light-skinned and could pass as Latina or "white" (9). Lorde elsewhere implies that her mother's silences led her to internalize the prevailing value system, its elevation of "white" over "black": "Somewhere I knew it was a lie that nobody else noticed color. Me, darker than my two sisters. My father, darkest of all. I was always jealous of my sisters because my mother thought they were such good girls" (*Sister Outsider*, 149).

5. Interestingly, Lorde seems to speak for all "black" women in this essay; as bell hooks points out: "Throughout 'Eye to Eye,' Lorde constructs a monolithic paradigm of black female experience that does not engage our differences. . . . To some extent Lorde's essay acts to shut down, close off, erase, and deny those black female experiences that do not fit the norm she constructs from the location of her experience. . . . By evoking this negative experience of black womanhood as 'commonly' shared, Lorde presents it in a way that suggests it represents 'authentic' black female reality" (*Black Looks*, 43). Although I agree with hooks, I would argue that this monolithic paradigm might be partially explained by the absence of an existing discourse that describes the varieties and nuances of U.S. "black" female experience, or what Hortense Spillers describes as "a first-order naming, words that express the experience of the community in diachronic time, in daily social relationships, in economic well-being, in the identity of a self" ("Interstices," 89).

6. I want to emphasize that Lorde's challenge is not gender-specific. See, for example, her warning in "Sexism: An American Disease in Blackface" (*Sister Outsider*, 60–65).

7. For another example of Lorde's performative language use, see her description of self-mothering in "Eye to Eye": "Mothering. Claiming some power over who we choose to be, and knowing that such power is relative within the realities of our lives. *Yet knowing that only through the use of that power can we effectively change those realities.* Mothering means the laying to rest of what is weak, timid, and damaged—without despisal—the protection and support of what is useful for survival and change, and our joint explorations of the difference" (*Sister Outsider*, 173–74; my emphasis).

8. Anna Wilson makes a similar comment concerning Lorde's

rejection and acceptance of her mother, or what she describes as "a sense of self that both acknowledges her mother and frees herself from her" (82–83).

9. Cornell bases her discussion of iterability on Derrida's; see *Transformations* (38–42). Iterability also plays an important role in Homi Bhabha's theory of cultural translation; see "The Commitment to Theory."

10. As Barbara Christian points out, Audre's relationship with Eudora enables her to "acknowledge that she is a lesbian with all the societal implications the word implies" (*Black Feminist Criticism*, 197). Similarly, Erin Carlston asserts that "[w]hen Audre leaves Eudora, . . . she realizes for the first time that her lesbianism extends beyond the fact of being involved in a sexual relationship with another woman" (231).

11. "Began" is hardly the correct term. As Spillers notes, this " 'beginning' . . . is really a rupture and a radically different kind of cultural continuation" ("Mama's Baby," 67).

12. There are additional similarities between these two episodes. In both, Lorde depicts transformational experiences reflecting an empowered use of language and an embodied spirituality that destabilize conventional boundaries between physical and nonphysical realities. Just as her transcendent experience occurred on the corner of Second Avenue, so Afrekete *"came out of a dream"* yet was *"always . . . hard and real"* (249).

13. As Drucilla Cornell notes, the distinction between *discovery* and *invention* blurs: "[B]ecause once we understand the metaphorical dimension of feminine reality, we can no longer completely separate discovery and invention. Our reality is in the process of being created in our very effort to 'discover' its meaning for us. This point about feminine reality should be understood within the context of a shifting understanding of the nature of reality itself, once we understand that what 'is' comes wrapped in language" (*Transformations*, 208, n. 69).

14. Actually, this Yoruban/Fon trickster has many names—Eshu, Esu, Ésú, Exú, Elegba, Elegbara, Echu-Elegua, Legba, Papa Legba, and Papa La Bas. I refer to this complex figure as Eshu/Legba, primarily because these are the names I was taught.

15. I can't help but wonder why, given Gates's acknowledgment of

Eshu/Legba's ambiguously gendered status, he consistently uses masculine pronouns to describe this orisha. Why not mix things up a bit? Uzo Esonwanne, for example, uses doubled pronouns—"his/her"—and Tejumola Olaniyan enfolds the masculine into the feminine—"h(is)er." Gates does, however, provide the following highly suggestive description of Eshu's transgendered nature. He explains that according to Ogundipe, a Yoruban woman scholar, "[Esu] certainly is not restricted to human distinctions of gender or sex; he is at once both male and female. Although his masculinity is depicted as visually and graphically overwhelming, his equally expressive femininity renders his enormous sexuality ambiguous, contrary, and genderless" (*Signifying Monkey*, 29).

16. My favorite dismissal is Donna Haraway's assertion, "Although both are bound in the spiral dance, I would rather be a cyborg than a goddess" ("Manifesto," 101).

17. For a biting critique of Daly's *Gyn/Ecology*, and the exclusionary, inflexible dimensions of her thought more generally, see Meaghan Morris's "A-Mazing Grace" in *Pirate's Fiancée*. Morris maintains that by focusing entirely on isolated signs, Daly cannot subvert the underlying phallocentric structures. She claims that "Daly pursues a politics of subverting isolated signs, not discourses. The 'word' is what carries, conveys and contains 'meaning' " (31). Rosi Braidotti makes a similar point in *Patterns of Dissonance*. She argues that Daly's "words modify nothing and offer absolutely no innovation in terms of the ideas of structuring the current moral and religious order. Daly simply indulges in a substitutive operation which puts women in the place of men, on earth as in heaven, thus preserving the state of things" (207).

18. Like Lorde and Allen, Irigaray maintains that earlier, prehistorical human societies were gynocratic and represented an epoch when, because "feminine" creativity was associated with female gods and cosmic rhythms, women were "both naturally and spiritually important." It was only with the rise of patriarchal social and religious systems and the corresponding sacrifice of the (female) body that creativity was appropriated by the masculine. See, for example, her arguments in "Equal to Whom?" and "Divine Women." I want to emphasize that Irigaray's call for a feminine divine does not represent the nostalgic desire to return to an earlier, more perfect gynocentric

era. Nor can it be seen as an attempt to escape or transcend female embodiment. As she explains in "Divine Women": "I am not suggesting that today we must once again deify ourselves as did our ancestors with their animal totems, that we have to regress to siren goddesses, who fight against men gods. Rather I think we must not merely instigate a return to the *cosmic*, but also ask ourselves why we have been held back from becoming *divine women*" (60; her emphasis).

19. The term dérélection is Irigaray's. As Margaret Whitford explains in *Luce Irigaray*, for Irigaray "dérélection" indicates women's current state because of the absence of symbolization; dérélection "connotes . . . the state of being abandoned by God or, in mythology, the state of an Ariadne, abandoned on Naxos, left without hope, without help, without refuge" (77–78). For a useful example of Irigaray's comments, see *je, tu, nous*: "The loss of divine representation has brought women to a state of dereliction, which is felt all the more because sensible representation is our primary method of figuration and communication. It has left us without a means of designating ourselves, of expressing ourselves between ourselves. It has also separated mothers from daughters, depriving them of mutually respectful mediums of exchange. It has subjected them to a reproductive order—natural and spiritual—that is governed symbolically by men" (111).

20. As Irigaray puts it, "[i]f God is always imagined to be a father, how can women find in Him a model of identity, a completed image or figure of themselves that could free them from the competition for measurable superiority?" ("Limits of Transference," 112).

21. See, for example, Irigaray's assertion in "Divine Women": "The (male) ideal other has been imposed upon women by men. Man is supposedly woman's more perfect other, her model, her essence. The most human and the most divine goal woman can conceive is to become *man*. If she is to become woman, if she is to accomplish her female subjectivity, woman needs a god who is a figure for the perfection of *her* subjectivity" (64; her emphasis).

22. In this essay, Irigaray contrasts the proliferation of masculinist images with the absence of representations of the feminine: "We live in a society of intermale bondings, which respects only the genealogy of the sons and the fathers and the competition among brothers. This means that our societies have subordinated women's genealogy to

men's. The daughters are separated physically and culturally from their mothers when they have to move into their husbands' families and male institutions" (188). As Whitford explains, Irigaray believes that without a maternal genealogy and the corresponding mother/daughter symbolizations, it is "difficult if not impossible for women to have an identity in the symbolic order that is distinct from the maternal function. . . . They remain 'residual,' 'defective men' " (*Luce Irigaray*, 77).

23. See, for example, "Eye to Eye." After exploring "black" U.S. women's inability to establish positive intersubjective relationships, Lorde asks: "Do we reenact these crucifixions upon each other, the avoidance, the cruelty, the judgments, because we have not been allowed Black goddesses, Black heroines, because we have not been allowed to see our mothers and our selves in their/our own magnificence until that magnificence became part of our blood and bone?" (*Sister Outsider*, 164–65).

24. Similarly, Lorde's definition of self-mothering indicates performative language use: "Claiming some power over who we choose to be, and knowing that such power is relative within the realities of our lives. Yet knowing that only through the use of that power can we effectively change those realities. Mothering means the laying to rest of what is weak, timid, and damaged—without despisal—the protection and support of what is useful for survival and change, and our joint explorations of the difference" (*Sister Outsider*, 173–74).

25. Ginger repeatedly uses this nickname for Lorde. See, for example, pages 129, 131, 135, and 184 in *Zami*.

26. In a related vein, Bonnie Zimmerman associates Kitty/Afrekete with Lorde's affirmation of a sexual identity. She suggests that the episode with Kitty illustrates "Audre's acceptance of her erotic self" (*Safe Sea*, 202).

27. The phrase "heterosexist logic" is Judith Butler's. In "The Lesbian Phallus" she distinguishes between Lacan's heterosexual, or "hegemonic Imaginary [that] constitutes itself through the naturalization of an exclusionary heterosexual morphology" and the development of "an alternative *Imaginary*" (164).

28. Although she does not associate Lorde's construction of a racialized identity with the "black"/"white" binary, Erin Carlston makes

a similar point: "Young Audre's intuitions about race make it appear as a given, a determining factor in her life from the moment of her birth. But the narrator's commentary reminds us that it is her culture's obsessive and constantly articulated awareness of race that allows her to be so aware herself. Skin color may be given, but race is constructed, both by a racist society and by the individual reacting to that society" (227).

29. Henry Louis Gates, Jr. *Loose Canons*, 75; his emphasis. For other discussions of racialist discourse, see Appiah, Omi and Winant, and Webster.

Works Cited

Alarcón, Norma. "The Theoretical Subject(s) of *This Bridge Called My Back* and Anglo-American Feminism." In *Making Face, Making Soul/Haciendo Caras: Creative and Critical Perspectives by Women of Color*, edited by Gloria Anzaldúa, 356–69. San Francisco: Aunt Lute Foundation, 1990.

Allen, Paula Gunn. "The Autobiography of a Confluence." In *I Tell You Now: Autobiographical Essays by Native American Writers*, edited by Brian Swann and Arnold Krupat, 143–54. Lincoln: University of Nebraska Press, 1987.

——. " 'Border' Studies: The Intersection of Gender and Color." In *Introduction to Scholarship in Modern Languages and Literatures*, edited by Joseph Gibaldi, 303–19. New York: Modern Languages Association, 1992.

——. "Bringing Home the Fact: Tradition and Continuity in the Imagination." In *Recovering the Word: Essays on Native American Literature*, edited by Brian Swann and Arnold Krupat, 563–79. Berkeley: University of California Press, 1987.

——. "Glastonbury Experience: Poem and Essay." *Religion and Literature* 26 (1994): 81–87.

——. *Grandmothers of the Light: A Medicine Woman's Sourcebook.* Boston: Beacon, 1991.

——. "Review of *This Bridge Called My Back.*" *Conditions* 5 (1982): 121–27.

——. *The Sacred Hoop: Recovering the Feminine in American Indian Traditions.* Boston: Beacon, 1986.

——. *Shadow Country.* Los Angeles: American Indian Studies Center, 1982.

——. *Skin and Bones; Poems 1979–87.* Albuquerque: West End, 1988.

——. "Some Like Indians Endure." In *Making Face, Making Soul/Haciendo Caras: Creative and Critical Perspectives by Women of Color*, edited by Gloria Anzaldúa, 298–99. San Francisco: Aunt Lute Foundation, 1990.

——, ed. *Voice of the Turtle: American Indian Literature, 1900–1970.* New York: Ballantine, 1994.

——. *The Woman Who Owned the Shadows.* San Francisco: Spinsters/Aunt Lute, 1983.

Annas, Pamela. "A Poetry of Survival: Naming and Renaming in the Poetry of Audre Lorde, Pat Parker, Sylvia Plath, and Adrienne Rich." *Colby Library Quarterly* 18 (1982): 9–25.

Anzaldúa, Gloria. *Borderlands/La Frontera: The New Mestiza.* San Francisco: Spinsters/Aunt Lute, 1987.

——. "Bridge, Drawbridge, Sandbar or Island: *Lesbians-of-Color Hacienda Alianzas.*" In *Bridges of Power: Women's Multicultural Alliances*, edited by Lisa Albrecht and Rose M. Brewer, 216–31. Philadelphia: New Society, 1990.

——. "*Del otro lado.*" In *Compañeras: Latina Lesbians (An Anthology)*, edited by Juanita Ramos. New York: Latina Lesbian History Project, 1987.

——. "En rapport, In Opposition: Cobrando cuentas a las nuestras." In *Making Face, Making Soul/Haciendo Caras: Creative and Critical Perspectives by Women of Color*, edited by Gloria Anzaldúa, 142–48. San Francisco: Aunt Lute Foundation, 1990.

——. "Haciendo caras, una entrada." *Making Face, Making Soul/Haciendo Caras: Creative and Critical Perspectives by Women of Color*, edited by Gloria Anzaldúa, xv–xxviii. San Francisco: Aunt Lute Foundation, 1990.

——. "La Prieta." In *This Bridge Called My Back: Writings by Radical Women of Color*, edited by Cherríe Moraga and Gloria Anzaldúa, 198–209. New York: Kitchen Table: Women of Color Press, 1983.

——, ed. *Making Face, Making Soul/Haciendo Caras: Creative and Critical Perspectives by Women of Color*. San Francisco: Aunt Lute Foundation, 1990.

——. "Metaphors in the Tradition of the Shaman." In *Conversant Essays: Contemporary Poets on Poetry*, edited by James McCorkle, 99–100. Detroit: Wayne State University Press, 1990.

——. *Prieta*. Forthcoming, San Francisco: Aunt Lute Foundation, 1996.

——. "She Ate Horses." In *Lesbian Philosophies and Cultures*, edited by Jeffner Allen, 371–88. New York: State University of New York, 1990.

——. "Speaking in Tongues: A Letter to Third World Women Writers." In *This Bridge Called My Back: Writings by Radical Women of Color*, edited by Cherríe Moraga and Gloria Anzaldúa, 165–74. New York: Kitchen Table: Women of Color Press, 1983.

——. "To(o) Queer the Writer—*Loca, escritora y chicana*." In *Inversions: Writing by Dykes, Queers, and Lesbians*, edited by Betsy Warland, 249–64. Vancouver: Press Gang, 1991.

Appiah, Kwame Anthony. "The Conservation of 'Race.'" *Black American Literature Forum* 23 (1989): 37–60.

——. *In My Father's House: Africa in the Philosophy of Culture*. New York: Oxford University Press, 1992.

Avi-ram, Amitai F. "*Apo Koinou* in Audre Lorde and the Moderns: Defining the Differences." *Callaloo* 9 (1986): 193–208.

Bádéjó, Dierdre L. "The Goddess Osun as a Paradigm for African Feminist Criticism." In *Sage: A Scholarly Journal on Black Women* 6 (Summer 1989): 27–32.

Baker, Houston A., Jr. *Blues, Ideology, and Afro-American Literature*. Chicago: University of Chicago Press, 1984.

——. "Caliban's Triple Play." *"Race," Writing, and Difference*, edited by Henry Louis Gates Jr., 381–95. Chicago: University of Chicago Press, 1995.

Ballinger, Franchot, and Brian Swann. "A MELUS Interview: Paula Gunn Allen." *MELUS* 10 (1983): 3–25.

Bannet, Eve Tavor. "The Feminist Logic of Both/And." *Genders* 15 (1992): 1–20.

Bar On, Bat-Ami. "Marginality and Epistemic Privilege." In *Feminist Epistemologies*, edited by Linda Alcoff and Elizabeth Potter, 83–100. New York: Routledge, 1993.

Bauman, Richard. *Verbal Art as Performance*. Prospect Heights, IL: Waveland Press, 1984.

Bhabha, Homi K. "The Commitment to Theory." In *Questions of Third Cinema*, edited by Jim Pines and Paul Willeman, 111–31. London: British Film Institute, 1989.

——. "Remembering Fanon: Self, Psyche, and The Colonial Condition." In *Remaking History*, edited by Barbara Kruger and Phil Mariani, 131–50. Seattle: Bay Press, 1989.

——. "The Third Space: Interview with Homi Bhabha." In *Identity: Community, Culture, Difference*, edited by Jonathan Rutherford, 207–21. London: Lawrence & Wishart, 1990.

Bordo, Susan. "Feminism, Postmodernism, and Gender-Scepticism." *Feminism/Postmodernism*, edited by Linda J. Nicholson, 133–56. New York: Routledge, 1990.

Bourne, Jenny. "Homelands of the Mind: Jewish Feminism and Identity Politics." *Race and Class* 29 (1987): 1–24.

Bracher, Mark. *Lacan, Discourse, and Social Change: A Psychoanalytic Cultural Criticism*. Ithaca: Cornell University Press, 1993.

Braidotti, Rosi. *Nomadic Subjects: Embodiment and Sexual Difference in Contemporary Feminist Theory*. New York: Columbia University Press, 1994.

——. *Patterns of Dissonance: A Study of Women in Contemporary Philosophy*. Translated by Elizabeth Guild. New York: Routledge, 1991.

Bredin, Renae. "Becoming Minor: Reading the Woman Who Owned the Shadows." *Studies in American Indian Literatures* 6 (1994): 36–50.

Bruchac, Joseph. *Survival This Way: Interviews with American Indian Poets*. Tucson: University of Arizona Press, 1987.

Butler, Judith. *Bodies That Matter: On the Discursive Limits of "Sex."* New York: Routledge, 1993.

——. "Contingent Foundations: Feminism and the Question of 'Postmodernism.'" In *Feminists Theorize the Political*, edited by Judith Butler and Joan Scott, 3–21. New York: Routledge, 1992.

——. "The Force of Fantasy: Feminism, Mapplethorpe, and Discursive Excess." *differences* 2 (1990): 105–25.

——. *Gender Trouble: Feminism and the Subversion of Identity*. New York: Routledge, 1989.

——. "The Lesbian Phallus and the Morphological Imaginary." *differences* 4 (1992): 132–71.

——. "Performative Acts and Gender Constitution: An Essay in Phenomenology and Feminist Theory." *Theatre Journal* 40 (1988): 519–31.

Calderón, Hector, and Jose David Saldívar, eds. *Criticism in the Borderlands: Studies in Chicano Literature, Culture, and Ideology*. Durham: Duke University Press, 1991.

Caputi, Jane. "Interview With Paula Gunn Allen." *Trivia* 16 (1990): 50–67.

Caraway, Nancie. *Segregated Sisterhood: Racism and the Politics of American Feminism*. Knoxville: University of Tennessee Press, 1991.

Carlston, Erin. "*Zami* and the Politics of Plural Identity." In *Sexual Practice, Textual Theory: Lesbian Cultural Criticism*, edited by Susan J. Wolfe and Julia Penelope, 237–50. Cambridge: Blackwell, 1993.

Certeau, Michel de. *The Practice of Everyday Life*. Translated by Steven Rendall. Berkeley: University of California Press, 1984.

Chambers, Ross. *Room for Maneuver: Reading (the) Oppositional (in) Narrative*. Chicago: University of Chicago Press, 1991.

Chinosole. "Audre Lorde and Matrilineal Diaspora: 'moving history beyond nightmare into structures for the future.'" In *Wild Women in the Whirlwind: Afra-American Culture and the Contemporary Literary Renaissance*, edited by Joanne M. Braxton and Andrée Nicola McLaughlin, 379–94. New Brunswick: Rutgers University Press, 1990.

Christ, Carol P. *Diving Deep and Surfacing: Women Writers on Spiritual Quest*. Boston: Beacon, 1980.

Christian, Barbara. *Black Feminist Criticism: Perspectives on Black Women Writers*. New York: Pergamon Press, 1985.

——. "The Race for Theory." In *Making Face, Making Soul/Haciendo Caras: Creative and Critical Perspectives by Women of Color*, edited by Gloria Anzaldúa, 335–45. San Francisco: Aunt Lute Foundation, 1990.

Cixous, Hélène. "The Laugh of the Medusa." Translated by K. Cohen and P. Cohen. In *New French Feminisms*, edited by Elaine Marks and I. de Courtivron, 334–49. New York: Shocken, 1981.

——. "Sorties." Translated by Betsy Wing. In *The Newly Born Woman*, edited by Hélène Cixous and Catherine Clément, 63–132. Minneapolis: University of Minnesota Press, 1988.

Cliff, Michelle. "Object into Subject: Some Thoughts on the Work of Black Women Artists." In *Making Face, Making Soul/Haciendo Caras: Creative and Critical Perspectives by Women of Color*, edited by Gloria Anzaldúa, 271–90. San Francisco: Aunt Lute Foundation, 1990.

Collins, Patricia Hill. *Black Feminist Thought: Knowledge, Consciousness, and the Politics of Empowerment*. Boston: Unwin Hymen, 1990.

Conley, Verena Andermatt. *Hélène Cixous: Writing the Feminine*. Lincoln: University of Nebraska Press, 1984.

Cornell, Drucilla. *Beyond Accommodation: Ethical Feminism, Deconstruction, and the Law*. New York: Routledge, 1991.

——. *The Philosophy of the Limit*. New York: Routledge, 1992.

——. *Transformations: Recollective Imagination and Sexual Difference*. New York: Routledge, 1993.

Dallery, Arleen B. "The Politics of Writing (the) Body: *Ecriture Feminine*." In *Gender/Body/Knowledge: Feminist Reconstructions of Being and Knowing*, edited by Alison Jaggar and Susan R. Bordo, 52–67. New Brunswick: Rutgers University Press, 1989.

Daly, Mary. *Beyond God the Father: Toward a Philosophy of Women's Liberation*. Boston: Beacon, 1973.

——. *Gyn/Ecology: The Metaethics of Radical Feminism*. Boston: Beacon, 1978.

——. *Pure Lust: Elemental Philosophy*. Boston: Beacon, 1984.

Danielson, Linda L. "Storyteller: *Grandmother Spider's Web*." *Journal of the Southwest* 13 (1988): 325–54.

Davis, Robert Con. "Woman as Oppositional Reader: Cixous on Discourse." In *Gender in the Classroom: Power and Pedagogy*, edited by Susan L. Gabriel and Isaiah Smithson, 96–111. Urbana: University of Illinois Press, 1990.

Defromont, Françoise. "Metaphorical Thinking and Poetic Writing in Virginia Woolf and Hélène Cixous." In *The Body and the Text: Hélène Cixous, Reading and Teaching*, edited by Helen Wilcox et al., 114–25. New York: St. Martin's, 1991.

Dent, Gina. "Black Pleasure, Black Joy: An Introduction." In *Black Popular Culture*, edited by Gina Dent, 1–19. Seattle: Bay Press, 1992.

Doty, William G. *Mythography: The Study of Myths and Rituals*. Tuscaloosa: University of Alabama Press, 1986.

DuPlessis, Rachel Blau. *Writing Beyond the Ending: Narrative Strategies of Twentieth-Century Women Writers*. Bloomington: Indiana University Press, 1985.

Esonwanne, Uzo. " 'Race' and Hermeneutics: Paradigm Shift—From Scientific to Hermeneutic Understanding of Race." *African American Review* 26 (1992): 565–82.

Eysturoy, Annie O. "Paula Gunn Allen." In *This Is About Vision: Interviews with Southwestern Writers* edited by John F. Crawford, William Balassi, and Annie O. Eysturoy, 95–107. Albuquerque: University of New Mexico, 1990.

Ferguson, Kathy E. *The Man Question: Visions of Subjectivity in Feminist Theory*. Berkeley: University of California Press, 1993.

Finke, Laurie A. "Rhetoric of Marginality: Why I Do Feminist Theory." *Tulsa Studies in Women's Literature* 5 (1986): 251–72.

Fischer, Michael. "Ethnicity and the Post-Modern Arts of Memory." In *Writing Culture: The Poetics and Politics of Ethnography*, edited by James Clifford and George E. Marcus, 194–233. Berkeley: University of California Press, 1986.

Flax, Jane. "The End of Innocence." In *Feminists Theorize the Political*, edited by Judith Butler and Joan Scott, 445–63. New York: Routledge, 1992.

Frye, Joanne S. *Living Stories, Telling Lives: Women and the Novel in Contemporary Experience*. Ann Arbor: University of Michigan Press, 1986.

Frye, Marilyn. *The Politics of Reality: Essays in Feminist Theory*. Freedom, CA: Crossing, 1983.

——. *Willful Virgin: Essays in Feminism, 1976–1992*. Freedom, CA: Crossing, 1992.

Fuss, Diana. *Essentially Speaking: Feminism, Nature and Difference*. New York: Routledge, 1989

Gadon, Elinor W. *The Once and Future Goddess: A Symbol for Our Time*. San Francisco: Harper & Row, 1989.

Gatens, Moira. "Power, Bodies, and Difference." In *Destabilizing Theory: Contemporary Feminist Debates*, edited by Michèle Barrett and Anne Phillips, 120–37. Stanford: Stanford University Press, 1992.

——. "Towards a Feminist Philosophy of the Body." In *Crossing Boundaries: Feminisms and the Critique of Knowledges*, edited by Barbara Caine, E. A. Grosz, and Marie de Lepervanche, 59–70. Sydney: Allen & Unwin, 1988.

Gates, Henry Louis, Jr. " 'Ethnic and Minority' Studies." In *Introduction to Scholarship in Modern Languages and Literatures*, edited by Joseph Gibaldi, 288–302. New York: Modern Languages Association, 1992.

——. *Loose Canons: Notes on the Culture Wars*. New York: Oxford University Press, 1992.

——. *The Signifying Monkey: A Theory of African-American Literary Criticism*. New York: Oxford University Press, 1988.

Gilbert, Sandra. "Introduction: A Tarantella of Theory." Translated by Betsy Wing. In *The Newly Born Woman*, edited by Hélène Cixous and Catherine Clément, ix–xviii. Minneapolis: University of Minnesota Press, 1988.

Ginzberg, Ruth. "Audre Lorde's (Nonessentialist) Lesbian Eros." *Hypatia* 7 (1992): 73–90.

Giroux, Henry. *Living Dangerously: Multiculturalism and the Politics of Difference*. New York: Peter Lang, 1993.

Grahn, Judy. *Another Mother Tongue: Gay Words, Gay Worlds*. Boston: Beacon Press, 1984.

Greene, Gail. *Changing the Story: Feminist Tradition and the Tradition*. Bloomington: Indiana University Press, 1991.

Grosz, E. A. "The In(ter)vention of Feminist Knowledges." In *Crossing Boundaries: Feminisms and the Critique of Knowledges*, edited by Barbara Caine, E. A. Grosz, and Marie de Lepervanche, 92–104. Sydney: Allen & Unwin, 1988.

Grosz, Elizabeth. "Bodies and Knowledges: Feminism and the Crisis of Reason." In *Feminist Epistemologies*, edited by Linda Alcoff and Elizabeth Potter, 187–215. New York: Routledge, 1993.

——. "Conclusion: A Note on Essentialism and Difference." In *Feminist Knowledge: Critique and Construct*, edited by Sneja Gunew, 332–44. New York: Routledge, 1990.

——. "Inscriptions and Body-Maps: Representation and the Real." In *Feminine, Masculine, and Representation*, edited by Terry Threadgold and Anne Cranny-Francis, 62–74. Sydney: Allen & Unwin, 1990.

——. *Jacques Lacan: A Feminist Introduction*. London and New York: Routledge, 1991.

——. "Philosophy." In *Feminist Knowledge: Critique and Construct*, edited by Sneja Gunew, 147–74. New York: Routledge, 1990.

——. *Sexual Subversions: Three French Feminists*. Sydney: Allen & Unwin, 1989.

Hall, Stuart. "Cultural Identity and Diaspora." In *Identity: Community, Culture, Difference*, edited by Jonathan Rutherford, 322–37. London: Lawrence & Wishart, 1990.

Hammond, Karla. "Audre Lorde: Interview." *Denver Quarterly* 16 (1981): 10–27.

Hanson, Elizabeth I. *Paula Gunn Allen*. Boise State University Western Writer Series. Boise: Boise State University, 1990.

Haraway, Donna. "A Manifesto for Cyborgs: Science, Technology, and Socialist Feminism in the 1980s." In *Feminism/Postmodernism*, edited by Linda J. Nicholson, 190–233. New York: Routledge, 1990.

Harris, Virginia R., and Trinity A. Ordona. "Developing Unity Among Women of Color: Crossing the Barriers of Internalized Racism and Cross-Racial Hostility." In *Making Face, Making Soul/Haciendo Caras: Creative and Critical Perspectives by Women of Color*, edited by Gloria Anzaldúa, 304–316. San Francisco: Aunt Lute Foundation, 1990.

Hart, Nett. "Lesbian Desire as Social Action." In *Lesbian Philosophies and Cultures*, edited by Jeffner Allen, 295–304. New York: State University of New York, 1990.

Hartman, Joan E. "Telling Stories: The Construction of Women's Agency." In *(En)Gendering Knowledge: Feminists in Academe*, edited by Joan Hartman and Ellen Messer-Davidow, 11–34. Knoxville: University of Tennessee Press, 1991.

Hekman, Susan J. *Gender and Knowledge: Elements of a Postmodern Feminism*. Boston: Northeastern University Press, 1990.

Hines, Darlene Clark. "Rape and the Inner Lives of Black Women in the Middle West: Preliminary Thoughts on the Culture of Dissemblance." In *Unequal Sisters: A Multicultural Reader in U.S. Women's History*, edited by Ellen Carol DuBois and Vicki L. Ruiz, 292–97. New York: Routledge, 1990.

Hirsch, Marianne, and Evelyn Fox Keller. *Conflicts in Feminism*. New York: Routledge, 1990.

Hodge, Joanna. "Subject, Body and the Exclusion of Women from Philosophy." In *Feminist Perspectives in Philosophy*, edited by Morwenna Griffiths and Margaret Whitford, 152–68. Bloomington: Indiana University Press, 1988.

Holloway, Karla F. C. *Moorings and Metaphors: Figures of Culture and Gender in Black Women's Literature*. New Brunswick: Rutgers University Press, 1992.

hooks, bell. *Black Looks: Race and Representation*. Boston: South End, 1992.

——. *Feminist Theory: From Margin to Center*. Boston: South End, 1984.

——. *Talking Back: Thinking Feminist, Thinking Black*. Boston: South End, 1989.

——. *Yearning: Race, Gender, and Cultural Politics*. Boston: South End, 1990.

Hull, Gloria. "Living on the Line: Audre Lorde and *Our Dead Behind Us*." In *Changing Our Own Words; Essays on Criticism, Theory, and Writing by Black Women*, edited by Cheryl A. Wallace, 150–72. New Brunswick: Rutgers University Press, 1989.

Irigaray, Luce. "A Chance for Life." Translated by Gillian Gill. In *Sexes and Genealogies*, 185–206. New York: Columbia University Press, 1993.

——. "Divine Women." Translated by Gillian Gill. In *Sexes and Genealogies*, 55–72. New York: Columbia University Press, 1993.

——. *Elemental Passions*. Translated by Joanne Collie and Judith Still. New York: Routledge, 1992.

——. "Equal to Whom?" Translated by Robert Mazolla. *differences* 1 (1989): 59–76.

——. *je, tu, nous: Toward a Culture of Difference*. Translated by Alison Martin. New York: Routledge, 1993.

——. "The Language of Man." 1978. Translated by Erin G. Carlston. *Cultural Critique* 13 (1989): 191–202.

——. "The Limits of Transference." In *The Irigaray Reader*, edited by Margaret Whitford, 105–17. Cambridge: Basil Blackwell, 1991.

——. *Marine Lover of Friedrich Nietzsche*. Translated by Gillian C. Gill. New York: Columbia University Press, 1991.

——. *Speculum of the Other Woman*. Translated by Gillian C. Gill. Ithaca: Cornell University Press, 1985.

——. *This Sex Which Is Not One*. Translated by Catherine Porter. Ithaca: Cornell University Press, 1985.

——. "The Universal as Mediation." Translated by Gillian Gill. In *Sexes and Genealogies*, 125–50. New York: Columbia University Press, 1993.

Jameson, Frederic. *Postmodernism, Or, The Cultural Logic of Late Capitalism*. Durham: Duke University Press, 1991.

Jardine, Alice A. *Gynesis: Configurations of Woman and Modernity*. Ithaca: Cornell University Press, 1985.

Johnson, Barbara. "Response to Henry Louis Gates, Jr." In *Afro-American Literary Study in the 1990s*, edited by Houston Baker and Patricia Redmond, 39–44. Chicago: University of Chicago Press.

Jones, Ann Rosalind. "Writing the Body: Toward an Understanding of *l'Écriture féminine*." In *The New Feminist Criticism: Essays on Women, Literature, and Theory*, edited by Elaine Showalter, 361–77. New York: Pantheon, 1985.

Jordan, June. *Civil Wars*. Boston: Beacon Press, 1981.

——. *On Call: Political Essays*. Boston: South End Press, 1987.

——. *Technical Difficulties: African-American Notions and the State of the Union*. New York: Pantheon, 1993.

Keating, AnnLouise. "Writing, Politics, and *las Lesberadas: Platicando con* Gloria Anzaldúa." *Frontiers: A Journal of Women Studies* 14 (1993): 105–30.

Kirby, Vicki. "Corporeal Habits: Addressing Essentialism Differently." *Hypatia* 6 (1991): 4–24.

Klein, Yvonne M. "Myth and Community in Recent Lesbian Auto-biographical Fiction." In *Lesbian Texts and Contexts: Radical Revisions*, edited by Karla Jay and Joanne Glasgow, 330–38. New York: New York University Press, 1990.

Krupat, Arnold. *Ethnocriticism: Ethnography, History, Literature*. Berkeley: University of California Press, 1992.

Laclau, Ernesto, and Chantal Mouffe. *Hegemony and Socialist Strategy: Towards a Radical Democratic Politics*. London: Verso, 1985.

Larsen, Jeanne. "Text and Matrix: Dickinson, H.D., and Woman's Voice." *Engendering the Word: Feminist Essays in Psychosexual Poetics*, edited by Temma F. Berg et al., 244–61. Urbana: University of Illinois Press, 1989.

Lauretis, Teresa de. "Feminist Studies/Critical Studies: Issues, Terms, and Contexts." In *Feminist Studies/Critical Studies*, edited by Teresa de Lauretis. Bloomington: Indiana University Press, 1986.

——. "Upping the Anti (sic) in Feminist Theory." In *Conflicts in Feminism*, edited by Marianne Hirsch and Evelyn Fox Keller, 255–70. New York: Routledge, 1990.

Lauter, Estella. "Re-visioning Creativity: Audre Lorde's Refiguration of Eros as the Black Mother Within." In *Writing the Woman Artist: Essays on Poetics, Politics, and Portraiture*, edited by Suzanne W. Jones, 398–418. Philadelphia: University of Pennsylvania Press, 1991.

Lincoln, Bruce. *Discourse and the Construction of Society: Comparative Studies of Myth, Ritual, and Classification*. New York: Oxford University Press, 1989.

Lionnet, Françoise. *Autobiographical Voices: Race, Gender, Self-Portraiture*. Ithaca: Cornell University Press, 1989.

Lorde, Audre. *The Black Unicorn*. New York: Norton, 1978.

——. *A Burst of Light*. Ithaca, N.Y.: Firebrand, 1988.

——. *The Cancer Journals*. San Francisco: Spinsters/Aunt Lute, 1980.

——. *Chosen Poems: Old and New*. New York: Norton, 1982.

——. *The Marvelous Distance of Arithmetic*. New York: Norton, 1993.

——. *Sister Outsider*. Freedom, CA: Crossing Press, 1984.

——. *Zami: A New Spelling of My Name*. Freedom, CA: Crossing Press, 1982.

Lugones, María, and Elizabeth V. Spelman. "Have We Got A Theory For You! Feminist Theory, Cultural Imperialism, and the Demand for 'the Woman's Voice.' " In *Hypatia Reborn*, edited by Azizah Y. al-Hibri and Margaret A. Simons, 18–33. Bloomington: Indiana University Press, 1990.

McGee, Patrick. *Telling the Other: The Question of Value in Modern and Postcolonial Writing*. Ithaca: Cornell University Press, 1992.

Martin, Biddy. "Lesbian Identity and Autobiographical Difference[s]." In *Life/Lines: Theorizing Women's Autobiography*, edited by Bella Brodzki and Celeste Schenck, 77–103. Ithaca: Cornell University Press, 1988.

Martin, Joan. "The Unicorn is Black: Audre Lorde in Retrospect." In *Black Women Writers 1950–1980: A Critical Evaluation*, edited by Mari Evans, 277–91. New York: Doubleday, 1984.

Mercer, Kobena. "Dark and Lovely Too: Black Gay Men in Independent Film." In *Queer Looks: Perspectives on Lesbian and Gay Film and Video*, edited by Martha Gever, John Greyson, and Pratibha Parmar, 238–56. New York: Routledge, 1993.

——. "Skin Head Sex Thing: Racial Difference and the Homoerotic Imaginary." In *How Do I Look? Queer Film and Video*, edited by Bad Object-Choices, 169–210. Seattle: Bay Press, 1991.

——. "Welcome to the Jungle: Identity and Diversity in Postmodern Politics." *Identity: Community, Culture, Difference*, edited by Jonathan Rutherford, 43–71. London: Lawrence & Wishart, 1990.

Mohanty, Chandra. "Introduction: Cartographies of Struggle: Third World Women and the Politics of Feminism." In *Third World Women and the Politics of Feminism*, edited by Chandra Talpade Mohanty, Ann Russo, and Lourdes Torres, 1–47. Bloomington: Indiana University Press, 1991.

Moi, Toril. "Patriarchal Thought and the Drive for Knowledge." In *Between Feminism and Psychoanalysis*, edited by Teresa Brennan, 189–205. New York: Routledge, 1991.

——. *Sexual/Textual Politics: Feminist Literary Theory*. New York: Routledge, 1983.

Moraga, Cherríe. "Algo secretamente amado." *Third Woman: The Sexuality of Latinas* 4 (1989): 151–56.

——. "La Güera." In *This Bridge Called My Back: Writings by Radical Women of Color*, edited by Cherríe Moraga and Gloria Anzaldúa, 27–34. New York: Kitchen Table: Women of Color Press, 1983.

Morris, Meaghan. *The Pirate's Fiancée: Feminism, Reading, Postmodernism*. London: Verso, 1988.

Mouffe, Chantal. "Radical Democracy: Modern or Postmodern?" In *Universal Abandon? The Politics of Postmodernism*, edited by Andrew Ross, 31–45. Minneapolis: University of Minnesota Press, 1988.

Mulvey, Laura. *Visual and Other Pleasures*. Bloomington: Indiana University Press, 1989.

Murray, David. *Forked Tongues: Speech, Writing, and Representation in North American Indian Texts*. Bloomington: Indiana University Press, 1991.

Navarro, Marta A. "Interview with Ana Castillo." In *Chicana Lesbians: The Girls Our Mothers Warned Us About*, edited by Carla Trujillo, 113–32. Berkeley: Third Woman, 1991.

Olaniyan, Tejumola. "African-American Critical Discourse and the Invention of Cultural Identities." *African American Review* 26 (1992): 533–45.

Omi, Michael, and Howard Winant. *Racial Formation in the United States from the 1960s to the 1980s*. New York: Routledge, 1986.

Orenstein, Gloria Feman. *The Reflowering of the Goddess*. New York: Pergamon, 1990.

Ostriker, Alicia. *Stealing the Language: The Emergence of Women's Poetry in America*. Boston: Beacon, 1986.

Parmar, Pratibha. "Black Feminism: the Politics of Articulation." *Identity: Community, Culture, Difference*, edited by Jonathan Rutherford, 101–27. London: Lawrence & Wishart, 1990.

Pelton, Robert D. *The Trickster in West Africa: A Study of Mythic Irony and Sacred Delight*. Berkeley: University of California Press, 1980.

Perreault, Jeanne. " 'That the Pain Not Be Wasted': Audre Lorde and the Written Self." *Auto/Biography Studies* 4 (1988): 1–16.

Pheterson, Gail. "Alliances Between Women: Overcoming Internalized Oppression and Internalized Domination." In *Bridges of Power: Women's Multicultural Alliances*, edited by Lisa Albrecht and Rose M. Brewer, 34–48. Philadelphia: New Society, 1990.

Rabuzzi, Kathryn Allen. *Motherself: A Mythic Analysis of Motherhood*. Bloomington: Indiana University Press, 1988.

Raynaud, Claudine. " 'A Nutmeg Nestled Inside Its Covering of Mace': Audre Lorde's *Zami*." In *Life/Lines: Theorizing Women's Autobiography*, edited by Bella Brodzki and Celeste Schenck, 221–42. Ithaca: Cornell University Press, 1988.

Ross, Andrew. "New Age Technoculture." In *Cultural Studies*, edited by Lawrence Grossberg, Cary Nelson, and Paula Treichler, 531–47. New York: Routledge, 1992.

Rubenstein, Roberta. *Boundaries of the Self: Gender, Culture, Fiction*. Urbana: University of Illinois Press, 1987.

Sanchez, Rosaura. "Ethnicity, Ideology and Academia." *The Americas Review* 15 (1987): 80–88.

Sanchez-Tranquilino, Marcos, and John Tagg. "The Pachuco's Flayed Hide: Mobility, Identity, and Buenas Garras." In *Cultural Studies*, edited by Lawrence Grossberg, Cary Nelson, and Paula Treichler, 556–70. New York: Routledge, 1992.

Sandoval, Chela. "Feminism and Racism: A Report on the 1981 National Women's Studies Association Conference." In *Making Face, Making Soul/Haciendo Caras: Creative and Critical Perspectives by Women of Color*, edited by Gloria Anzaldúa, 55–71. San Francisco: Aunt Lute Foundation, 1990.

———. "U.S. Third World Feminism: The Theory and Method of Oppositional Consciousness in the Postmodern World." *Genders* 10 (Spring 1991): 1–25.

Shiach, Morag. *Hélène Cixous: A Politics of Writing*. London: Routledge, 1991.

———. " 'Their "symbolic" exists, it holds power—we, the sowers of disorder, know it only too well.' " In *Between Feminism and Psychoanalysis*, edited by Teresa Brennan, 153–67. New York: Routledge, 1991.

Singer, Linda. "True Confessions: Cixous and Foucault on Sexuality and Power." In *The Thinking Muse: Feminism and Modern French Philosophy*, edited by Jeffner Allen and Iris Marion Young, 136–55. Bloomington: Indiana University Press, 1989.

Smith, Barbara, ed. *Home Girls: A Black Feminist Anthology*. New York: Kitchen Table, Women of Color, 1983.

——. "Racism and Women's Studies." In *Making Face, Making Soul/ Haciendo Caras: Creative and Critical Perspectives by Women of Color*, edited by Gloria Anzaldúa, 25–28. San Francisco: Aunt Lute Foundation, 1990.

Smith, Paul. *Discerning the Subject*. Minneapolis: University of Minnesota Press, 1988.

Smith, Sidonie. *Subjectivity, Identity, and the Body: Women's Autobiographical Practices in the Twentieth Century*. Bloomington: Indiana University Press, 1993.

Sojourner, Sabrina. "From the House of Yemanja: The Goddess Heritage of Black Women." In *The Politics of Women's Spirituality: Essays on the Rise of Spiritual Power Within the Feminist Movement*, edited by Charlene Spretnak, 57–63. New York: Doubleday, 1982.

Spelman, Elizabeth V. *Inessential Woman: Problems of Exclusion in Feminist Thought*. Boston: Beacon, 1988.

Spillers, Hortense. "Interstices: A Small Drama of Words." In *Pleasure and Danger: Exploring Female Sexuality*, edited by Carole S. Vance, 73–100. Boston: Routledge & Kegan Paul, 1984.

——. "Mama's Baby, Papa's Maybe: An American Grammar Book." *Diacritics* (1987): 65–81.

——. "An Order of Constancy: Notes on Brooks and the Feminine." In *Reading Black, Reading Feminist: A Critical Anthology*, edited by Henry Louis Gates Jr., 244–71. New York: Meridian, 1990.

——. " 'The Permanent Obliquity of an In(pha)llibly Straight': In the Time of the Daughters and the Fathers." In *Changing Our Own Words; Essays on Criticism, Theory, and Writing by Black Women*, edited by Cheryl A. Wallace. New Brunswick: Rutgers University Press, 1989.

Spivak, Gayatri Chakravorty. *In Other Worlds: Essays in Cultural Politics*. New York: Metheun, 1987.

——. *Outside in the Teaching Machine*. New York: Routledge, 1993.

Stanton, Domna C. "Difference on Trial: A Critique of the Maternal Metaphor in Cixous, Irigaray, and Kristeva." In *The Poetics of Gender*, edited by Nancy K. Miller, 157–82. New York: Columbia University Press, 1986.

Stone, Merlin. *When God Was a Woman*. San Diego: Harcourt Brace Jovanovich, 1976.

Stuart, Andrea. "Feminism: Dead or Alive?" In *Identity: Community, Culture, Difference*, edited by Jonathan Rutherford, 28–42. London: Lawrence & Wishart, 1990.

Suleri, Sara. "Woman Skin Deep: Feminism and the Postcolonial Condition." *Critical Inquiry* 18 (1992): 756–69.

Tate, Claudia. *Black Women Writers at Work*. New York: Continuum, 1983.

Teish, Luisah. *Jambalaya: The Natural Woman's Book of Personal Charms and Practical Rituals*. San Francisco: Harper & Row, 1985.

Tijerina, Aletícia. "Notes on Oppression and Violence." In *Making Face, Making Soul/Haciendo Caras: Creative and Critical Perspectives by Women of Color*, edited by Gloria Anzaldúa. San Francisco: Aunt Lute Foundation, 1990. 170–73.

Torres, Lourdes. "The Construction of Self in U.S. Latina Autobiographies." In *Third World Women and the Politics of Feminism*, edited by Chandra Talpade Mohanty, Ann Russo, and Lourdes Torres, 271–87. Bloomington: Indiana University Press, 1991.

Trinh T. Minh-ha. *When the Moon Waxes Red: Representation, Gender and Cultural Politics*. New York: Routledge, 1991.

——. *Woman Native Other: Writing Postcoloniality and Feminism*. Bloomington: Indiana University Press, 1989.

Turner, Victor. *The Ritual Process: Structure and Anti-Structure*. Chicago: Aldine, 1969.

Tyler, Stephen. "Post-Modern Ethnography: From Document of the Occult to Occult Document." In *Writing Culture: The Poetics and Politics of Ethnography*, edited by James Clifford and George E. Marcus, 122–41. Berkeley: University of California Press, 1986.

Uttal, Lynet. "Inclusion without Influence: The Continuing Tokenism of Women of Color." In *Making Face, Making Soul/Haciendo Caras: Creative and Critical Perspectives by Women of Color*, edited by Gloria Anzaldúa, 42–44. San Francisco: Aunt Lute Foundation, 1990.

Van Dyke, Annette. "The Journey Back to Female Roots: A Laguna Pueblo Model." In *Lesbian Texts and Contexts: Radical Revisions*, edited by Karla Jay Joanne Glasgow, 339–54. New York: New York University Press, 1990.

Walker, Alice. "Definition of Womanist." In *Making Face, Making*

Soul/Haciendo Caras: Creative and Critical Perspectives by Women of Color, edited by Gloria Anzaldúa, 356–70. San Francisco: Aunt Lute Foundation, 1990.

Walker, Nancy. "Language, Irony, and Fantasy in the Contemporary Novel by Women." *LIT: Literature Interpretation Theory* 1 (December 1989): 31–57.

Watson, Julia. "Unspeakable Differences: The Politics of Gender in Lesbian and Heterosexual Women's Autobiographies." In *De/Colonizing the Subject: The Politics of Gender in Women's Autobiography*, edited by Sidonie Smith and Julia Watson, 139–68. Minneapolis: University of Minnesota Press, 1992.

Webster, Yehudi O. *The Racialization of America*. New York: St. Martin's Press, 1992.

Wenzel, Hélène Vivienne. "The Text as Body/Politics: An Appreciation of Monique Wittig's Writings in Context." *Feminist Studies* 7 (1981): 264–87.

Whitford, Margaret. *Luce Irigaray: Philosophy in the Feminine*. New York: Routledge, 1991.

——. "Luce Irigaray's Critique of Rationality." In *Feminist Perspectives in Philosophy*, edited by Morwenna Griffiths and Margaret Whitford, 109–30. Bloomington: Indiana University Press, 1988.

Wilson, Anna. "Audre Lorde and the African-American Tradition: When the Family is Not Enough." In *Lesbian Criticism: Literary and Cultural Readings*, edited by Sally Munt, 75–94. New York: Columbia University Press, 1992.

Wittig, Monique. *The Straight Mind and Other Essays*. Boston: Beacon, 1992.

Wolff, Janet. *Feminine Sentences: Essays on Women and Culture*. Berkeley: University of California Press, 1990.

Wood, Deborah. "Interview With Audre Lorde." In *In Memory and Spirit of Frances, Zora, and Lorraine: Essays and Interviews on Black Women and Writing*, edited by Juliette Bowles, 11–22. Washington, D.C.: Institute for the Arts and Humanities, 1979.

Wynter, Sylvia. "On Disenchanting Discourse: 'Minority' Literary Criticism and Beyond." In *The Nature and Context of Minority Discourse*, edited by Abdul R. JanMohamed and David Lloyd, 432–69. New York: Oxford University Press, 1990.

Yamato, Gloria. "Something about the Subject Makes It Hard to Name." In *Making Face, Making Soul/Haciendo Caras: Creative and Critical Perspectives by Women of Color*, edited by Gloria Anzaldúa, 20–24. San Francisco: Aunt Lute Foundation, 1990.

Zimmerman, Bonnie. "Lesbians Like This and That: Some Notes on Lesbian Criticism for the Nineties." In *Lesbian Criticism: Literary and Cultural Readings*, edited by Sally Munt, 1–15. New York: Columbia University Press, 1992.

——. *The Safe Sea of Women: Lesbian Fiction 1969–1989*. Boston: Beacon, 1990

——. "Seeing, Reading, Knowing: The Lesbian Appropriation of Literature." In *(En)Gendering Knowledge: Feminists in Academe*, edited by Joan Hartman and Ellen Messer-Davidow, 85–99. Knoxville: University of Tennessee Press, 1991.

Index